THE ADULT LEARNER

LEARNER

FIFTH EDITION

FIFTH EDITION

THE ADULT LEARNER

The Definitive Classic in
Adult Education and
Human Resource Development

MALCOLM S. KNOWLES ▪ ELWOOD F. HOLTON III
RICHARD A. SWANSON

Gulf Publishing Company
Houston, Texas

The Adult Learner
Fifth Edition

Copyright © 1973, 1978, 1984, 1990, 1998 by Gulf Publishing Company, Houston, Texas. All rights reserved. This book, or parts thereof, may not be reproduced in any form without permission of the publisher.

Gulf Publishing Company
Book Division
P.O. Box 2608 ☐ Houston, Texas 77252-2608

10   9   8   7   6   5   4   3   2   1

Library of Congress Cataloging-in-Publication Data
    Knowles, Malcolm Shepherd, 1913–1997
    The adult learner : the definitive classic in adult education and human resource development / Malcolm S. Knowles, Elwood F. Holton, Richard A. Swanson. — 5th ed.
        p.   cm.
    Includes bibliographical references and index.
    ISBN 0-88415-115-8 (alk. paper)
    1. Adult learning.   2. Adult education.   3. Training.
I. Holton, Elwood F., 1957–   .   II. Swanson, Richard A., 1942–
III. Title.
LC5225.L42K56 1998
374—dc21   98-6788
                                                                 CIP

Printed on Acid-Free Paper (∞).

Printed in the United States of America.

DEDICATION

Malcolm S. Knowles
1913-1997

Malcolm S. Knowles, the Father of Andragogy in the United States, died on November 27, 1997.

Malcolm was one of the world's leading scholar-practitioners of adult learning. He was a member of a generation that experienced the fullest range of character-building phases the United States has known: a massive influx of immigrants, several wars, an economic depression, waves of technological advances, the civil rights movement, the dominance of the knowledge worker, and an optimism about the human spirit. While Malcolm participated in all this, he was one of the thinkers and doers rising above the milieu and pointing the way for a dynamic democracy. Equivalent leaders of his generation, in such areas as economics, quality improvement, religion, and psychology, have finished their work and their legacy lives on in the next generation. Malcolm's early understanding of the importance of adult learning has provided insight that will guide the professions dedicated to adult learning into the next millennium.

This revised fifth edition of Malcolm's 1973 book is a testimony to his own learning journey and his personal confidence in the individual learner. In honor of Malcolm S. Knowles, the Academy of Human Resource Development has named its doctoral-dissertation-of-the-year award in his name. Those wishing to make a donation to this student-award endowment should contact the Academy.

Elwood F. Holton, III, Ed.D., is associate professor of human resource development and adult education at Louisiana State University. He is the author and editor of numerous books and articles on learning and human resource development. He is an expert on adult learning applications in public and private settings and consults extensively with organizations in both sectors.

Richard A. Swanson, Ed.D., is professor of human resource development and adult education at the University of Minnesota. He also directs the University of Minnesota Human Resource Development Research Center. He has 30 years of teaching and consulting experience and has written extensively in the areas of learning and human resource development. Swanson is a leading authority on how to develop and unleash human potential in organizations.

Contents

Preface

Welcome to the newest edition of *The Adult Learner*. It is an honor for us to join with Malcolm Knowles in this updated and revised fifth edition. *The Adult Learner* has stood as a core work on adult learning for over a quarter of a century. Our goal has been for it to remain a classic in the field of adult learning.

We approached the task of updating this classic book with care and thoughtfulness. The sad part of this effort is that it represents the passing of an era. Malcolm Knowles' health no longer allowed him to take on the work of revision and updating.

In shaping this revision, we decided that it was important to preserve Malcolm's words and thoughts as close to their original form as possible. Thus, you will find that Part 1 of this edition (chapters 2–5), entitled "The Roots of Andragogy," are nearly identical to chapters 1–4 of the fourth edition of *The Adult Learner*. We have done only minor copy editing and formatting to preserve Malcolm's original thinking. Chapter 1 and Part 2 (chapters 6–8), entitled "Advancements in Adult Learning" are our new contributions to the book. In addition, Part 3, "Practice in Adult Learning" has been updated.

Each of the three parts of *The Adult Learner* have their own style. While the voices are varied, the messages are harmonious. The messages of lifelong learning, faith in the human spirit, and the role that adult learning professionals play in the adult learning process come through chapter by chapter.

Our hope is that this new edition of *The Adult Learner,* and its potential to advance adult learning wherever it is practiced, is realized and that Malcolm Knowles' vision moves into the next century.

We would like to thank several colleagues for their help at various points in this effort. Sharon Naquin provided many hours of careful critique and research that were invaluable. We also appreciate the advice from our colleagues Reid A. Bates, Harold Stubblefield, Richard J. Torraco, and Albert K. Wiswell for critiquing the manuscript. Finally, thanks to our families who continue to believe that our work is important and worth the sacrifices.

Elwood F. Holton III
Louisiana State University

Richard A. Swanson
University of Minnesota

CHAPTER 1

Introduction

In the early 1970s when andragogy and the concept that adults and children learn differently was first introduced in the United States by Malcolm Knowles, the idea was groundbreaking and sparked much subsequent research and controversy. Since the earliest days, adult educators have debated what andragogy really is. Spurred in large part by the need for a defining theory within the field of adult education, andragogy has been extensively analyzed and critiqued. It has been alternately described as a set of guidelines (Merriam, 1993), a philosophy (Pratt, 1993), a set of assumptions (Brookfield, 1986), or a theory (Knowles, 1989). The disparity of these positions is indicative of the perplexing nature of the field of adult learning; but regardless of what it is called, "it is an honest attempt to focus on the learner. In this sense, it does provide an alternative to the methodology-centered instructional design perspective" (Feur and Gerber, 1988). Merriam, in explaining the complexity and present condition of adult-learning theory, offers the following:

"It is doubtful that a phenomenon as complex as adult learning will ever be explained by a single theory, model or set of principles. Instead, we have a case of the proverbial elephant being described differently depending on who is talking and on which part of the animal is examined. In the first half of this century, psychologists took the lead in explaining learning behavior; from the 1960s onward, adult educators began formulating their own ideas about adult learning and, in particular, about how it might differ from learning in childhood. Both of these approaches are still operative. Where we are headed, it seems, is toward a multifaceted understanding of adult learning, reflecting the inherent richness and complexity of the phenomenon."

Despite years of critique, debate, and challenge, the core principles of adult learning advanced by andragogy have endured (Davenport and Davenport, 1985; Hartree, 1984; Pratt, 1988), and few adult learning scholars would disagree with the observation that Knowles' ideas sparked a revolution in adult education and training (Feur and Gerber, 1988). Brookfield, positing a similar view, asserts that andragogy is the "single most popular idea in the education and training of adults" (1986). Adult educators, particularly beginning ones, find them invaluable in shaping the learning process to be more conducive to adults.

It is beyond the scope of this introductory book to address the many dimensions of the theoretical debate raised in academic circles. Our position is that andragogy presents core principles of adult learning that in turn enable those designing and conducting adult learning to build more effective learning processes for adults. It is a transactional model in that it speaks to the characteristics of the learning transaction, not to the goals and aims of that transaction. As such, it is applicable to any adult learning transaction, from community education to human resource development in organizations.

Care must be taken to avoid confusing core principles of the adult learning transaction with the goals and purposes for which the learning event is being conducted. They are conceptually distinct, though as a practical matter may overlap considerably. Critiques of andragogy point to missing elements that keep it from being a defining theory of the *discipline of adult education* (Davenport and Davenport, 1985; Grace, 1996; Hartree, 1984), not of *adult learning*. Grace, for example, criticizes andragogy for focusing solely on the individual and not operating from a critical social agenda or debating the relationship of adult education to society (Grace, 1996). This criticism reflects the goals and purposes of adult education. Human resource developers in organizations will have a different set of goals and purposes, which andragogy does not embrace either. Community health educators may have yet another set of goals and purposes that are not embraced.

Therein lies the strength of andragogy: it is a set of core adult learning principles that apply to all adult learning situations. The goals and purposes for which the learning is offered are a separate issue. Adult education (AE) professionals should develop and debate models of adult learning separately from models of the goals and purposes of their respective fields that use adult learning. Human resource development (HRD), for example, embraces organizational performance as one of its core goals, while adult education may focus more on individual growth.

Having said that, these core principles are also incomplete in terms of learning decisions. Figure 1-1, Andragogy in Practice, graphically shows that andragogy is a core set of adult learning principles. The six principles of andragogy, 1) the learner's need to know, 2) self-concept of the learner, 3) prior experience of the learner, 4) readiness to learn, 5) orientation to learning, and 6) motivation to learn, are listed in the center of the model. As we shall see in this and subsequent chapters, there are a variety of other factors that affect adult learning in any particular situation and may cause adults to behave more or less closely to the core principles. These include individual learner differences, situational differences, and goals and purposes of learning, shown in the two outer rings of the model. Andragogy works best in practice when it is adapted to fit the uniqueness of the learners and the learning situation. We see this not as a weakness of the principles, but as a strength. That is, their strength is that these core principles apply to all adult learning situations, provided they are considered in concert with other factors that are present in that situation.

This fifth edition of *The Adult Learner* provides a journey from theory to practice in adult learning. Figure 1-1 provides a snapshot summary of the journey in displaying the six core adult learning principles surrounded by the context of individual and situational differences, and the goals and purposes of learning. The following chapters will reveal the substance and subtleties of this holistic model of andragogy in practice.

PLAN FOR THE BOOK

The first part of the book, "The Roots of Andragogy" (chapters 2–5), presents the core principles of adult learning: andragogy. It traces the development of the theory and focuses on the core unique characteristics of adults as learners.

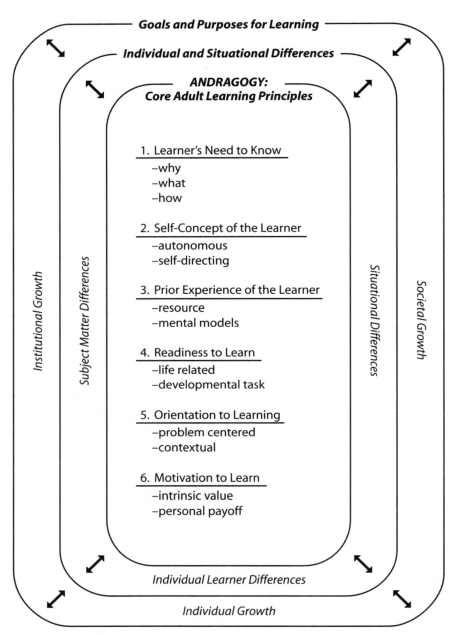

Figure 1-1. Andragogy in practice (Knowles, Holton, and Swanson, 1998).

Part 2, "Advances in Adult Learning," (chapters 6–9) addresses the two outer rings. Chapters 6 discusses adult learning as practiced within human resource development. Chapter 7 focuses on new thinking about andragogy and elaborates on applying the core principles to different learners. Chapter 8 discusses new advancements in our understanding of adult learning that enable facilitators to further tailor application of the core principles. Chapter 9 summarizes these two sections and elaborates on how andragogy is applied in practice.

Part 3, "Practices in Adult Learning" (chapters 10–17), presents selected readings that elaborate on specific aspects of andragogy in practice. These include strategies to implement the core assumptions, to tailor learning to individual differences, and to implement adult learning in organizations.

PART 1

The Roots of Andragogy

*History and Principles of Classic
Andragogical Adult Learning Theory*

CHAPTER 2

Exploring the World of Learning Theory

WHY EXPLORE LEARNING THEORY?

This is a good question. Perhaps you shouldn't. If you have no questions about the quality of learning in your organization, if you are sure it's the best it can be, we suggest that you cancel your order for this book and get a refund. However, if you're a policy-level executive, a change agent, a learning specialist, or a consultant, you should seriously consider exploring learning theory. Doing so will increase your understanding of various theories and your chances for achieving your desired results.

Policy-level executives may have such questions as: Are our HRD interventions based on assumptions about human nature and organizational life that are congruent with the assumptions on which our management policies are based? Is our HRD program contributing to long-run gains in our human capital, or only short-run cost reduction? Why do our HRD personnel make the decisions they do concerning priorities, activities, methods and techniques, materials, and the use of outside resources (consultants, package programs, hardware, software, and university courses)? Are these the best decisions?

How can I assess whether or not, or to what degree, the program is producing the results I want?

Managers may have all of the above questions plus others such as: Which learning theory is most appropriate for which kind of learning, or should our entire program be faithful to a single learning theory? How do I find out what learning theories are being followed by the various consultants, package programs, and other outside resources available to us? What difference might their theoretical orientation make in our program? What are the implications of the various learning theories for our program development, selection and training of instructional personnel, administrative policies and practices, facilities, and program evaluation?

Learning specialists (instructors, curriculum builders, and methods, materials, and media developers), may have some of the above questions in addition to the following: How can I increase my effectiveness as a learning specialist? Which techniques will be most effective for particular situations? Which learning theories are most congruent with my own view of human nature and the purpose of education? What are the implications of the various learning theories for my own role and performance?

Consultants (change agents, experts, advocates) may have some of the above questions plus others such as: Which learning theory should I advocate under what circumstances? How shall I explain the nature and consequences of the various learning theories to my clients? What are the implications of the various learning theories for total organizational development? Which learning theory is most consistent with my conception of the role of consultant?

A good theory should provide explanations of phenomena as well as guidelines for action. But theories about human behavior also carry with them assumptions about human nature, the purpose of education, and desirable values. Understandably then, a better understanding of the various learning theories will result in better decisions regarding learning experiences and more desirable outcomes.

WHAT IS A THEORY?

It seems that most writers in this field don't expressly define the term theory, but expect their readers to derive its meaning from their use of the term. Torraco (1997, p. 115) informs us that "a theory simply explains what a phenomenon is and how it works."

Webster's Seventh New Intercollegiate Dictionary gives five definitions: (1) the analysis of a set of facts in their relation to one another; (2) the general or abstract principles of a body of fact, a science, or an art; (3) a plausible or scientifically acceptable general principle or body of principles offered to explain phenomena; (4) a hypothesis assumed for the sake of argument or investigation; (5) abstract thought. Learning theorists use all five of these definitions in one way or another, but with wide variations in their usage:

Here, for example, are some definitions by usage in context.

The research worker needs a set of assumptions as a starting point to guide what he/she does, to be tested by experiment, or to serve as a check on observations and insights. Without any theory, researcher activities may be as aimless and as wasteful as the early wanderings of the explorers in North America . . . knowledge of theory always aids practice (Kidd, 1959, pp. 134–135).

A scientist, with the desire to satisfy his/her curiosity about the facts of nature, has a predilection for ordering his/her facts into systems of laws and theories. He/she is interested not only in verified facts and relationships, but in neat and parsimonious ways of summarizing these facts (Hilgard and Bower, 1966, pp. 1–2).

Every managerial act rests on assumptions, generalizations, and hypotheses—that is to say, on theory (McGregor, 1960, p. 6).

"Few people, other than theorists, ever get excited about theories. Theories, like vegetables and televised golf tournaments, don't trigger provocative reactions from people. Most theories, except those that are truly revolutionary, such as the contributions of Newton, Einstein, and Darwin, just do their jobs quietly behind the scenes. They may increase our understanding of a real-world event or behavior or they may help us predict what will happen in a given situation. But they do so without a lot of fanfare" (Torraco, 1997, p. 114).

From these excerpts and perspectives we can see that a theory can be a guiding set of assumptions (Kidd), an ordering system that neatly summarizes the facts (Hilgard and Bower), and/or assumptions, generalizations, and hypotheses (McGregor). And, as Torraco points out, theories can be tacit. Yet, we must examine another important perspective, the fact that there are some psychologists who don't believe in theories at all. For example, Skinner objects to theories on the score that the hypothesis-formulation-and-testing procedures they generate are wasteful and misleading. "They usually send the investigator down the wrong paths, and even if the scientific logic makes them self-correcting, the paths back are strewn with discarded theories" (Hilgard, 1966, p. 143). Skinner believes that the end result of scientific investigation is a "described functional relationship demonstrated in the data." After reviewing the classical theories, he comes to the conclusion that "such theories are now of historical interest only, and unfortunately, much of the work which was done to support them is also of little current value. We may turn instead to a more adequate analysis of the changes which take place as a student learns" (Skinner, 1968, p. 8).

Similarly, Gagne writes, "I do not think learning is a phenomenon which can be explained by simple theories, despite the admitted intellectual appeal that such theories have" (Gagne, 1965, p. v). He goes on to explain, however, that a number of useful generalizations can be made about classes of performance change, which he describes as conditions of learning.

Where does all this leave us in answering the question, What is a theory? Perhaps the only realistic answer is that a theory is what a given author says it is. If you want to understand his or her thinking you have to go along with his or her definitions. So here is our definition: *A theory is a comprehensive, coherent, and internally consistent system of ideas about a set of phenomena.*

WHAT IS LEARNING?

Any discussion of a definition of learning must be prefaced with an important and frequently made distinction—the one between education and learning.

Education is an activity undertaken or initiated by one or more agents that is designed to effect changes in the knowledge, skill, and attitudes of individuals, groups, or communities. The term emphasizes the educator, the agent of change who presents stimuli and rein-forcement for learning and designs activities to induce change.

The term *learning*, by contrast, emphasizes the person in whom the change occurs or is expected to occur. Learning is the act or process by which behavioral change, knowledge, skills, and attitudes are acquired (Boyd, Apps, *et al.*, 1980, pp. 100–101).

Having made this distinction, we can proceed with our definition of learning. However, defining learning, like defining theory, can prove complicated. Some learning theorists assert that defining learning is difficult, while still others maintain that there is no basic dis-agreement about the definition of learning between the theories. Smith summarizes the difficulty of defining learning in these words:

It has been suggested that the term learning defies precise defini-tion because it is put to multiple uses. Learning is used to refer to (1) the acquisition and mastery of what is already known about something, (2) the extension and clarification of meaning of one's experience, or (3) an organized, intentional process of testing ideas relevant to problems. In other words, it is used to describe a product, a process, or a function (Smith, 1982, p. 34).

In contrast, Ernest Hilgard, one of our most distinguished contem-porary interpreters of learning theory, concludes that the debate cen-ters on interpretation and not definition.

While it is extremely difficult to formulate a satisfactory defini-tion of learning so as to include all the activities and processes which we wish to include and eliminate all those which we wish to exclude, the difficulty does not prove to be embarrassing because it is not a source of controversy as between theories. The controversy is over fact and interpretation, not over defini-tion (Hilgard and Bower, 1966, p. 6).

This generalization appears to hold with regard to those learning theorists who dominated the field until recently, although there are striking variations in the degree of precision among them. Let's start with three definitions by different authors as presented in *Readings in Human Learning*.

Learning involves change. It is concerned with the acquisition of habits, knowledge, and attitudes. It enables the individual to make both personal and social adjustments. Since the concept of change is inherent in the concept of learning, any change in behavior implies that learning is taking place or has taken place. Learning that occurs during the process of change can be referred to as the *learning process* (Crow and Crow, 1963b, p. 1).

Learning is a change in the individual, due to the interaction of that individual, and his environment, which fills a need and makes him more capable of dealing adequately with his environment (Burton, 1963, p. 7).

There is a remarkable agreement upon the definition of learning as being reflected in a change in behavior as the result of experience (Haggard, 1963, p. 20).

The last notion implies that we don't directly know what learning is, but can only infer what it is. This idea is supported by Cronbach who stated, "Learning is shown by a change in behavior as a result of experience" (Cronbach, 1963, p. 71). Harris and Schwahn go back to, "Learning is essentially change due to experience," but then go on to distinguish among *learning as product,* which emphasizes the end result or outcome of the learning experience, *learning as process,* which emphasizes what happens during the course of a learning experience in attaining a given learning product or outcome, and *learning as function,* which emphasizes certain critical aspects of learning, such as motivation, retention, and transfer, which presumably make behavioral changes in human learning possible (Harris and Schwahn, 1961, pp. 1-2).

Others take care to distinguish between planned learning and natural growth.

Learning is a change in human disposition or capability, which can be retained, and which is not simply ascribable to the process of growth (Gagne, 1965, p. 5).

Learning is the process by which an activity originates or is changed through reacting to an encountered situation, provided that the characteristics of the change in activity cannot be explained on the basis of native response tendencies, maturation, or temporary states of the organism (e.g., fatigue, drugs, etc.) (Hilgard and Bower, 1966, p. 2).

The concepts of control and shaping lie at the heart of Skinner's treatment of learning: (1) "Recent improvements in the conditions which control behavior in the field of learning are of two principal sorts. The Law of Effect has been taken seriously; we have made sure that effects do occur under conditions which are optimal for producing changes called learning" [control] and (2) Once we have arranged the particular type of consequence called a reinforcement, our techniques permit us to shape the behavior of an organism almost at will (Skinner, 1968, p. 10).

Clearly, these learning theorists (and most of their precursors and many of their contemporaries) see learning as a process by which behavior is changed, shaped, or controlled. Other theorists prefer to define learning in terms of growth, development of competencies, and fulfillment of potential. Jerome Bruner, for example, observes, "It is easy enough to use one's chosen theory for explaining modifications in behavior as an instrument for describing growth; there are so many aspects of growth that any theory can find something that it can explain well." He then lists these "benchmarks about the nature of intellectual growth against which to measure one's efforts at explanation":

1. Growth is characterized by increasing independence of response from the immediate nature of the stimulus.

2. Growth depends upon internalizing events into a "storage system" that corresponds to the environment.

3. Intellectual growth involves an increasing capacity to say to oneself and others, by means of words or symbols, what one has done or what one will do.

4. Intellectual development depends upon a systematic and contingent interaction between a tutor and a learner.

5. Teaching is vastly facilitated by the medium of language, which ends by being not only the medium for exchange but the instrument that the learner can then use himself in bringing order into the environment.

6. Intellectual development is marked by increasing capacity to deal with several alternatives simultaneously, to tend to several sequences during the same period of time, and to allocate time and attention in a manner appropriate to these multiple demands (Bruner, 1966, pp. 4–6).

Still other theorists feel that even this emphasis on growth, with its focus on cognitive development, is too narrow to explain what learning is really about. For instance, Jones objects to Bruner's underemphasis on emotional skills, his exclusive attention to extra-psychic stimuli, the equating of symbolism with verbalism, and his preoccupation with the processes of concept attainment to the seeming exclusion of the processes of concept formation or invention (Jones, 1968, pp. 97–104).

Nevertheless, Bruner is moving away from the perception of learning as a process of controlling, changing, or shaping behavior and putting it more in the context of competency-development. One of the most dynamic and prolific developments in the field of psychology, *humanistic psychology,* has recently exploded on the scene (the Association of Humanistic Psychology was founded in 1963) and has carried this trend of thought much farther. Carl Rogers is one of its exponents. The elements of humanistic psychology include:

1. *Personal involvement.* The whole person, including his or her feelings and cognitive aspects, are involved in the learning event.
2. *Self-initiation.* Even when the impetus or stimulus comes from the outside, the sense of discovery, of reaching out, of grasping and comprehending, comes from within.
3. *Pervasiveness.* Learning makes a difference in the behavior, attitudes, perhaps even the personality of the learner.
4. *Evaluation by the learner.* The learner knows whether the learning meets personal need, whether it leads toward what the individual wants to know, whether it illuminates the dark area of ignorance the individual is experiencing. The locus of evaluation, we might say, resides definitely in the learner.
5. *Its essence is meaning.* When such learning takes place, the element of meaning to the learner is built into the whole experience (Rogers, 1969, p. 5).

Maslow sees the goal of learning to be self-actualization, ". . . the full use of talents, capacities, potentialities, etc." (Maslow, 1970, p. 150). He conceives of growth toward this goal as being determined by the relationship of two sets of forces operating within each individual. "One set clings to safety and defensiveness out of fear, tending to regress backward, hanging on to the past. . . . The other set of forces impels him forward toward wholeness to Self and uniqueness of Self, toward full functioning of all his capacities. . . . We grow forward when the delights of growth and anxieties of safety are greater than the anxieties of growth and the delights of safety" (Maslow, 1972, pp. 44–45).

Building on the notion that "insights from the behavioral sciences have expanded the perception of human potential, through a re-casting of the image of man from a passive, reactive recipient, to an active, seeking, autonomous, and reflective being," Sidney Jourard develops the concept of *independent learning.*

> . . . That independent learning is problematic is most peculiar, because man always and only learns by himself. . . . Learning is not a task or problem; it is a way to be in the world. Man learns as he pursues goals and projects that have meaning for him. He is always learning something. Perhaps the key to the problem of independent learning lies in the phrase 'the learner has the need and the capacity to assume responsibility for his own continuing learning' (Jourard, 1972, p. 66).

Other educational psychologists question the proposition that learning can be defined as a single process. For example, Gagne identifies five *domains of the learning process,* each with its own praxis:

1. *Motor skills,* which are developed through practice.
2. *Verbal information,* the major requirement for learning being its presentation within an organized, meaningful context.
3. *Intellectual skills,* the learning of which appears to require prior learning of prerequisite skills.
4. *Cognitive strategies,* the learning of which requires repeated occasions in which challenges to thinking are presented.

5. *Attitudes,* which are learned most effectively through the use of human models and "vicarious reinforcement" (Gagne, 1972, pp. 3–41).

Tolman distinguished six "types of connections or relations" to be learned: (1) cathexes, (2) equivalence beliefs, (3) field expectancies, (4) field-cognition modes, (5) drive discriminations, and (6) motor patterns (Hilgard and Bower, 1966, pp. 211–213).

Bloom and his associates identified three domains of educational objectives: (1) cognitive, "which deal with the recall or recognition of knowledge and the development of intellectual abilities and skills"; (2) affective, "which describe changes in interest, attitudes, and values, and the development of appreciations and adequate adjustment"; and (3) psychomotor (Bloom, 1956, p. 7). Later scholars expanded on the psychomotor domain to include all the human senses and their dimensions.

It is certainly clear by now that learning is an elusive phenomenon. And, as we shall see next, the way people define it greatly influences how they theorize and go about effecting it. Until recently, educators of adults have been wallowing around in this same morass, and after wallowing around in it a bit more ourselves, we'll see how adult educators are beginning to extricate themselves.

SUMMARY

Exploring learning theory can be beneficial to policy-level executives, managers, learning specialists, and consultants by providing information that will allow better decisions and, ultimately more desirable learning experiences. However, doing so is not a simple task. In order to explore learning theory, we must understand several key concepts including the definition of theory, the distinction between learning and education, and the complexities involved in defining learning. We know that some learning theorists consider a theory to be a guiding set of assumptions, an ordering system that neatly summarizes the facts, and/or assumptions, generalizations, and hypotheses. Some psychologists, however, oppose the concept of learning theories. For instance, Gagne asserts that despite the "intellectual appeal," learning cannot be readily explained by theories. Analyzing the changes that occur as a student learns, according to Skinner, produces more valuable information than the "wasteful" and "misleading" procedures generated by theories. Despite these objections, we conclude that a theory is a comprehensive, coherent, and internally consistent system of ideas about a set of phenomena. We also acknowledge the distinction between education and learning. Education emphasizes the educator while learning emphasizes the person in whom the change occurs or is expected to occur. While this distinction is easily understood, developing a working definition of learning is much more complex. Key components of learning theorists' definitions of learning serve as the foundation for our discussion of the definition of learning. These include change; filling a need; learning as product; learning as process; learning as function; natural growth; control; shaping; development of competencies; fulfillment of potential; personal involvement; self-initiated; learner-evaluated; independent learning; and learning domains. We define learning as the process of gaining knowledge and/or expertise.

CHAPTER 3

Theories of Learning

Traditionally, we have known more about how animals learn than about how children learn; and we know much more about how children learn than about how adults learn. Perhaps this is because the study of learning was taken over early by experimental psychologists whose canons require the control of variables. And it is obvious that the conditions under which animals learn are more controllable than those under which children learn; and the conditions under which children learn are much more controllable than those under which adults learn.

The fact is that many of the "scientific" theories of learning have been derived from the study of learning by animals and children.

PROPOUNDERS AND INTERPRETERS

In general, there are two types of literature about learning theory: that produced by propounders of theories (who tend to be single-minded), and that produced by interpreters of theories (who tend to be reconciliatory). Admittedly, the distinction between propounders and interpreters is not absolute. For instance, some theorists, such as Pressey, Estes, Lorge, Gagne, Hilgard and Huhlen, have made contributions of both sorts.

Table 3-1 presents a historic list of the major propounders and interpreters in the literature of learning theory. To keep the list reasonably short, we have defined "major" as those who have made the greatest impact on the thinking of others. Those making contributions of both sorts have been placed in the column representing their major work. To provide a sense of historical development, the theorists are listed more or less in the order of appearance in the evolving body of literature.

Table 3-1
Propounders and Interpreters of Learning Theory

Propounders	Interpreters
Ebbinghaus (1885)	
Thorndike (1898)	
Angell (1896)	
Dewey (1896)	
Pavlov (1902)	
Woodworth (1906)	
Watson (1907)	
Judd (1908)	
Freud (1911)	
Kohler (1917)	
Tolman (1917)	
Wertheimer (1923)	
Koffka (1924)	Kilpatrick (1925)
Pressey (1926)	
Guthrie (1930)	Rugg (1928)
Skinner (1931)	Hilgard (1931)
Hall (1932)	
McGeoch (1932)	
Lewin (1933)	
Piaget (1935)	
Miller (1935)	
Spence (1936)	
Mowrer (1938)	
Katona (1940)	Bode (1940)
Maslow (1941)	Melton (1941)
Festinger (1942)	Cronbach (1943)
Rogers (1942)	Brunner (1943)
Estes (1944)	Lorge (1944)
Krech (1948)	
McClelland (1948)	
Sheffield (1949)	
Underwood (1949)	
Dollard (1950)	Schaie (1953)
Tyler (1950)	Garry (1953)
	Koch (1954)
	McKeachie (1954)
	Birren (1954)

(table continued on next page)

Table 3-1. Continued

Propounders	Interpreters
Bloom (1956)	Getzels (1956)
Bruner (1956)	Bugelski (1956)
Erikson (1959)	Kuhlen (1957)
Crowder (1959)	Kidd (1959)
Lumsdaine (1959)	Botwinick (1960)
Combs and Snygg (1959)	Miller (1960)
Ausubel (1960)	Glaser (1962)
Glaser (1962)	Flavell (1963)
Gagne (1963)	
	Hill (1963)
	Gage (1963)
	McDonald (1964)
Jourard (1964)	Goldstein (1965)
Suchman (1964)	Reese and Overton (1970)
Crutchfield (1969)	Goble (1971)
Friere (1970)	
Knowles (1970)	
Tough (1971)	
Houle (1972)	
Dave (1973)	
Loevinger (1976)	
Cross (1976)	
Botwinick (1977)	Howe (1977)
Gross (1977)	Knox (1977)
Srinivasan (1977)	
Cropley (1980)	Chickering (1981)
Mezirow (1981)	Darkenwald (1982)
Smith (1982)	Merriam (1982)
Wlodkowski (1985)	Brookfield (1986)
Daloz (1986)	

TYPES OF THEORIES

The proliferation of propounders has presented a major challenge to the interpreters in their quest to bring some sort of order to learning theories. Researchers have exerted considerable effort in their attempts to structure the system. However, no single, unified classification emerged from their early efforts. For instance, Hilgard and

Bower identify eleven categories of theories; whereas, McDonald identifies six, and Gage names three. Hilgard and Bower's eleven categories are:

Thorndike's Connectionism

Pavlov's Classical Conditioning

Guthrie's Contiguous Conditioning

Skinner's Operant Conditioning

Hull's Systematic Behavior Theory

Tolman's Purposive Behaviorism

Gestalt Theory

Freud's Psychodynamics

Functionalism

Mathematical Learning Theory

Information Processing Models

McDonald breaks the theories down into six categories in his analysis:

Recapitulation (Hull)

Connectionism (Thorndike)

Pragmatism (Dewey)

Gestalt and field theory (Ogden, Hartman, Lewin)

Dynamic psychology (Freud)

Functionalism (Judd) [McDonald, 1964, pp. 1–26]

Gage identifies three families of learning theories: (1) conditioning, (2) modeling, and (3) cognitive (Gage, 1972, p. 19). Kingsley and Garry provide two sets: (1) association or stimulus-response (Thorndike, Guthrie, and Hull), and (2) field theories (Lewin, Tolman, and the gestalt psychologists) (Kingsley and Garry, 1957, p. 83). Taba agrees with the two-family set, but uses different labels: (1) associationist or behaviorist theories, and (2) organismic, gestalt, and field theories (Taba, 1962, p. 80).

The work of Hilgard and Bower is perhaps the most comprehensively interpretive work to date. Their frustration in arranging the disparate categories of theories into a pattern is clearly expressed in their work.

Learning theories fall into two major families: *behaviorist/connectionist theories* and *cognitive/gestalt theories,* but not all theories belong to these two families. The behaviorist theories include such diverse theories as those of Thorndike, Pavlov, Guthrie, Skinner, and Hull. The cognitive theories include at least those of Tolman and the classical gestalt psychologists. Not completely and clearly classifiable in these terms are the theories of functionalism, psychodynamics, and the probabilistic theories of the model builders. The distinctions between the two families of theories are based not only on differences within learning theories: there are other specific issues upon which theories within one family may differ (Hilgard and Bower, 1966, p. 8).

Obviously, the interpreters had not succeeded up to this point in organizing the field of learning theories in a really fundamental way—at least not in a way that satisfied most of them, and certainly not Knowles. Then, in 1970, two developmental psychologists, Hayne W. Reese and Willis F. Overton, presented a way to conceptualize the theories in terms of larger models: mechanistic or elemental and organismic or holistic models. Then, the mist began to clear.

The Concept of Part and Whole Models of Development

Reese and Overton propose that, "Any theory presupposes a more general model according to which the theoretical concepts are formulated." The most general models are the world views or metaphysical systems that constitute basic models of the essential characteristics of man and indeed of the nature of reality (Reese and Overton, 1970, p. 117).

Two systems that have been pervasive in both the physical and the social sciences are the elemental world view, the basic metaphor of which is the machine, and the holistic world view, the basic metaphor of which is the organism—the living, organized system presented to experience in multiple forms. See Table 3-2.

Table 3-2
World Views or Metaphysical Systems

Elemental Model	Holistic Model
Represents the universe as a machine composed of discrete pieces operating in a spatio-temporal field: reactive and adaptive model of man.	Represents the world as a unitary, interactive, developing organism: active and adaptive model of man.

The *elemental model* represents the universe as a system composed of discrete pieces operating in a spatio-temporal field. These pieces—elementary particles in motion—and their relations form the basic reality to which all other more complex phenomena are ultimately reducible. When forces are applied in the operation of the system, a chain-like sequence of events results; and, since these forces are the only efficient or immediate causes of the events, complete prediction is possible—in principle. As Reese and Overton point out, ". . . consequently of the universe represented in this way, is that it is eminently susceptible to quantification" (Reese and Overton, p. 131).

The *holistic model* represents the universe as a unitary, interactive, developing organism. The essence of substance it perceives to be activity, rather than the static elementary particle. From such a point of view, one element can never be like another, and as a consequence, the logic of discovering reality according to the analytical ideal of reducing the many qualitative differences to the one is repudiated. In its place is substituted a search for unity among the many; that is, a pluralistic universe is substituted for a monistic one, and it is the diversity which constitutes the unity. Thus, unity is found in multiplicity, being is found in becoming, and constancy is found in change (Reese and Overton, p. 133).

The whole is therefore organic rather than mechanical in nature. "The nature of the whole, rather than being the sum of its parts, is presupposed by the parts and the whole constitutes the condition of the meaning and existence of the parts" (Reese and Overton). Accordingly, efficient cause is replaced by formal cause—cause by the essential nature of the form. Thus, the possibility of a predictive and quantifiable universe is precluded.

When applied to the sphere of epistemology and psychology, this world view results in an inherently and spontaneously active organism model of humans. It sees people as an active organism rather than a reactive organism, as a source of acts, rather than as a collection of acts initiated by external forces. It also represents individuals as an organized entity.

> . . . a configuration of parts which gain their meaning, their function, from the whole in which they are imbedded. From this point of view, the concepts of psychological structure and function, or means and ends, become central rather than derived. Inquiry is directed toward the discovery of principles of organization, toward the explanation of the nature and relation of parts and wholes, structures and functions, rather than toward the derivation of these from elementary processes.

> The individual who accepts this model will tend to emphasize the significance of processes over products, and qualitative change over quantitative change. . . . In addition, he/she will tend to emphasize the significance of the role of experience in facilitating or inhibiting the course of development, rather than the effect of training as the source of development. (Reese and Overton, pp. 133–134).

With this and the preceding set of concepts as a frame of reference, let us turn to a brief examination of the theories about learning derived from the study of learning in animals and children.

Theories Based on a Elemental Model

While John B. Watson (1878-1958) is considered the father of behaviorism, Edward L. Thorndike conducted the first systematic investigation in this country of the phenomenon we call learning. It was a study of learning in animals, first reported in his *Animal Intelligence*, published in 1898.

Thorndike conceived inexperienced learners to be empty organisms who more or less responded to stimuli randomly and automatically. A specific response is *connected* to a specific stimulus when it is reward-ed. In this situation, the stimulus, S, is entirely under the control of the experimenter (or teacher), and in large measure so is the response, R, for all the experimenter has to do to connect the particular R to a par-ticular S is to reward the R when the organism happens to make it. This association between sense impressions and impulses to action came to be known as a bond or a connection. Thus, Thorndike's sys-tem has sometimes been called bond psychology or *connectionism,* and was the original stimulus-response (or S-R) psychology of learning.

Thorndike developed three laws that he believed governed the learning of animals and human beings:

1. *the law of readiness* (the circumstances under which a learner tends to be satisfied or annoyed, to welcome or to reject);
2. *the law of exercise* (the strengthening of connections with prac-tice); and
3. *the law of effect* (the strengthening or weakening of a connection as a result of its consequences).

In the course of a long and productive life (he died in 1949), and with help from many collaborators, both friendly and critical, Thorndike's system of thought became greatly refined and elaborated. It provided the subfoundation of the behaviorist theories of learning.

While Thorndike conducted his work on connections in this coun-try, the Russian physiologist Ivan Pavlov (1849–1936) conducted his experiments that resulted in the concept of conditioned reflexes. Hil-gard describes his classical experiment.

When meat powder is placed in a dog's mouth, salivation takes place; the food is the *unconditioned stimulus* and salivation is the *unconditioned reflex.* Then some arbitrary stimulus, such as a light, is combined with the presentation of the food. Eventual-ly, after repetition and if time relationships are right, the light will evoke salivation independent of the food; the light is the *conditioned stimulus* and the response to it is the *conditioned reflex* (Hilgard and Bower, 1966, p. 48).

Pavlov's work resulted in a system that has been termed *classical conditioning* to distinguish it from later developments in *instrumental conditioning* and *operant conditioning*. In his system, he developed several concepts and accompanying techniques that have since been incorporated into the behaviorist system. These concepts are reinforcement, extinction, generalization, and differentiation. In *reinforcement,* a conditioned reflex becomes fixed by providing the conditioned stimulus and following it repeatedly with the unconditioned stimulus and response at appropriate time intervals. *Extinction* occurs when reinforcement is discontinued and the conditioned stimulus is presented alone, unaccompanied by the unconditioned stimulus. The conditioned response gradually diminishes and disappears. It becomes "extinct." In *generalization,* a conditioned reflex evoked to one stimulus can also be elicited by other stimuli, not necessarily similar to the first. A fourth basic concept Pavlov developed was *differentiation.* In differentiation, the initial generalization is overcome by the method of contrasts in which one of a pair of stimuli is regularly reinforced and the other is not; in the end, the conditioned reflex occurs only to the positive (reinforced) stimulus and not to the negative (nonreinforced) stimulus.

> The behaviorists, then and now, had and have in common the conviction that a science of psychology must be based upon a study of that which is overtly observable: physical stimuli, the muscular movements and glandular secretions which they arouse, and the environmental products that ensue. The behaviorists have differed among themselves as to what may be inferred in addition to what is measured, but they all exclude self-observation (Hilgard and Bower, 1966, p. 75).

Watson placed emphasis on kinesthetic stimuli as the integrators of animal learning and, applying this concept to human beings, conjectured that thought was merely implicit speech—that sensitive enough instruments would detect tongue movements or other movements accompanying thinking.

Edward R. Guthrie (1886–1959) built on the works of Thorndike, Pavlov, and Watson and added the *principle of contiguity of cue and response.* He stated his only law of learning, "from which all else about learning is made comprehensible," as follows: "A combination of stimuli which has accompanied a movement will on its recurrence tend to be followed by that movement" (Hilgard and Bower, 1966, p. 77). In his later work, Guthrie placed increasing emphasis on the part played by the learner in selecting the physical stimuli to which it would respond; hence, the *attention or scanning behavior* that goes on before association takes place became important.

Guthrie's system of thought was further clarified and formalized by his students, Voeks and Sheffield, but the next major advance in behaviorist psychology was the result of the work of B. E. Skinner and his associates. It is from their work that the educational technology of *programmed instruction* and teaching machines so popular in the 1960s has been derived. Skinner's ideas are summarized in Chapter 4.

Another development in behaviorist psychology occurring during the middle decades of the twentieth century was the construction of Clark L. Hull's *systematic behavior theory* and its elaboration by Miller, Mowrer, Spence, and others. Hull's theory is a conceptual descendant of Thorndike's, inasmuch as he adopted reinforcement as an essential characteristic of learning. Hull constructed an elaborate *mathematico-deductive* theory revolving around the central notion that there are intervening variables in the organism that influence what response will occur following the onset of a stimulus. He developed sixteen postulates regarding the nature and operation of these variables, and stated them in such precise terms that they were readily subjected to quantitative testing. Hilgard's assessment of the effect of Hull's work follows.

It must be acknowledged that Hull's system, for its time, was the best there was—not necessarily the one nearest to psychological reality, not necessarily the one whose generalizations were the most likely to endure—but the one worked out in the greatest detail, with the most conscientious effort to be quantitative throughout and at all points closely in touch with empirical tests. . . . Its primary contribution may turn out to lie not in its substance at all, but rather in the ideal it set for a genuinely systematic and quantitative psychological system far different from the schools which so long plagued psychology (Hilgard and Bower, p. 187).

Undoubtedly, Hull's work also stimulated the rash of mathematical models of learning which were developed after 1950 by Estes, Burke, Bush, Mosteller and others. It should be pointed out that these are not themselves learning theories, but mathematical representations of substantive theories.

Theories Based on an Holistic Model

John Dewey, in 1896, launched the first direct protest against the elemental model of the associationists. Although his work falls into the category of educational philosophy rather than learning theory, his emphasis on the role of interest and effort and on the child's motivation to solve his own problems became the starting point for a line of theorizing that has been given the label *functionalism*. Translated into schoolroom practices, functionalism provided the conceptual basis for progressive education, which, as Hilgard states, "at its best was an embodiment of the ideal of growth toward independence and self-control through interaction with an environment suited to the child's developmental level" (Hilgard and Bower, 1966, p. 299).

The spirit of experimentalism fostered by functionalism is reflected in the work of such learning theorists as Woodworth, Carr, McGeogh, Melton, Robinson, and Underwood. The essence of functionalism is summarized by Hilgard:

1. The functionalist is tolerant but critical.
2. The functionalist prefers continuities over discontinuities or typologies.
3. The functionalist is an experimentalist.
4. The functionalist is biased toward associationism and environmentalism (Hilgard and Bower, 1966, pp. 302-304).

In a sense, Edward C. Tolman (1886–1959) represents a bridge between the elemental and the holistic models. His system was behavioristic in that he rejected introspection as a method for psychological science, but it was *molar* rather than *molecular* behaviorism—an act of behavior has distinctive properties all its own, to be identified and described irrespective of the muscular, glandular, or neural processes that underlie it. But most importantly, he saw behavior as purposive—as being regulated in accordance with objectively determined ends. Purpose is, of course, an organismic concept. Tolman rejected the idea that learning is the association of particular responses to particular stimuli. In contrast to the associationists, who believed that it is the response or sequence of responses resulting in reward that is learned, Tolman believed it is the route to the goal that is learned. He believed that organisms, at their respective levels of ability, are capable of recognizing and learning the relationships between signs and desired goals; in short, they perceive the significance of the signs (Kingsley and Garry, 1957, p. 115). Tolman called his theory *purposive behaviorism.*

The most complete break with behaviorism occurred at the end of the first quarter of the twentieth century with the importation of the notion of insight learning in the gestalt theories of the Germans Wertheimer, Koffka, and Kohler. These theorists took issue with the proposition that all learning consisted of the simple connection of responses to stimuli, insisting that experience is always structured, that we react not to just a mass of separate details, but to a complex pattern of stimuli. And we need to perceive stimuli in organized wholes, not in disconnected parts. The learner tends to organize his or her perceptual field according to four laws:

1. *The law of proximity.* The parts of a stimulus pattern that are close together or near each other tend to be perceived in groups; therefore, the proximity of the parts in time and space affects the learner's organization of the field.

2. *The law of similarity and familiarity.* Objects similar in form, shape, color, or size tend to be grouped in perception; familiarity with an object facilitates the establishing of a figure-ground pattern. (Related to this law is the gestaltists' view of memory as the persistence of traces in the brain that allows a carryover from previous to present experiences. They view these traces not as static, but as modified by a continual process of integration and organization.)

3. *The law of closure.* Learners try to achieve a satisfying endstate of equilibrium; incomplete shapes, missing parts, and gaps in information are filled in by the perceiver. (Kingsley and Garry observe that "closure is to Gestalt psychology what reward is to association theory") (1957, p. 109).

4. *The law of continuation.* Organization in perception tends to occur in such a manner that a straight line appears to continue as a straight line, a part circle as a circle, and a three-sided square as a complete square.

Gestalt psychology is classified by most interpreters as within the family of *field theories*—theories which propose that the total pattern or field of forces, stimuli, or events determine learning.

Kurt Lewin (1890–1947) developed what he referred to specifically as a field theory. Using the topological concepts of geometry, Lewin conceptualized each individual as existing in a *life space* in which many forces are operating. The life space includes features of the environment to which the individual reacts—material objects encountered and manipulated, people met, and private thoughts, tensions, goals, and fantasies. Behavior is the product of the interplay of these forces, the direction and relative strength of which can be portrayed by the geometry of vectors. Learning occurs as a result of a change in cognitive structures produced by changes in two types of forces: (1) change in the structure of the cognitive field itself, or (2) change in the internal needs or motivation of the individual. Because of its emphasis on the immediate field of forces, field theory places more emphasis on motivation than on any of the preceding theories. Lewin felt that success was a more potent motivating force than reward and gave attention to the concepts of ego-involvement and level of aspiration as forces affecting success. He saw change in the relative attractiveness of one goal over another, which he called *valence,* as another variable affecting motivation. Since some of the strongest forces affecting an individual's psychological field are other people, Lewin became greatly interested in group and institutional dynamics; and, as we shall see later, it is in this dimension of education that his strongest influence has been felt.

Developments in the field-theoretical approach have more recently appeared under several labels: phenomenological psychology, perceptual psychology, humanistic psychology, and third-force psychology. Since the bulk of the work with this approach has been with adults, major attention to it will be reserved for a later section. Since phenomenologists are concerned with the study of the progressive development of the mind—or, as our contemporaries would insist, the person—they see man as an organism forever seeking greater personal adequacy. The urge for self-actualization is the driving force motivating all human behavior.

Two phenomenologists, Arthur Combs and Donald Snygg, have focused on the learning of children and the role of their educators, and their findings have important implications for learning theories. The flavor of Combs and Snygg's system of thought can be caught from statements from Pittenger and Gooding (1971).

- Man behaves in terms of what is real to him and what is related to his self at the moment of action (p. 130).

- Learning is a process of discovering one's personal relationship to and with people, things, and ideas. This process results in and from a differentiation of the phenomenal field of the individual (p. 136).

- Further differentiation of the phenomenological field occurs as an individual recognizes some inadequacy of a present organization. When a change is needed to maintain or enhance the phenomenal self, it is made by the individual as the right and proper thing to do. The role of the teacher is to facilitate the process (p. 144).

- Given a healthy organism, positive environmental influences, and a nonrestrictive set of percepts of self, there appears to be no forseeable end to the perceptions possible for the individual (pp. 150–1511).

- Transfer is a matter of taking current differentiations and using them as first approximations in the relationship of self to new situations (p. 157).

- Learning is permanent to the extent that it generates problems that may be shared by others and to the degree that continued sharing itself is enhancing (p. 165).

Two other contemporary psychologists, Jean Piaget and Jerome Bruner, have had great impact on thinking about learning, although they are not literally learning theorists. Their focus is on cognition and the theory of instruction. Piaget has conceptualized the process of the development of cognition and thought in evolutionary stages. According to Piaget, the behavior of the human organism starts with the organization of sensory-motor reactions and becomes more intelligent as coordination between the reactions to objects becomes progressively more interrelated and complex. Thinking becomes possible after language develops, and with it a new mental organization. This development involves the following evolutionary periods:

1. The formation of the symbolic or semiotic function (ages two to seven or eight)—which enables the individual to represent objects or events that are not at the moment perceptible by evoking them through the agency of symbols or differentiated signs.
2. The formation of concrete mental operations (ages seven or eight to eleven or twelve)—linking and dissociation of classes, the sources of classification; the linking of relations; correspondences, etc.
3. The formation of conceptual thought, or formal operations (ages eleven or twelve through adolescence)—"This period is characterized by the conquest of a new mode of reasoning, one that is no longer limited exclusively to dealing with objects or directly representable realities, but also employs 'hypotheses' . . ." (Piaget, 1970, pp. 30–33).

Some reservations have been expressed about the rigid age scale and minimization of individual differences in Piaget's schema, but his conception of evolutionary stages adds a dimension that is not generally given much attention in the established learning theories.

Jerome Bruner has also been interested in the process of intellectual growth, and his benchmarks were described in Chapter 2. His main interest, however, has been in the structuring and sequencing of knowledge and translating this into a *theory of instruction*. But Bruner does have a basic theory about the act of learning, which he views as involving three almost simultaneous processes: (1) acquisition of new information, often information that runs counter to or is a replacement of what the person has previously known, but which at the very least is a refinement of previous knowledge; (2) transformation, or the process of manipulating knowledge to make it fit new tasks; and (3) evaluation, or checking whether the way we have manipulated information is adequate to the task (Bruner, 1960, pp. 48-49). We shall return to this theory of instruction in a later chapter.

The main criticism of Piaget, Bruner, and other cognitive theorists by other adherents to the holistic model is that they are unbalanced in their overemphasis on cognitive skills at the expense of emotional development; that they are preoccupied with the aggressive, agentic, and autonomous motives to the exclusion of the homonymous, libidinal, and communal motives; and that they concern themselves with concept attainment to the exclusion of concept formation or invention (Jones, 1968, p. 97).

In the years following Piaget's pronouncements, new avenues opened in such learning-related fields of inquiry as neurophysiology (M. Boucouvalas, K. H. Pribrain, G. A. Miller, J. E. Delefresnaye, H. E. Harlow, D. P. Kimble, W. G. Walter, D. E. Wooldridge, J. Z. Young); mathematical modeling (R. C. Atkinson, R. R. Bush, W. K. Estes, R. D. Luce, E. Restle); information processing and cybernetics (H. Borko, E. A. Feigenbaum, B. E. Green, W. R. Reitman, K. M. Sayre, M. Yovitts, J. Singh, K. O. Smith); creativity (J. P. Guilford, R. P. Crawford, J. E. Drevdahl, A. Meadow, S. J. Parnes, J. W. Getzels, P. W. Jackson); and ecological psychology (R. G. Barker, P. V. Gump, H. E. Wright, E. P. Willems, H. L. Raush).

SUMMARY

Learning theory literature falls into two general types—that produced by propounders and that produced by interpreters. Many propounders of theories have made a concerted effort to impose order on the system of learning theory. Among these are Hilgard and Bower, McDonald, and Gage. It was Reese and Overton, however, who successfully conceptualized the theories within a larger construct—the concept of models of development. Reese and Overton postulated that "any theory presupposes a more general model according to which the theoretical concepts are formulated." Building upon this premise, they developed the elemental model and the holistic models of individuals. Among the theories based on the elemental model are Thorndike's connectionism, Pavlov's classical conditioning, and Watson's behaviorism. Other theories within this category were those developed by Guthrie, which both resulted in the principle of contiguity of cue and response and emphasized the importance of attention behavior. It was Guthrie's work that spawned additional research by Voeks, Sheffield, B. F. Skinner, and Hull's systematic behavior theory. Behaviorism was uniquely American and mirrored the philosophy of the turn-of-the century notion that all people could achieve great accomplishments given the opportunity (stimulus), individual initiative (response), and fair treatment (rewards).

Paralleling this effort were the holistic models. And, it was Dewey's work that initiated a line of theorizing called functionalism. Tolman, however, bridged the gap between cognitive and behavioral psychologies with a theory that he called purposive behaviorism. Gestalt theories, classified by most interpreters as within the family of field theories, paralleled behaviorism. The notable field theorist Lewin was intensely interested in group and institutional dynamics, and greatly influenced this educational dimension. Recent developments in the field-theoretical approach have appeared under the labels of phenomenological psychology, perceptual psychology, humanistic psychology, and cognitive psychology.

CHAPTER 4

A Theory of Adult Learning: Andragogy

Until fairly recently, there has been relatively little thinking, investigating, and writing about adult learning. This is a curious fact considering that the education of adults has been a concern of the human race for such a long time. Yet, for many years, the adult learner was indeed a neglected species.

The lack of research in this field is especially surprising in view of the fact that all of the great teachers of ancient times—Confucius and Lao Tse of China, the Hebrew prophets and Jesus in Biblical times, Aristotle, Socrates, and Plato in ancient Greece, and Cicero, Evelid, and Quintillian in ancient Rome—were all teachers of adults, not of children. Because their experiences were with adults, they developed a very different concept of the learning/teaching process from the one that later dominated formal education. They perceived learning to be a process of mental inquiry, not passive reception of transmitted content. Accordingly, they invented techniques for engaging learners in inquiry. The ancient Chinese and Hebrews invented what we now call the case method, in which the leader or one of the group members describes a situation, often in the form of a parable, and together with the group explores its characteristics and possible resolutions. The Greeks invented what we now call the Socratic dialogue, in which the leader or a group member poses a question or dilemma and the group members pool their thinking and experience to seek an answer or solution. The Romans were more confrontational: they used challenges that forced group members to state positions and then defend them.

In the seventh century in Europe, schools were organized for teaching children, primarily for preparing young boys for the priesthood. Hence, they became known as cathedral and monastic schools. Since the indoctrination of students in the beliefs, faith, and rituals of the church was the principal mission of these teachers, they developed a set of assumptions about learning and strategies for teaching that came to be labeled "pedagogy," literally meaning "the art and science of teaching children" (since the term is derived from the Greek words "paid," meaning "child," and "agogus," meaning "leader of"). This model of education persisted through the ages well into the twentieth century and was the basis of organization for our educational system.

Shortly after the end of World War I, both in this country and in Europe, a growing body of notions about the unique characteristics of adult learners began emerging. But only in the past few decades have these notions evolved into an integrated framework of adult learning. It is fascinating to trace this evolutionary process in this country.

TWO STREAMS OF INQUIRY

Beginning with the founding of the American Association for Adult Education in 1926 and the provision of substantial funding for research and publications by the Carnegie Corporation of New York, two streams of inquiry are discernible. One stream can be classified as the *scientific stream* and the other the *artistic or intuitive/reflective stream.* The scientific stream seeks to discover new knowledge through rigorous (and often experimental) investigation, and was launched by Edward L. Thorndike with the publication of his *Adult Learning* in 1928. The title is misleading, however, for Thorndike was not concerned with the processes of adult learning but rather with learning ability. His studies demonstrated that adults could learn, and that was important because it provided a scientific foundation for a field that had previously been based on the mere faith that adults could learn. Additions to this stream in the next decade included Thorndike's *Adult Interests* in 1935 and Herbert Sorenson *Adult Abilities* in 1938. By the onset of World War II, therefore, adult educators had scientific evidence that adults could learn and that they possessed interests and abilities that were different from those of children.

On the other hand, the artistic stream, which seeks to discover new knowledge through intuition and the analysis of experience, was concerned with how adults learn. This stream of inquiry was launched with the publication of Eduard C. Lindeman's *The Meaning of Adult Education* in 1926. Strongly influenced by the educational philosophy of John Dewey, Lindeman laid the foundation for a systematic theory about adult learning with such insightful statements as these:

> . . . the approach to adult education will be via the route of situations, not subjects. Our academic system has grown in reverse order: subjects and teachers constitute the starting point, students are secondary. In conventional education the student is required to adjust himself to an established curriculum; in adult education the curriculum is built around the student's needs and interests. Every adult person finds himself in specific situations with respect to his work, his recreation, his family life, his community life, etc.—situations which call for adjustments. Adult education begins at this point. Subject matter is brought into the situation, is put to work, when needed. Texts and teachers play a new and secondary role in this type of education; they must give way to the primary importance of the learners (Lindeman, 1926, pp. 8–9).

> . . . the resource of highest value in adult education is the learner's experience. If education is life, then life is also education. Too much of learning consists of vicarious substitution of someone else's experience and knowledge. Psychology is teaching us, however, that we learn what we do, and that therefore all genuine education will keep doing and thinking together. . . . Experience is the adult learner's living textbook (pp. 9–10).

> Authoritative teaching, examinations which preclude original thinking, rigid pedagogical formulae—all these have no place in adult education. . . . Small groups of aspiring adults who desire to keep their minds fresh and vigorous, who begin to learn by confronting pertinent situations, who dig down into the reservoirs of their experience before resorting to texts and secondary

facts, who are led in the discussion by teachers who are also searchers after wisdom and not oracles: this constitutes the setting for adult education, the modern quest for life's meaning (pp. 10–11).

Adult learning theory presents a challenge to static concepts of intelligence, to the standardized limitations of conventional education and to the theory which restricts educational facilities to an intellectual class. Apologists for the status quo in education frequently assert that the great majority of adults are not interested in learning, are not motivated in the direction of continuing education; if they possessed these incentives, they would, naturally, take advantage of the numerous free educational opportunities provided by public agencies. This argument begs the question and misconceives the problem. We shall never know how many adults desire intelligence regarding themselves and the world in which they live until education once more escapes the patterns of conformity. Adult education is an attempt to discover a new method and create a new incentive for learning; its implications are qualitative, not quantitative. Adult learners are precisely those whose intellectual aspirations are least likely to be aroused by the rigid, uncompromising requirements of authoritative, conventionalized institutions of learning (pp. 27–28).

Adult education is a process through which learners become aware of significant experience. Recognition of significance leads to evaluation. Meanings accompany experience when we know what is happening and what importance the event includes for our personalities (p. 1691).

Two excerpts from other Lindeman writings elaborate on these ideas:

I am conceiving adult education in terms of a new technique for learning, a technique as essential to the college graduate as to the unlettered manual worker. It represents a process by which the adult learns to become aware of and to evaluate his experience. To do this he cannot begin by studying "subjects" in the hope that some day this information will be useful. On the contrary, he begins by giving attention to situations in which he finds himself, to problems which include obstacles to his self-fulfillment. Facts and information from the differentiated spheres of knowledge are used, not for the purpose of accumulation, but because of need in solving problems. In this process the teacher finds a new function. He is no longer the oracle who speaks from the platform of authority, but rather the guide, the pointer-out who also participates in learning in proportion to the vitality and relevance of his facts and experiences. In short, my conception of adult education is this: a cooperative venture in nonauthoritarian, informal learning, the chief purpose of which is to discover the meaning of experience; a quest of the mind which digs down to the roots of the preconceptions which formulate our conduct; a technique of learning for adults which makes education coterminous with life and hence elevates living itself to the level of adventurous experiment (Gessner, 1956, p. 160).

One of the chief distinctions between conventional and adult education is to be found in the learning process itself. None but the humble become good teachers of adults. In an adult class the student's experience counts for as much as the teacher's knowledge. Both are exchangeable at par. Indeed, in some of the best adult classes it is sometimes difficult to discover who is learning most, the teacher or the students. This two-way learning is also reflected by shared authority. In conventional education the pupils adapt themselves to the curriculum offered, but in adult education the pupils aid in formulating the curricula. . . . Under democratic conditions authority is of the group. This is not an easy lesson to learn, but until it is learned democracy cannot succeed (p. 166).

These excerpts from the pioneering theorist are sufficient to portray a new way of thinking about adult learning, yet it is important to note that Lindeman (1926) also identified several key assumptions about adult learners. His assumptions, listed below and summarized in Table 4-1, have been supported by later research and constitute the foundation of adult learning theory:

1. Adults are motivated to learn as they experience needs and interests that learning will satisfy; therefore, these are the appropriate
   starting points for organizing adult learning activities.

2. Adults' orientation to learning is life-centered; therefore, the
   appropriate units for organizing adult learning are life situations,
   not subjects.

3. Experience is the richest resource for adults' learning; therefore,
   the core methodology of adult education is the analysis of experience.

4. Adults have a deep need to be self-directing; therefore, the role
   of the teacher is to engage in a process of mutual inquiry with
   them rather than to transmit his or her knowledge to them and
   then evaluate their conformity to it.

5. Individual differences among people increase with age; therefore,
   adult education must make optimal provision for differences in
   style, time, place, and pace of learning.

Table 4-1
Summary of Lindeman's Key Assumptions About Adult Learners

1. Adults are motivated to learn as they experience needs and interests that
   learning will satisfy.
2. Adults' orientation to learning is life-centered.
3. Experience is the richest source for adults' learning.
4. Adults have a deep need to be self-directing.
5. Individual differences among people increase with age.

It is interesting to note that Lindeman did not dichotomize adult
versus youth education, but rather adult versus "conventional" education. The implication here is that youths might learn better, too,
when their needs and interests, life situations, experience, self-concepts, and individual differences are taken into account. The artistic
stream of inquiry that Lindeman launched in 1926 flowed on through
the pages of the *Journal of Adult Education,* the quarterly publication
of the American Association for Adult Education, which between
February 1929 and October 1941, provided the most distinguished
body of literature yet produced in the field of adult education. The
following excerpts from its articles reveal the growing collection of

insights about adult learning gleaned from the experience of successful practitioners.

By Lawrence P. Jacks, principal of Manchester College, Oxford,
England:

> Earning and living are not two separate departments or opera-
> tions in life. They are two names for a continuous process looked
> at from opposite ends. . . . A type of education based on this
> vision of continuity is, obviously, the outstanding need of our
> times. Its outlook will be lifelong. It will look upon the industry
> of civilization as the great "continuation school" for intelligence
> and for character, and its object will be, not merely to fit men and
> women for the specialized vocations they are to follow, but also
> to animate the vocations themselves with ideals of excellence
> appropriate to each. At the risk of seeming fantastic I will venture
> to say that the final objective of the New Education is the grad-
> ual transformation of the industry of the world into the universi-
> ty of the world; in other words, the gradual bringing about of a
> state of things in which "breadwinning" and "soulsaving"
> instead of being, as now, disconnected and often opposed opera-
> tions, shall become a single and continuous operation (*Journal of
> Adult Education*, I, 1, February 1929, pp. 7–10).

By Robert D. Leigh, president of Bennington College:

> At the other end of the traditional academic ladder the adult
> educational movement is forcing recognition of the value and
> importance of continuing the learning process indefinitely . . . .
> But among the far-seeing leaders of the movement in the United
> States it is recognized not so much as a substitute for inadequate
> schooling in youth as an educational opportunity superior to
> that offered in youth—superior because the learner is motivated
> not by the artificial incentives of academic organization, but by
> the honest desire to know and to enrich his experience, and
> because the learner brings to his study relevant daily experience,
> and consequently the new knowledge takes root firmly, strikes
> deep, and feeds on what the day's life brings it.

There is gradually emerging, therefore, a conception of education as a lifelong process beginning at birth and ending only with death, a process related at all points to the life experiences of the individual, a process full of meaning and reality to the learner, a process in which the student is active participant rather than passive recipient (*Journal of Adult Education*, II, 2, April 1930, p. 123).

By David L. Mackaye, director of the Department of Adult Education, San Jose, California, public schools:

A person is a good educator among adults when he has a definite conviction about life and when he can present intelligent arguments on behalf of it; but primarily he does not qualify as an adult educator at all until he can exist in a group that collectively disputes, denies, or ridicules his conviction, and continues to adore him because he rejoices in them. That is tolerance, an exemplification of Proudhon's contention that to respect a man is a higher intellectual feat than to love him as one's self. . . . there is positive evidence that no adult education system will ever make a success of collegiate methods of instruction to adults in the cultural fields. Something new in the way of content and method must be produced as soon as possible for adult education, and probably it will have to grow up in the field. No teacher-training-college hen can lay an adult education egg (*Journal of Adult Education*, III, 3, June 1931, pp. 293-294).

By Maria Rogers, volunteer worker, New York City Adult Education Council:

One type of adult education merits particular consideration and wider use by educators seeking new methods. Though meagerly publicized, it has proved effective in numerous instances. It has undertaken a far more difficult task than that assumed by the institutions for adult education which confine their concept of method to the sequence of procedure established for adults who enter classrooms to learn something already set up to be learned. Its prime objective is to make the group life of adults yield educational value to the participants. . . .

The educator who uses the group method of education takes ordinary, gregarious human beings for what they are, searches out the groups in which they move and have their being, and then helps them to make their group life yield educational values (*Journal of Adult Education*, X, October 1938, pp. 409–411).

By Ruth Merton, director of the Education Department, Milwaukee Y.W.C.A.:

In a day school, where the students are usually children or young adolescents, a learned teacher-ignorant pupil relationship is almost inevitable, and frequently it has its advantages. But in a night school the situation is entirely different. Here, so far as the class is concerned, the teacher is an authority upon one subject only, and each of the students has, in his own particular field, some skill or knowledge that the teacher does not possess. For this reason, there is a spirit of give and take in a night-school class that induces a feeling of comradeship in learning, stimulating to teacher and students alike. And the quickest way to achieve this desirable state is through laughter in which all can join.

And so I say again that, if we are really wise, we teachers in night schools will, despite taxes or indigestion, teach merrily! (*Journal of Adult Education*, XI, April 1939, p. 178).

By Ben M. Cherrington, chief of the Division of Cultural Relations, United States Department of State:

Authoritarian adult education is marked throughout by regimentation demanding obedient conformity to patterns of conduct handed down from authority. Behavior is expected to be predictable, standardized. . . . Democratic adult education employs the method of self-directing activity, with free choice of subject matter and free choice in determining outcomes. Spontaneity is welcome. Behavior cannot with certainty be predicted and therefore is not standardized. Individual, critical thinking is perhaps the best description of the democratic method and it is here that the gulf is widest between democracy and the authoritarian system (*Journal of Adult Education*, XI, 3, June 1939, pp. 244–245).

By Wendell Thomas, author of *Democratic Philosophy* and a teacher of adult education teachers in New York City:

> On the whole, adult education is as different from ordinary schooling as adult life, with its individual and social responsibilities, is different from the protected life of the child. . . . The adult normally differs from the child in having both more individuality and more social purpose.
>
> Adult education, accordingly, makes special allowance for individual contributions from the students, and seeks to organize these contributions into some form of social purpose (*Journal of Adult Education, XI, 4, October 1939, pp. 365–366*).

By Harold Fields, acting assistant director of Evening Schools, Board of Education, New York City:

> Not only the content of the courses, but the method of teaching also must be changed. Lectures must be replaced by class exercises in which there is a large share of student participation. "Let the class do the work" should be adopted as a motto. There must be ample opportunity for forums, discussions, debates. Newspapers, circulars, and magazines as well as textbooks should be used for practice in reading. Extracurricular activities should become a recognized part of the educational process. . . . These are some of the elements that must be incorporated in a program of adult education for citizens if it is to be successful (*Journal of Adult Education*, XII, January 1940, pp. 44–45).

By 1940 most of the elements required for a comprehensive theory of adult learning had been discovered, but they had not yet been brought together into a unified framework; they remained as isolated insights, concepts, and principles. During the 1940s and 1950s these elements were clarified, elaborated on, and added to in a veritable explosion of knowledge from the various disciplines in the human sciences. (It is interesting to note that during this period there was a gradual shift in emphasis in research away from the highly quantitative, fragmentary, experimental research of the 1930s and 1940s to more holistic longitudinal case studies with a higher yield of useful knowledge.)

CONTRIBUTIONS FROM THE SOCIAL SCIENCES

Clinical Psychology

Some of the most important contributions to learning theory have come from the discipline of psychotherapy. After all, psychotherapists are primarily concerned with reeducation, and their subjects are overwhelmingly adults. (See Table 4-2 for summary.)

Sigmund Freud has influenced psychological thinking more than any other individual, but he did not formulate a theory of learning as such. His major contribution was no doubt in identifying the influence of the subconscious mind on behavior. Some of his concepts such as anxiety, repression, fixation, regression, aggression, defense mechanism, projection, and transference (in blocking or motivating learning) have had to be considered by learning theorists. Freud was close to the behaviorists in his emphasis on the animalistic nature of man, but he saw the human being as a dynamic animal that grows and develops through the interaction of biological forces, goals, purposes, conscious and unconscious drives, and environmental influences. This is a concept more in keeping with the organismic model.

Carl Jung advanced a more holistic concept of human consciousness, introducing the notion that it possesses four functions or four ways to extract information from experience to achieve internalized understanding: sensation, thought, emotion, and intuition. His plea for the development and use of all four functions in balance laid the groundwork for the concepts of the balanced personality and the balanced curriculum.

Erik Erikson provided the "eight ages of man," the last three occurring during the adult years, as a framework for understanding the stages of personality development:

1. Oral-sensory, in which the basic issue is trust vs. mistrust.

2. Muscular-anal, in which the basic issue is autonomy vs. shame.

3. Locomotion-genital, in which the basic issue is initiative vs. guilt.

4. Latency, in which the basic issue is industry vs. inferiority.

5. Puberty and adolescence, in which the basic issue is identity vs. role confusion.

6. Young adulthood, in which the basic issue is intimacy vs. isolation.

7. Adulthood, in which the basic issue is generativity vs. stagnation.

8. The final stage, in which the basic issue is integrity vs. despair.

In fact, the central role of self-concept in human development (and learning) received increasing reinforcement from the entire field of psychiatry as it moved away from the medical model toward an educational model in its research and practice. (See especially the works of Erich Fromm and Karen Horney.)

But it is the clinical psychologists, especially those who identify themselves as humanistic, who have concerned themselves most deeply with problems of learning. The humanistic psychologists speak of themselves as "third-force psychologists." In Goble's words, "By 1954 when Maslow published his book *Motivation and Personality,* there were two major theories dominant" in the behavioral sciences, Freudianism and behaviorism, in which "Freud placed the major motivational emphasis on deep inner drives (and) urges and the behaviorists placed the emphasis on external, environmental influences." But "like Freud and like Darwin before him, the behaviorists saw man as merely another type of animal, with no essential differences from animals and with the same destructive, anti-social tendencies" (Goble, 1971, pp. 3-8). Third-force psychologists are concerned with the study and development of fully functioning persons (to use Rogers' term) or self-actualizing persons (to use Maslow's). They are critical of the atomistic approach common in physical science and among the behaviorists, breaking things down into their component parts and studying them separately.

Most behavioral scientists have attempted to isolate independent drives, urges, and instincts and study them separately. Maslow found this to be generally less productive than the holistic approach that holds that the whole is more than the sum of the parts (Goble, 1971, p. 22).

Growth takes place when the next step forward is subjectively more delightful, more joyous, more intrinsically satisfying than the previous gratification with which we have become familiar and even bored; that the only way we can ever know that it is right for us is that it feels better subjectively than any alternative. The new experience validates itself rather than by any outside criterion (Maslow, 1972, p. 43).

Maslow placed special emphasis on the role of safety, which the following formulation of the elements in the growth process illustrates:

1. The healthily spontaneous [person], in his spontaneity, from within out, reaches out to the environment in wonder and interest, and expresses whatever skills he has.

2. He does this to the extent that he is not crippled by fear and to the extent that he feels safe enough to dare.

3. In this process, that which gives him the delight-experience is fortuitously encountered, or is offered to him by helpers.

4. He must be safe and self-accepting enough to be able to choose and prefer these delights, instead of being frightened by them.

5. If he can choose these experiences, which are validated by the experience of delight, then he can return to the experience, repeat it, savor it to the point of repletion, satiation, or boredom.

6. At this point, he shows the tendency to go on to richer, more complex experiences and accomplishments in the same sector (if he feels safe enough to dare).

7. Such experiences not only mean moving on, but have a feedback effect on the Self, in the feeling of certainty ("This I like; that I don't for sure"), of capability, mastery, self-trust, self-esteem.

8. In this never ending series of choices of which life consists, the choice may generally be schematized as between safety (or, more broadly, defensiveness) and growth, and since only that [person] doesn't need safety who already has it, we may expect the growth choice to be made by the safety-need gratified [individual].

9. In order to be able to choose in accord with his own nature and to develop it, the [individual] must be permitted to retain the subjective experiences of delight and boredom, as the criteria of the correct choice for him. The alternative criterion is making the choice in terms of the wish of another person. The Self is lost when this happens. Also this constitutes restricting the choice to safety alone, since the [individual] will give up trust in his own delight criterion out of fear (of losing protection, love, etc.).

10. If the choice is really a free one, and if the [individual] is not crippled, then we may expect him ordinarily to choose progression forward.

11. The evidence indicates that what delights the healthy [person], what tastes good to him, is also, more frequently than not, "best" for him in terms of far goals as perceivable by the spectator.

12. In this process the environment [parents, teachers, therapists] is important in various ways, even though the ultimate choice must be made by the individual.

    a. It can gratify his basic needs for safety, belongingness, love and respect, so that he can feel unthreatened, autonomous, interested and spontaneous and thus dare to choose the unknown;

    b. It can help by making the growth choice positively attractive and less dangerous, and by making regressive choice less attractive and more costly.

13. In this way the psychology of Being and the psychology of Becoming can be reconciled, and the [person], simply being himself, can yet move forward and grow (Maslow, 1972, pp. 50–51).

Carl R. Rogers, starting with the viewpoint that "in a general way, therapy is a learning process," (1951, p. 132) developed nineteen propositions for a theory of personality and behavior which were evolved from the study of adults in therapy (pp. 483–524) and then sought to apply them to education. This process led him to conceptualize *student-centered teaching* as parallel to client-centered therapy (pp. 388–391).

Rogers' student-centered approach to education was based on five "basic hypotheses," the first of which was: *We cannot teach another person directly; we can only facilitate his learning.* This hypothesis stems from the propositions in his personality theory that "Every individual exists in a continually changing world of experience of which he is the center," and "The organism reacts to the field as it is experienced and perceived." It requires a shift in focus from what the teacher does to what is happening in the student.

His second hypothesis was: *A person learns significantly only those things which he perceives as being involved in the maintenance of, or enhancement of, the structure of self.* This hypothesis underlines the importance of making the learning relevant to the learner, and puts into question the academic tradition of required courses.

Rogers grouped his third and fourth hypotheses together: *Experience which, if assimilated, would involve a change in the organization of self, tends to be resisted through denial or* distortion of symbolization, and *the structure and organization of self appear to become more* rigid under threats and to relax its boundaries when completely free from threat. Experience that is perceived as inconsistent with the self can only be assimilated if the current organization of self is relaxed and expanded to include it. These hypotheses acknowledge the reality that significant learning is often threatening to an individual, and suggest the importance of providing an acceptant and supportive climate, with heavy reliance on student responsibility.

Rogers' fifth hypothesis extends the third and fourth to educational practice. *The educational situation which most effectively promotes significant learning is one in which (a) threat to the self of the learner is reduced to a minimum, and (b) differentiated perception of the field is facilitated.* He points out that the two parts of this hypothesis are almost synonymous, since *differentiated perception* is most likely when the self is not being threatened. Rogers defined undifferentiated perception as an individual's "tendency to see experience in absolute and unconditional terms, to anchor his reactions in space and time, to confuse fact and evaluation, to rely on ideas rather than upon reality testing," in contrast to differentiated perception as the tendency "to see things in limited, differentiated terms, to be aware of the space-time anchorage of facts, to be dominated by facts, not concepts, to evaluate in multiple ways, to be aware of different levels of abstraction, to test his inferences and abstractions by reality, in so far as possible" (p. 1441).

Rogers sees learning as a completely internal process controlled by the learner and engaging his whole being in interaction with his environment as he perceives it. But he also believes that learning is as natural—and as required—a life process as breathing. His Proposition IV states: *The organism has one basic tendency and striving—to actualize, maintain, and enhance the experiencing organism.* (p. 497). This central premise is summarized in the following statement:

> Clinically, I find it to be true that though an individual may remain dependent because he has always been so, or may drift into dependence without realizing what he is doing, or may temporarily wish to be dependent because his situation appears desperate. I have yet to find the individual who, when he examines his situation deeply, and feels that he perceives it dearly, deliberately chooses dependence, deliberately chooses to have the integrated direction of himself undertaken by another. When all the elements are clearly perceived, the balance seems invariably in the direction of the painful but ultimately rewarding path of self-actualization and growth (p. 490).

Both Maslow and Rogers acknowledge their affinity with the works of Gordon Allport (1955, 1960, 1961) in defining growth not as a process of "being shaped," but a process of becoming. The essence of their conception of learning is captured in this brief statement by Rogers: I should like to point out one final characteristic of these individuals as they strive to discover and become themselves. It is that the individual seems to become more content to be a process rather than a product (1961, p. 122).

Developmental Psychology

The discipline of developmental psychology has contributed a growing body of knowledge about changes with age through the life span in such characteristics as physical capabilities, mental abilities, interests, attitudes, values, creativity, and life styles. Pressey and Kuhlen (1957) pioneered in the collection of research findings on human development and laid the foundation for a new field of spe-

Table 4-2
Major Contributions of Clinical Psychologists

Sigmund Freud	Identified influence of subconscious mind on behavior
Carl Jung	Introduced notion that human consciousness possesses four functions: sensation, thought, emotion, and intuition
Erik Erikson	Provided "Eight Ages of Man": Oral-sensory, muscular-anal, locomotion-genital, latency, puberty and adolescene, young adulthood, adulthood, and final stage
Abraham Maslow	Emphasized the role of safety
Carl Rogers	Conceptualized a student-centered approach to education based on five "basic hypotheses": 1. We cannot teach another person directly, we can only facilitate his learning 2. A person learns significantly only those things which he perceives as being involved in the maintenance of, or enhancement of, the structure of self 3. Experience which, if assimilated would involve a change in the organization of self, tends to be resisted through denial or distortion of symbolization 4. The structure and organization of self appear to become more rigid under threat and to relax its boundaries when completely free from threat. Experience which is perceived as inconsistent with the self can only be assimilated if the current organization of self is relaxed and expanded to include it 5. The educational situation which most effectively promotes significant learning is one in which (a) threat to the self of the learner is reduced to a minimum, and (b) differentiated perception of the field is facilitated.

cialization in psychology—life-span developmental psychology—which has been built on by such contemporary scholars as Bischof (1969) and Goulet and Baltes (1970). Havighurst (1972) identified the developmental tasks associated with different stages of growth that give rise to a person's readiness to learn different things at different times and create "teachable moments." Sheehy (1974) provided a popular portrayal of the "Predictable Crises of Adult Life" and Knox

(1977) provided a more scholarly summary of research findings on adult development and learning. (See also Stevens-Long, 1979; Stokes, 1983.) Closely related to this discipline is gerontology, which has produced a large volume of research findings regarding the aging process in the later years (Birren, 1964; Botwinick, 1967; Donahue and Tibbitts, 1957; Grabowski and Mason, 1974; Granick and Patterson, 1971; Gubrium, 1976; Kastenbaum, 1964 and 1965; Neugarten, 1964 and 1968; Woodruff and Birren, 1975) and their implications for learning and teaching (Burnside, 1978; Hendrickson, 1973; John, 1987; Long, 1972).

Sociology and Social Psychology

The disciplines of sociology and social psychology have contributed a great deal of new knowledge about the behavior of groups and larger social systems, including the forces that facilitate or inhibit learning and change (Argyris, 1964; Bennis, 1966; Bennis, Benne and Chin, 1968; Bennis and Slater, 1968; Etzioni, 1961 and 1969; Hare, 1969; Knowles and Knowles, 1972; Lewin, 1951; Lippitt, 1969; Schein and Bennis, 1965; Schlossberg, Lynch, and Chickering, 1989; Zander, 1982) and about environmental influences, such as culture, race, population characteristics, and density, on learning. (Barker, 1963, 1968, 1978; Bronfenbrenner, 1979; Moos, 1974, 1976, 1979; Jensen, et al, 1964, pp. 113–175; Harris and Moran, 1996; Moran and Harris, 1982).

Philosophy

Philosophical issues have been prominent in the literature of the adult education movement in this country since its beginning. Eduard Lindeman laid the foundation of this theme in his *The Meaning of Adult Education* in 1926 (See also Gessner, 1956), and it was reinforced by Lyman Bryson in his *Adult Education* in 1936 and *The Next America* in 1952. But many of the articles in the periodicals of the American Association for Adult Education between 1926 and 1948 were also philosophical treatises, with the aims and purposes of adult education as a social movement as the predominant issue. The underlying premise of the argument was that achieving a unified and potent adult education movement required a common goal among all programs in all institutions—one side holding that this goal should be the improvement of individuals, and the other holding that it should be the improvement of society. Two attempts were made in the mid-fifties, under the sponsorship of the Fund for Adult Education of the Ford Foundation, to sway argument in favor of the latter position with the publication of Hartley Grattan's *In Quest of Knowledge* (1955) and John Walker Powell's *Learning Comes of Age* (1956). However, this issue and arguments over other issues continued to embroil the field.

Professional philosopher, Kenneth Benne, president of the newly formed Adult Education Association of the USA in 1956, dedicated his efforts to bringing some order to the polemics. One of his first acts as president was to convene a national conference on the "Philosophy of Adult Education," in North Andover, Massachusetts, in which thirteen philosophers and adult educators from across the country spent three days addressing these issues:

- What is the purpose of adult education—adult education for what?
- What is the relationship between content and method in instruction?
- Should individual interests and desires prescribe the curricula of adult education, or should the needs of society play a determining role in the creation of educational programs?
- What implications do different theories of knowledge, or of the nature of man and society, have for the planning and operation of adult education programs?

The 1956 conference did not resolve these issues, but it produced three positive results:

1. It uncovered some tool concepts that would prove useful in working through the strife of tongues and the maze of special interests and moved the emphasis toward areas of genuine agreement and disagreement.
2. It revealed the importance of philosophizing as a necessary and continuing ingredient of all policy formulation and program determination.

3. It furnished an example of the pains and tribulations that men from many disciplines and from many special vantage points in adult education encounter as they venture seriously and thoughtfully to seek common ground in their chosen field (Sillars, 1958, p. 5).

Clearly, it stimulated continuing discussion of the philosophical issues in adult education, as evidenced by numerous articles in the periodical literature and at least four major books by the following authors: Benne, 1968; Bergevin, 1967; Elias and Merriam, 1980; and Darkenwald and Merriam, 1982. It probably also influenced the publication of one book on philosophy for adult learners (Buford, 1980) and one book on the use of philosophical approaches to the improvement of practice in continuing education (Apps, 1985).

CONTRIBUTIONS FROM ADULT EDUCATION

Most scholars in the field of adult education itself have addressed the problem of learning by trying to adapt theories about child learning to the "differences in degree" among adults. (For example, Bruner, 1959; Kidd, 1959; Kempfer, 1955; Verner and Booth, 1964.) For the most part, Howard McClusky followed this line, but began to map out directions for the development of a "differential psychology of the adult potential" in which the concepts of margin (the power available to a person over and beyond that required to handle his load), commitment, time perception, critical periods, and self concept are central.

Cyril O. Houle began a line of investigations in the 1950s at the University of Chicago that has been extended by Allen Tough at the Ontario Institute for Studies in Education that has to yield better understanding about the process of adult learning. Their approach was a study through in-depth interviews of a small sample of adults who were identified as continuing learners.

Houle's study of twenty-two subjects was designed to discover primarily why adults engage in continuing education, but it also sheds some light on how they learn. Through an involved process of the analysis of the characteristics uncovered in the interviews, he found that his subjects could be fitted into three categories. As Houle points out, "These are not pure types; the best way to represent them pictorially would be by three circles which overlap at their edges. But the central emphasis of each subgroup is clearly discernible" (Houle, 1961, p. 16). The criterion for classifying the individuals into subgroups was the major conception they held about the purposes and values of continuing education for themselves. The three types are:

1. The *goal-oriented learners,* who use education for accomplishing fairly clear-cut objectives. These individuals usually did not make any real start on their continuing education until their middle twenties and after—sometimes much later.

   The continuing education of the goal-oriented is in episodes, each of which begins with the realization of a need or the identification of an interest. There is no even, steady, continuous flow to the learning of such people, though it is an ever-recurring characteristic of their lives. Nor do they restrict their activities to any one institution or method of learning. The need or interest appears and they satisfy it by taking a course, or joining a group, or reading a book or going on a trip (p. 181).

2. The *activity-oriented,* who take part because they find in the circumstances of the learning a meaning which has no necessary connection—and often no connection at all—with the content or the announced purpose of the activity. These individuals also begin their sustained participation in adult education at the point when their problems or their needs become sufficiently pressing.

   All of the activity-oriented people interviewed in this study were course-takers and group-joiners. They might stay within a single institution or they might go to a number of different places, but it was social contact that they sought and their selection of any activity was essentially based on the amount and kind of human relationships it would yield (pp. 23–24).

3. The *learning-oriented,* who seek knowledge for its own sake. Unlike the other types, most learning-oriented adults have been engrossed in learning as long as they can remember. What they do has a continuity, a flow and a spread which establish the basic nature of their participation in continuing education. For the most part, they are avid readers and have been since childhood; they join groups and classes and organizations for educational reasons; they select the serious programs on television and

radio; when they travel . . . they make a production out of it, being sure to prepare adequately to appreciate what they see; and they choose jobs and make other decisions in life in terms of the potential for growth which they offer (pp. 24–25).

Tough's investigation was concerned not only with what and why adults learn, but how they learn and what help they obtain for learning. Tough found that adult learning is a very pervasive activity.

Almost everyone undertakes at least one or two major learning efforts a year, and some individuals undertake as many as 15 or 20. . . . It is common for a man or woman to spend 700 hours a year at learning projects. . . . About 70 percent of all learning projects are planned by the learner himself, who seeks help and subject matter from a variety of acquaintances, experts, and printed resources (Tough, 1979, p. 1).

Tough found that his subjects organized their learning efforts around "projects . . . defined as a series of related episodes, adding up to at least seven hours. In each episode more than half of the person's total motivation is to gain and retain certain fairly clear knowledge and skill, or to produce some other lasting change in himself" (p. 6).

He found that in some projects the episodes may be related to the desired knowledge and skill. For example, the learner may want to learn more about India. In one episode he/she reads about the people of India; in another episode the learner discusses the current economic and political situation with an Indian graduate student; in a third, he or she watches a television program describing the life of an Indian child. The episodes can also be related by the use to which the knowledge and skill will be put. For instance, one person might engage in a project consisting of a number of learning experiences to improve parenting skills; another project might consist of episodes aimed at obtaining the knowledge and skills necessary for building a boat.

Tough was interested in determining what motivated adults to begin a learning project, and overwhelmingly found that his subjects anticipated several desired outcomes and benefits. Some of the benefits are immediate: satisfying a curiosity, enjoying the content itself, enjoying practicing the skill, enjoying the activity of learning; others are long-run: producing something, imparting knowledge or skill to others, understanding what will happen in some future situation, etc. Clearly, pleasure and self-esteem were critical elements in the motivation of Tough's subjects.

Tough concluded that adult learners proceed through several phases in the process of engaging in a learning project, and speculated that helping them gain increased competence in dealing with each phase might be one of the most effective ways of improving their learning effectiveness.

The first phase is deciding to begin. Tough identified twenty-six possible steps the learner might take during this phase, including setting an action goal, assessing interests, seeking information regarding certain opportunities, choosing the most appropriate knowledge and skill, establishing a desired level or amount, and estimating the cost and benefits.

A second phase is choosing the planner, which may be the learner, an object (e.g., programmed text, workbook, tape recording), an individual learning consultant (e.g., instructor, counselor, resource person), or a group. Competence in choosing a planner and proactively, rather than reactively, using the planner in a collaborative rather than dependent manner were found to be crucial in this phase.

Finally, the learner engages in learning episodes sketched out in the planning process. The critical elements here are the variety and richness of the resources, their availability, and the learner's skill in making use of them.

Tough emerged from his study with this challenging vision regarding future possibilities in adult learning:

> The last 20 years have produced some important new additions to the content of adult learning projects. Through group and individual methods, many adults now set out to increase their self-insight, their awareness and sensitivity with other persons and their interpersonal competence. They learn to "listen to themselves," to free their bodies and their conversations from certain restrictions and tensions, to take a risk, to be open and congruent. Attempting to learn this sort of knowledge and skill seemed incredible to most people 20 years ago. Great changes in our conception of what people can and should set out to learn

have been created by T-groups, the human potential movement, humanistic psychology, and transpersonal psychology.

Perhaps the next 20 years will produce several important additions to what we try to learn. In 1990, when people look back to our conception of what adults can learn, will they be amused by how narrow it is (pp. 43–44)?

Tough's prediction in the final paragraph has been borne out. Since he made it, a rising volume of research on adult learning has been reported. Most of this research builds on, reinforces, and refines the research of Tough's "last 20 years," especially in regard to the developmental stages of the adult years. Predictions are that the major new discoveries in the next decade will be related to the physiology and chemistry of learning, with special implications for the acceleration of learning and the efficiency of information processing.

THE ROOTS OF ANDRAGOGY—AN INTEGRATIVE CONCEPT

Attempts to bring the isolated concepts, insights, and research findings regarding adult learning together into an integrated framework began as early as 1949, with the publication of Harry Overstreet's *The Mature Mind*. Other related publications followed including *Informal Adult Education* (Knowles, 1950), *An Overview of Adult Education Research* (Bruner, 1959), *How Adults Learn* (Kidd, 1973), J.R. Gibb's chapter on "Learning Theory in Adult Education" in the *Handbook of Adult Education* in the United States in 1960, and *Teaching and Learning in Adult Education* (Miller, 1964). However, these turned out to be more descriptive listings of concepts and principles than comprehensive, coherent, and integrated theoretical frameworks. What was needed was an integrative and differentiating concept.

Such a concept had been evolving in Europe for some time—the concept of an integrated framework of adult learning for which the label *andragogy* had been coined to differentiate it from the theory of youth learning, *pedagogy*. Dusan Savicevic, a Yugoslavian adult educator, first introduced the concept and label into the American culture in 1967, and Knowles wrote the article, "Androgogy, Not Pedagogy," in *Adult Leadership* in April, 1968. (Note the misspelling which was ultimately corrected through correspondence with the publishers of Merriam-Webster dictionaries.) Since this label has now become widely adopted in the literature, it may be worthwhile to trace the history of its use.

A Dutch adult educator, Ger van Enckevort, has made an exhaustive study of the origins and use of the term andragogy. A summary of his findings follows.* The term (Andragogik) was first coined, so far as he could discover, by a German grammar school teacher, Alexander Kapp, in 1833. Kapp used the word in a description of the educational theory of the Greek philosopher Plato, although Plato never used the term himself. A few years later the better-known German philosopher Johan Friedrich Herbart acknowledged the term by strongly opposing its use. Van Enckevort observes that "the great philosopher had more influence than the simple teacher, and so the word was forgotten and disappeared for nearly a hundred years."

Van Enckevort found the term used again in 1921 by the German social scientist Eugen Rosenstock, who taught at the Academy of Labor in Frankfort. In a report to the Academy in 1921 he expressed the opinion that adult education required special teachers, special methods, and a special philosophy. "It is not enough to translate the insights of education theory [or pedagogy] to the situation of adults . . . the teachers should be professionals who could cooperate with the pupils; only such a teacher can be, in contrast to a "pedagogue," an "andragogue." Incidentally, Rosenstock believed that he invented the term until 1962, when he was informed of its earlier use by Kapp and Herbart. Van Enckevort reports that Rosenstock used the term on a number of occasions, and that it was picked up by some of his colleagues, but that it did not receive general recognition.

The Dutch scholar next finds the term used by a Swiss psychiatrist, Heinrich Hanselmann, in a book published in 1951, *Andragogy: Nature, Possibilities and Boundaries of Adult Education,* which dealt with the nonmedical treatment or reeducation of adults. Only six years later, in 1957, a German teacher, Franz Poggeler, published a book entitled *Introduction to Andragogy: Basic Issues in Adult Education.* About this time, other Europeans began using the term. In

---

*Ger van Enckevort, "Andragology: A New Science," Nederlands Centrum Voor Volksontwikkeling, Amersfoort, The Netherlands, April, 1971 (mimeographed.)

1956, M. Ogrizovic published a dissertation in Yugoslavia on "peno-logical andragogy," and in 1959 a book entitled *Problems of Andra-gogy*. Soon other leading Yugoslavian adult educators, including Samolovcev, Filipovic, and Savicevic, began speaking and writing about andragogy, and faculties of andragogy offering doctorates in adult education were established at the universities of Zagreb and Belgrade in Yugoslavia and the universities of Budapest and Debrecen in Hungary.

In the Netherlands, Professor T. T. ten Have, in lectures in 1954, began to use the term andragogy. In 1959 he published the outline for a science of andragogy. Since 1966 the University of Amsterdam has had a doctorate for andragogues, and in 1970 a department of peda-gogical and andragogical sciences was established in the faculty of social sciences. Current Dutch literature distinguishes between "andr-agogy," "andragogics," and "andragology." "Andragogy" is any intentional and professionally guided activity that aims at a change in adult persons; "andragogics" is the background of methodological and ideological systems that govern the actual process of andragogy; and "andragology" is the scientific study of both andragogy and andragogics.

During the past decade, andragogy has increasingly been used by adult educators in France (Bertrand Schwartz), England (J. A. Simp-son), Venezuela (Felix Adam), and Canada (a Bachelor of Andragogy degree program was established at Concordia University in Montreal in 1973).

To date, several major expositions of the theory of andragogy and its implications for practice have appeared in this country (e.g., God-bey, 1978; Knowles, 1970, rev. 1980; Ingalls and Arceri, 1972; Knowles, 1973, 1975, and 1984); a number of journal articles have been published reporting on applications of the andragogical frame-work to social work education, religious education, undergraduate and graduate education, management training, and other spheres; and an increasing volume of research on hypotheses derived from andragogical theory is being reported. There is a growing evidence, too, that the use of andragogical theory is making a difference in the way programs of adult education are being organized and operated, in the way teachers of adults are being trained, and in the way adults are being helped to learn. There is even evidence that concepts of andragogy are beginning to make an impact on the theory and practice of elementary, secondary, and collegiate education. *Andragogy in Action* (Knowles, 1984) provides case descriptions of a variety of programs based on the andragogical model.

AN ANDRAGOGICAL THEORY OF ADULT LEARNING

Efforts to formulate a theory that considers what we know from experience and research about the unique characteristics of adult learners have been underway for more than four decades. An early attempt, *Informal Education* (1950), organized ideas around the notion that adults learn best in informal, comfortable, flexible, nonthreatening settings. Then, in the mid1960s a Yugoslavian adult educator attending a summer workshop at Boston University exposed participants to the term andragogy, and it seemed to be a more adequate organizing concept. It meant the art and science of helping adults learn, and was ostensibly the antithesis of the pedagogical model. (In fact, the subtitle of the 1970 edition of *The Modern Practice of Adult Education* was "Andragogy Versus Pedagogy.") Accordingly, an explanation of the meaning of pedagogy is required to fully elaborate on the meaning of andragogy.

First There Was Pedagogy

Pedagogy is derived from the Greek words paid, meaning "child" (the same stem from which "pediatrics" comes) and agogus, meaning "leader of." Thus, pedagogy literally means the art and science of teaching children. The pedagogical model of education is a set of beliefs. As viewed by many traditional teachers, it is an ideology based on assumptions about teaching and learning that evolved between the seventh and twelfth centuries in the monastic and cathedral schools of Europe out of their experience in teaching basic skills to young boys. As secular schools organized in later centuries, and public schools in the nineteenth century, the pedagogical model was the only existing educational model Thus, our entire educational enterprise, including higher education, was frozen into this model. Systematic efforts to establish adult education programs in this country, initiated after World War I, also used this model because it was the only model teachers had. As a result, until fairly recently, adults have by and large been taught as if they were children.

The pedagogical model assigns to the teacher full responsibility for making all decisions about what will be learned, how it will be learned, when it will be learned, and if it has been learned. It is teacher-directed education, leaving to the learner only the submissive role of following a teacher's instructions. Thus, it is based on these assumptions about learners:

1. *The need to know.* Learners only need to know that they must learn what the teacher teaches if they want to pass and get promoted; they do not need to know how what they learn will apply to their lives.

2. *The learner's self-concept.* The teacher's concept of the learner is that of a dependent personality; therefore, the learner's self-concept eventually becomes that of a dependent personality.

As individuals mature, their need and capacity to be self-directing, to use their experience in learning, to identify their own readiness to learn, and to organize their learning around life problems increases steadily from infancy to preadolescence, and then increases rapidly during adolescence. (See Bruner, 1961; Erikson, 1950, 1959, 1964; Getzels and Jackson, 1962; Bower and Hollister, 1967; Cross, 1981; Iscoe and Stevenson, 1960; Smith, 1982; White, 1959).

In Figure 4-1 this rate of natural maturation is represented as a decrease in dependency, (as represented by the solid line). Thus, pedagogical assumptions are realistic—and pedagogy is practiced appropriately—because of the high degree of dependency during the first year. Yet, they become decreasingly appropriate in the second, third, fourth, and subsequent years—(as represented by the area with the vertical lines). Seemingly, American culture (home, school, religious institutions, youth agencies, governmental systems) assumes—and therefore permits—a growth rate that is much slower (as represented by the broken line). Accordingly, pedagogy is practiced increasingly inappropriately (as represented by the shaded area between the solid and broken lines). The problem is that the culture does not nurture the development of the abilities required for self-direction, while the increasing need to be self-directing continues to develop organically. The result is a growing gap between the need and the ability to be

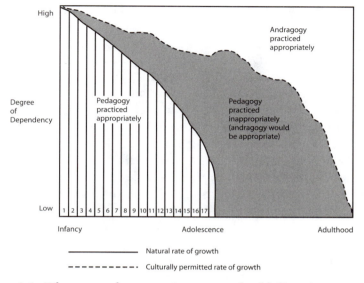

High

Degree
of
Dependency

Andragogy
practiced
appropriately

Pedagogy
practiced
appropriately

Pedagogy
practiced
inappropriately
(andragogy would
be appropriate)

Low | 1 | 2 | 3 | 4 | 5 | 6 | 7 | 8 | 9 |10|11|12|13|14|15|16|17|

Infancy   Adolescence   Adulthood

———————— Natural rate of growth

– – – – – – – – – – · Culturally permitted rate of growth

Figure 4-1. *The natural maturation toward self-direction as compared with the culturally permitted rate of growth of self-direction.*

self-directing, which produces tension, resistance, resentment, and often rebellion in the individual.

3. *The role of experience.* The learner's experience is of little worth as a resource for learning; the experience that counts is that of the teacher, the textbook writer, and the audio-visual aids producer. Therefore, transmittal techniques (e.g., lectures, assigned readings, etc.) are the backbone of pedagogical methodology.

4. *Readiness to learn.* Learners become ready to learn what the teacher tells them they must learn if they want to pass and get promoted.

5. *Orientation to learning.* Learners have a subject-centered orientation to learning; they see learning as acquiring subject-matter content. Therefore, learning experiences are organized according to the logic of the subject-matter content.

6. *Motivation.* Learners are motivated to learn by external motivators (e.g., grades, the teacher's approval or disapproval, parental pressures).

And Then Came Andragogy

Before describing the andragogical assumptions about learners and learning, it is helpful to look at what is meant by adult. There are at least four viable definitions of adult. First, the biological definition: we become adult biologically when we reach the age at which we can reproduce—which at our latitude is in early adolescence. Second, the legal definition: we become adult legally when we reach the age at which the law says we can vote, get a driver's license, marry without consent, and the like. Third, the social definition: we become adult socially when we start performing adult roles, such as the role of full-time worker, spouse, parent, voting citizen, and the like. Finally, the psychological definition: we become adult psychologically when we arrive at a self-concept of being responsible for our own lives, of being self-directing. With regard to learning, it is the psychological definition that is most crucial. But it seems that the process of gaining a self-concept, of self-directedness, starts early in life and grows cumulatively as we biologically mature, start performing adult-like roles, and take increasing responsibility for making our own decisions. So we become adult by degree as we move through childhood and adolescence, and the rate of increase by degree is probably accelerated if we live in homes, study in schools, and participate in youth organizations that foster our taking increasing responsibilities. But most of us probably do not have full-fledged self-concepts of self-directedness until we leave school or college, get a full-time job, marry, and start a family.

The Andragogical Model

The andragogical model is based on several assumptions that are different from those of the pedagogical model:

1. *The need to know.* Adults need to know why they need to learn something before undertaking to learn it. Tough (1979) found that when adults undertake to learn something on their own, they will invest considerable energy in probing into the benefits they will gain from learning it and the negative consequences of not learning it. Consequently, one of the new aphorisms in adult education is that the first task of the facilitator of learning is to

help the learners become aware of the "need to know." At the very least, facilitators can make an intellectual case for the value of the learning in improving the effectiveness of the learners' performance or the quality of their lives. Even more potent tools for raising the level of awareness of the need to know are real or simulated experiences in which the learners discover for themselves the gaps between where they are now and where they want to be. Personnel appraisal systems, job rotation, exposure to role models, and diagnostic performance assessments are examples of such tools. Paolo Freire, the great Brazilian adult educator, developed an elaborate process for what he calls the "consciousness-raising" of peasants in developing countries in his *The Pedagogy of the Oppressed* (1970).

2. *The learners' self-concept.* Adults have a self-concept of being responsible for their own decisions, for their own lives. Once they have arrived at that self-concept they develop a deep psychological need to be seen by others and treated by others as being capable of self-direction. They resent and resist situations in which they feel others are imposing their wills on them. This presents a serious problem in adult education: the minute adults walk into an activity labeled "education," "training," or anything synonymous, they hark back to their conditioning in their previous school experience, put on their dunce hats of dependency, fold their arms, sit back, and say "teach me." This assumption of required dependency and the facilitator's subsequent treatment of adults students as children creates a conflict within them between their intellectual model—learner equals dependent— and the deeper, perhaps subconscious, psychological need to be self-directing. And the typical method of dealing with psychological conflict is to try to flee from the situation causing it—which probably accounts in part for the high dropout rate in much voluntary adult education. As adult educators become aware of this problem, they make efforts to create learning experiences in which adults are helped to make the transition from dependent to self-directing learners. *Self-Directed Learning: A Guide for Learners and Teachers* (Knowles, 1975) is a collection of such experiences.

3. *The role of the learners' experiences.* Adults come into an educational activity with both a greater volume and a different quality

of experience from youths. By virtue of simply having lived longer, they have accumulated more experience than they had as youths. But they also have had a different kind of experience. This difference in quantity and quality of experience has several consequences for adult education.

It assures that in any group of adults there will be a wider range of individual differences than is the case with a group of youths. Any group of adults will be more heterogeneous in terms of background, learning style, motivation, needs, interests, and goals than is true of a group of youths. Hence, greater emphasis in adult education is placed on individualization of teaching and learning strategies.

It also means that for many kinds of learning, the richest resources for learning reside in the adult learners themselves. Hence, the emphasis in adult education is on experiential techniques—techniques that tap into the experience of the learners, such as group discussion, simulation exercises, problem-solving activities, case method, and laboratory methods instead of transmittal techniques. Also, greater emphasis is placed on peer-helping activities.

But the fact of greater experience also has some potentially negative effects. As we accumulate experience, we tend to develop mental habits, biases, and presuppositions that tend to cause us to close our minds to new ideas, fresh perceptions, and alternative ways of thinking. Accordingly, adult educators try to discover ways to help adults examine their habits and biases and open their minds to new approaches. Sensitivity training, value clarification, meditation, and dogmatism scales are among the techniques that are used to tackle this problem.

There is another, more subtle reason for emphasizing the experience of the learners; it has to do with the learner's self-identity. Young children derive their self-identity largely from external definers—who their parents, brothers, sisters, and extended families are; where they live; and what churches and schools they attend. As they mature, they increasingly define themselves in terms of the experiences they have had. To children, experience is something that happens to them; to adults, their experience is who they are. The implication of this fact for adult education is that in any situation in which the participants' experiences are ignored or devalued, adults will perceive this as rejecting not only their experience, but rejecting themselves as persons.

4. *Readiness to learn*. Adults become ready to learn those things they need to know and be able to do in order to cope effectively with their real-life situations. An especially rich source of "readiness to learn" is the developmental tasks associated with moving from one developmental stage to the next. The critical implication of this assumption is the importance of timing learning experiences to coincide with those developmental tasks. For example, a sophomore girl in high school is not ready to learn about infant nutrition or marital relations, but let her get engaged after graduation and she will be very ready.

Bench workers are not ready for a course in supervisory training until they have mastered doing the work they will supervise and have decided that they are ready for more responsibility.

It is not necessary to sit by passively and wait for readiness to develop naturally, however. There are ways to induce readiness through exposure to models of superior performance, career counseling, simulation exercises, and other techniques.

5. *Orientation to learning*. In contrast to children's and youths' subject-centered orientation to learning (at least in school), adults are life-centered (or task-centered or problem-centered) in their orientation to learning. Adults are motivated to learn to the extent that they perceive that learning will help them perform tasks or deal with problems that they confront in their life situations. Furthermore, they learn new knowledge, understandings, skills, values, and attitudes most effectively when they are presented in the context of application to real-life situations.

This point is so critical that reinforcement is required:

For many years, we sought to reduce illiteracy in this country by teaching courses in reading, writing, and arithmetic, and our record was terribly disappointing. The dropout rate was high, motivation to study was low, and achievement scores were poor. When researchers started to discover what was wrong, they quickly found that the words presented in the standard vocabulary lists in the reading and writing courses were not the words

these people used in their life situations and that the mathematical problems presented in their arithmetic courses were not the
problems they had to be able to solve when they went to the
store, the bank, or the shop. As a result, new curriculums organized around life situations and the acquisition of coping skills
(e.g., coping with the world of work, of local government and
community services, of health, of the family, of consuming) were
constructed. Many of the problems encountered in the traditional courses disappeared or were greatly reduced.

A second example is from university extension. For many
years, it was the practice of universities to offer late afternoon or
evening courses for adults that were exactly the same courses
taught to teenagers in the day. Then in the 1950s, the evening
programs changed. A course titled "Composition I" in the day
program became "Writing Better Business Letters" in the
evening program; "Composition II" became "Writing for Pleasure and Profit"; and "Composition III" became "Improving
Your Professional Communications." And it wasn't just the
titles that changed; the way the courses were taught also
changed. While students in "Composition I" still memorized
rules of grammar, students in "Writing Better Business Letters"
immediately began writing business letters and then extracted
principles of grammatical writing from an analysis of what they
had written.

6. *Motivation.* While adults are responsive to some external motivators (better jobs, promotions, higher salaries, and the like), the
most potent motivators are internal pressures (the desire for
increased job satisfaction, self-esteem, quality of life, and the
like). Tough (1979) found in his research that all normal adults
are motivated to keep growing and developing, but this motivation is frequently blocked by such barriers as negative self-concept as a student, inaccessibility of opportunities or resources,
time constraints, and programs that violate principles of adult
learning.

It is important to note that the number of assumptions has grown
from 4 to 6 over the years. Originally, andragogy presented four
assumptions, numbers 2–5 (Knowles 1980, 1978, 1975). Assumption

number 6, motivation to learn, was added in 1984 (Knowles, 1984), and assumption number 1, the need to know, in more recent years (Knowles, 1989, 1990).

Putting the Pedagogical and Andragogical Models in Perspective

So far, the treatment of these two models may suggest that they are antithetical, that pedagogy is bad and andragogy is good, and that pedagogy is for children and andragogy is for adults. This is pretty much the way the models were presented in the first edition of *The Modern Practice of Adult Education: Andragogy Versus Pedagogy* in 1970. But during the next decade, a number of teachers in elementary and secondary schools and in colleges reported that they were experimenting with applying the andragogical model, and that children and youths seemed to learn better in many circumstances when some features of the andragogical model were applied. So, in the revised edition of *The Modern Practice of Adult Education (1980),* the subtitle was changed to "From Pedagogy to Andragogy." Also, a number of trainers and teachers of adults described situations in which they found that the andragogical model did not work.

Therefore, putting the two models into perspective requires making a distinction between an ideology and a system of alternative assumptions. It seems that the pedagogical model has taken on many of the characteristics of an ideology, ideology being defined as a systematic body of beliefs that requires loyalty and conformity by its adherents. Consequently, teachers often feel pressure from the educational system to adhere to the pedagogical model. For example, the best motivator of performance, teachers are told, is competition for grades; and, therefore, grades must be on a curve of normal distribution—only so many "A"s are allowed and there must be some failures. The pedagogical ideology is typically sanctified by the shibboleth "academic standards." (Giving too many "A"s violates academic standards.)

What this means in practice is that we educators now have the responsibility to check out which assumptions are realistic in a given situation. If a pedagogical assumption is realistic for a particular learner in regard to a particular learning goal, then a pedagogical strategy is appropriate, at least as a starting point. Examples of this occur when learners are indeed dependent (such as when entering into a totally strange content area), when they have in fact had no previous experience with a content area, when they do not understand the relevance of a content area to their life tasks or problems, when they do need to accumulate a given body of subject matter in order to accomplish a required performance, and when they feel no internal need to learn that content. But there is one big difference between how an ideological pedagog and an andragog would go from here. The pedagog, perceiving the pedagogical assumptions to be the only realistic assumptions, will insist that the learners remain dependent on the teacher. On the other hand, the andragog, perceiving that movement toward the andragogical assumptions is a desirable goal, will do everything possible to help the learners take increasing responsibility for their own learning.

Even dyed-in-the-wool pedagogical instructors have reported that their teaching has become more effective when they adapted some of the andragogical concepts to the pedagogical model; some ways they do this are by providing a climate in which the learners feel more respected, trusted, unthreatened, and cared about; by exposing them to the need to know before instructing them; by giving them some responsibility in choosing methods and resources; and by involving them in sharing responsibility for evaluating their learning.

Chapter 6 explores the implications for applying these assumptions to planning and conducting programs of adult education and human resources development.

CHAPTER SUMMARY

Despite the fact that educating adults has been a concern for centuries, there has been relatively little research in the area of adult learning until recently. Only after World War I, did a growing body of assumptions about the unique characteristics of adult learners emerge. Within the study of adult learning, there are two streams of inquiry, scientific and artistic, that are distinguishable. Initiated by Thorndike, the scientific stream uses rigorous investigation to discover new information. In contrast, the artistic stream, launched by Lindeman's *The Meaning of Adult Education,* uses intuition and analysis of experience to discover new information. A pioneering theorist, Lindeman laid the foundation for a systematic theory of adult education and identified key assumptions about adult learners. These include the following concepts: adults are motivated to learn as they experience needs and interests that learning will satisfy; adults' orientation to learning is life-centered; experience is the richest resource for adults' learning; adults have a deep need to be self-directing; and individual differences among people increase with age.

Subsequent to the 1926 publication of *The Meaning of Adult Education*, interest in the field became evident and other related articles began appearing in the *Journal of Adult Education*. By 1940, most of the elements required for a conceptualization of adult learning had been discovered. However, these fragmented elements were not yet incorporated into an integrated framework. During the 1950s, the social sciences seized upon adult learning and more intensive research began. These social science disciplines include clinical psychology, developmental psychology, sociology and social psychology, and philosophy. Noted clinical psychologists such as Freud, Jung, Erikson, Maslow, and Rogers made significant contributions to the study of adult learning. Freud identified the influence of the subconscious on behavior; Jung introduced the idea that human consciousness possesses four functions: sensation, thought, emotion, and intuition; Erikson provided the "eight ages of man"; Maslow emphasized the importance of safety; and Rogers conceptualized a student-centered approach to education based on five "basic hypotheses." Developmental psychologists provided knowledge of characteristics associated with age (i.e., physical capabilities, mental abilities, interests, attitudes, values, creativity, and life styles), whereas sociology and social psychology provided knowledge about group and social system behavior including factors that facilitate or inhibit learning.

The label and concept of andragogy greatly enhanced the efforts to create a conceptual framework of adult learning. Although the term was first used in 1833, Americans were not introduced to it until 1967. Since then, a number of journal articles have been published reporting on applications of the andragogical frameworks to social work education, religious education, undergraduate and graduate education, management training, and other spheres; and there is an increasing volume of research on hypotheses derived from the andragogical model.

A distinction between the concepts of pedagogy and andragogy is required to fully grasp the concept of andragogy. The pedagogical model, designed for teaching children, assigns to the teacher full responsibility for all decision making about the learning content, method, timing, and evaluation. Learners play a submissive role in the educational dynamics. In contrast, the andragogical model focuses on the education of adults and is based on the following precepts: adults need to know why they need to learn something; adults maintain the concept of responsibility for their own decisions, their own lives; adults enter the educational activity with a greater volume and more varied experiences than do children; adults have a readiness to learn those things that they need to know in order to cope effectively with real-life situations; adults are life-centered in their orientation to learning; and, adults are more responsive to internal motivators than external motivators. The pedagogical model is an ideological model that excludes the andragogical assumptions. The andragogical model is a system of assumptions that includes the pedagogical assumptions. The andragogical model, is not an ideology; it is a system of alternative sets of assumptions, a *transactional* model that speaks to those characteristics of the learning situation.

CHAPTER 5

Theories of Teaching

PRINCIPLES OF TEACHING FROM THEORIES OF LEARNING

Typically, theories of learning are only useful to adult learning practitioners when they are somehow applied to the facilitation of learning, a function assigned usually in our society to a person designated as teacher.

A distinction must be made between theories of learning and theories of teaching. While theories of learning deal with the ways in which an organism learns, theories of teaching deal with the ways in which a person influences an organism to learn (Gage, 1972, p. 56).

Presumably, the learning theory subscribed to by a teacher will influence his or her teaching theory.

Hilgard, resisting this fragmentation of learning theory, identified twenty principles he believed to be universally acceptable from three different families of theories: *Stimulus-Response* (S-R) *theory, cognitive theory,* and *motivation and personality theory.* These principles are summarized in Table 5-1.

It is important for us to note Hilgard's conviction in his belief that his twenty principles would be "in large part acceptable to all parties"—a conviction that is grounded in his verification process. Hilgard limited the "parties" with whom he checked these principles out to control-oriented theorists. In spite of their differences about the internal mechanics of learning, these theorists are fairly close in their conceptualization of the role of the teacher.

Table 5-1
Summary of Hilgard's Principles

Principles emphasized in S-R theory	1. The learner should be an *active*, rather than a passive listener or viewer.
	2. *Frequency of repetition* is still important in acquiring skill and for retention through overlearning.
	3. *Reinforcement* is important; that is, repetition's desirable and correct responses should be rewarded.
	4. *Generalization* and *discrimination* suggest the importance of practice in varied contexts, so that learning will become (or remain) appropriate to a wider (or more restricted) range of stimuli.
	5. *Novelty* in behavior can be enhanced through imitation of models, through cueing, through shaping, and is not inconsistent with a liberalized S-R approach.
	6. *Drive* is important in learning, but all personal-social motives do not conform to the drive-reduction principles based on food-deprivation experiments.
	7. *Conflicts and frustrations* arise inevitably in the process of learning difficult discriminations and in social situations in which irrelevant motives may be aroused. Hence we must recognize and provide for their resolution or accommodation.
Principles emphasized in cognitive theory	1. *The perceptual features* of the problems given the learner are important conditions of learning—figure-ground relations, directional signs, sequence, organic interrelatedness. Hence a learning problem should be so structured and presented that the essential features are open to the inspection of the learner.
	2. *The organization of knowledge* should be an essential concern of the teacher or educational planner so that the direction from simple to complex is not from arbitrary, meaningless parts to meaningful wholes, but instead from simplified wholes to more complex wholes.
	3. Learning *is culturally relative,* and both the wider culture and the subculture to which the learner belongs may affect his learning.

4. *Cognitive feedback* confirms correct knowledge and corrects faulty learning. The learner tries something provisionally and then accepts or rejects what he/she does on the basis of its consequences. This is, of course, the cognitive equivalent of reinforcement in S-R theory, but cognitive theory tends to place more emphasis upon a kind of hypothesis testing through feedback.

5. *Goal-setting* by the learner is important as motivation for learning and personal successes and failures determine how individuals set future goals.

Principles from motivation and personality theory

1. The learner's *abilities* are important, and provisions have to be made for slower and more rapid learners, as well as for those with specialized abilities.

2. *Postnatal development* may be as important as hereditary and congenital determiners of ability and interest. Hence, the learner must be understood in terms of the influences that have shaped his/her development.

3. Learning is *culturally relative,* and both the wider culture and the subculture to which the learner belongs may affect learning.

4. *Anxiety level* of the individual learner may determine the beneficial or detrimental effects of certain kinds of encouragements to learn.

5. The same objective situation may tap *appropriate motives* for one learner and not for another, as for example, in the contrast between those motivated by affiliation and those motivated by achievement.

6. The *organization of motives and values* within the individual is relevant. Some long-range goals affect short-range activities. Thus college students of equal ability may do better in courses perceived as relevant to their majors than in those perceived as irrelevant.

7. The *group atmosphere* of learning (competition vs cooperation, authoritarianism vs democracy, individual isolation vs group identification) will affect satisfaction in learning as well as the products of learning (Hilgard and Bower, 1966, pp. 562–564).

TEACHING CONCEPTS DERIVED FROM LEARNING THEORIES ABOUT ANIMALS AND CHILDREN

Let's examine the concepts of a variety of theories about the nature of teaching and the role of the teacher. First, we'll look at the members of Hilgard's jury. These include Thorndike, Guthrie, Skinner, Hull, Tolman, and Gagne.

Thorndike essentially saw teaching as the control of learning by the management of reward. The teacher and learner must know the characteristics of a good performance in order that practice may be appropriately arranged. Errors must be diagnosed so that they will not be repeated. The teacher is not primarily concerned with the internal states of the organism, but with structuring the situation so that rewards will operate to strengthen desired responses. The learner should be interested, problem-oriented, and attentive. However, the best way to obtain these conditions is to manipulate the learning situation so that the learner accepts the problem posed because of the rewards involved. Attention is maintained and appropriate stimulus-response connections are strengthened through the precise application of rewards toward the goals set by the teacher. A teacher's role is to cause appropriate S-R bonds to be built up in the learner's behavior repertoire (Hilgard and Bower, 1966, pp. 22–23; Pittenger and Gooding, 1971, pp. 82–83).

Hilgard summarizes Guthrie's suggestions for teaching as follows:

1. If you wish to encourage a particular kind of behavior or discourage another, *discover the cues leading to the behavior in question.* In the one case, arrange the situation so that the desired behavior occurs when those cues are present; in the other case, arrange it so that the undesired behavior does not occur in the presence of the cues. This is all that is involved in the skillful use of reward and punishment. A student does not learn what was in a lecture or a book. He learns only what the lecture or book caused him to do.

2. *Use as many stimulus supports for desired behavior as possible,* because any ordinary behavior is a complex of movements to a complex of stimuli. The more stimuli there are associated with

the desired behavior, the less likely that distracting stimuli and competing behavior will upset the desirable behavior (Hilgard and Bower, 1966, pp. 86–87).

From B. F. Skinner's vantage point, "Teaching is simply the arrangement of contingencies of reinforcement" (1968, p. 5). Subsequent statements in *The Technology of Teaching* throw further light on his position:

Some promising advances have recently been made in the field of learning. Special techniques have been designed to arrange what are called *contingencies of reinforcement*—the relations which prevail between behavior on the one hand and the consequences of behavior on the other—with the result that a much more effective control of behavior has been achieved (p. 9).

Comparable results have been obtained with pigeons, rats, dogs, monkeys, human children and psychotic subjects. In spite of great phylogenic differences, all these organisms show amazingly similar properties of the learning process. It should be emphasized that this has been achieved by analyzing the effects of reinforcement with considerable precision. Only in this way can the behavior of the individual organism be brought under such precise control (p. 14).

The human organism does, of course, learn without being taught. It is a good thing that this is so, and it would no doubt be a good thing if more could be learned in that way. . . . But discovery is no solution to the problems of education. A culture is no stronger than its capacity to transmit itself. It must impart an accumulation of skills, knowledge, and social and ethical practices to its new members. The institution of education is designed to serve this purpose. . . . It is dangerous to suggest to the student that it is beneath his dignity to learn what others already know, that there is something ignoble (and even destructive of "rational powers") in memorizing facts, codes, formulae, or passages from literary works, and that to be admired he must think in original ways. It is equally dangerous to forego teaching important facts and principles in order to give the student a chance to discover them for himself (p. 110).

Hull was primarily concerned with the development of a systematic behavior theory that would improve the laboratory study of learning, and so he gave little attention to its implications for teaching. In assessing the significance of his work for education, Kingsley and Garry point out:

> Systematic order and arrangement would characterize the classroom patterned after Hull's theory. The development of habits and skills would proceed from the simple to the complex with a clear understanding of the stimuli and responses to be associated. The program would have to be dynamic and stimulating in view of the central position that reinforcement holds, inasmuch as aroused drives which can be reduced by satisfying outcomes are an essential condition of learning. . . . Practice would be presented for the purpose of building the desired habits and maintaining them, but would not proceed to the point at which the increase in inhibition from repeating the same response would make the child reluctant to respond (1957, pp. 104–105).

Tolman was also principally concerned with the laboratory study of learning, and Kingsley and Garry point out that "the fact that Tolman accepts different forms of learning makes it more difficult to infer how an educational program which followed his theory literally would operate." But the teacher's task would be concerned primarily with "the creating of stimulus-conditions which make it possible for the learner to perceive clearly what leads to what, and to understand the different means by which a given goal can be reached. Emphasis would be placed upon making vivid the relationships between the parts and the whole. . . . Because of variations in capacity with age, previous experience, etc., it would be necessary to select learning tasks which can be perceived as wholes" (Kingsley and Garry, 1957, pp. 119–120).

The gestalt psychologists saw the teacher's task as being essentially to help the individual see significant relationships and to manage instruction in order to organize his experiences into functional patterns. Through verbal explanations, showing pictures, putting words on chalkboards, presenting reading matter, and many other teaching activities, the teacher provides stimulating situations.

For this reason, careful lesson planning with due regard for suit-able arrangement and orderly presentation is essential for good teaching. Practices conducive to the establishment of appropri-ate relations and organization include starting with the familiar, basing each step on those already taken, putting together facts which belong together, grouping items according to their natural connections, placing subtopics under the topic to which they belong, using illustrations based on the learner's experience, giv-ing major emphasis to essentials, centering supporting details around the main points, and avoiding irrelevant details (Kings-ley and Garry, 1957, pp. 111–112).

Furthermore, all the divisions and topics of each subject must be integrated, and all the various subjects of a course or program must be related to one another.

Robert Gagne in *The Conditions of Learning* (1965) agrees with these learning theorists that teaching means the arranging of condi-tions that are external to the learner (p. 26), but he disagrees that learning is a phenomenon which can be explained by simple theories. He believes that there are eight distinct types of learning, each with its own set of required conditions. These are summarized in Table 5-2.

Gagne further believed that the most important class of conditions that distinguishes one form of learning from another is its prerequi-sites, since the types are in hierarchical order, as follows:

Problem solving (type 8) requires as prerequisites:

Principles (type 7), which require as prerequisites:

Concepts (type 6), which require as prerequisites:

Multiple discriminations (type 5), which require as prerequisites:

Verbal associations (type 4) or other chains (type 3), which require as prerequisites:

Stimulus-response connections (type 2) (p. 60).

Gagne specifies eight component functions of the instructional situ-ation that represent the ways in which the learner's environment acts on him and that must be managed by the teacher:

Table 5-2
Gagne's Eight Distinctive Types of Learning

Type 1	*Signal Learning.* The individual learns to make a general, diffuse response to a signal. This is the classical conditioned response of Pavlov.
Type 2	*Stimulus-Response Learning.* The learner acquires a precise response to a discriminated stimulus. What is learned is a connection (Thorndike) or a discriminated operant (Skinner), sometimes called an instrumental response (Kimble).
Type 3	*Chaining.* What is acquired is a chain of two or more stimulus-response connections. The conditions for such learning have been described by Skinner and others.
Type 4	*Verbal Association.* Verbal association is the learning of chains that are verbal. Basically, the conditions resemble those for other (motor) chains. However, the presence of language in the human being makes this a special type because internal links may be selected from the individual's previously learned repertoire of language.
Type 5	*Multiple Discrimination.* The individual learns to make different identifying responses to as many different stimuli, which may resemble each other in physical appearance to a greater or lesser degree.
Type 6	*Concept Learning.* The learner acquires a capability to make a common response to a class of stimuli that may differ from each other widely in physical appearance. He or she is able to make a response that identifies an entire class of objects or events.
Type 7	*Principle Learning.* In simplest terms, a principle is a chain of two or more concepts. It functions to control behavior in the manner suggested by a verbalized rule of the form "If A, then B," which, of course, may also be learned as Type 4.
Type 8	*Problem Solving.* Problem solving is a kind of learning that requires the internal events usually called thinking. Two or more previously acquired principles are somehow combined to produce a new capability that can be shown to depend on a "higher-order" principle (pp. 58–59).

1. *Presenting the stimulus.* Every type of learning requires a stimulus, and usually these stimuli must be located within the learning environment, outside the learner. If a chain is being learned, an external cue must be provided for each link, even though these may become unnecessary later. If multiple discrimination is to be accomplished, the stimuli to be discriminated must be displayed so that correct connections can become differentiated from incorrect ones. If concepts are being learned, a suitable variety of objects or events representing a class must be displayed. If principles are being acquired, the stimulus objects to which they are expected to apply must somehow be represented to the student. And if problem solving is undertaken, the "problem situation" must similarly be represented in many different ways by objects already in the learner's environment, or by means of pictures, printed books, or oral communication.

2. *Directing attention and other learner activities.* Environmental components also act on the learner by directing attention to certain stimuli or aspects of stimulus objects and events. In very young children, vivid or suddenly changing stimulation may be used for this purpose. Very soon these can be supplanted by oral commands, and later still by printed directions such as, "Notice the number of electrons in the outer ring," or "Look at the graph in Figure 23." As implied by the statements, "Remember how a line is defined," or "Complete the following sentence," activities other than attention may also be directed by such instructions. These activities are not themselves learning. They are simply actions that must be taken by the learner in order to create the proper conditions for learning. Verbal directions that have these purposes can be presented either orally or in printed form.

3. *Providing a model for terminal performance.* The importance of the function of informing the learner about the general nature of the performance to be acquired has been emphasized previously on several occasions. There is no single way to do this, and many different components of the instructional situation may be employed. Most commonly, the "model" of performance to be expected following learning is conveyed by oral or printed communication.

4. *Furnishing external prompts.* In learning chains, as well as multiple discriminations, cues may be provided in the instructional sit-

uation to establish a proper sequence of connections or to increase the distinctiveness of stimuli. As learning proceeds, these extra cues may be made to "vanish" when they are no longer needed. Stimuli that function as extra cues may take a variety of forms. For example, they may be pictorial, as when a sequence is depicted in a diagram reading from left to right. Or they may be auditory, as in emphasizing the differences in sound of such French words as *rue* and *rouge*. Verbal stimuli are often employed for both these purposes, as well as for the purpose of furnishing distinctive "coding links" in verbal chains. For example, when learning color coding for resistors, the word "penny" is used to link "brown" and "one;" the word "nothingness" is used to link "black" and "zero."

5. *Guiding the direction of thinking.* When principles are being learned, and particularly when learning takes the form of problem solving, instructions from the learner's environment may guide the direction of recalled internal connections (thoughts). As described previously, such guidance is presumed to increase the efficiency of learning by reducing the occurrence of irrelevant "hypotheses." Generally, instructions having this function of "hinting" and "suggesting" take the form of oral or printed prose statements.

6. *Inducing transfer of knowledge.* Transferring of learned concepts and principles to novel situations may be accomplished in a number of ways. Discussion is one of the most convenient. Obviously, this is a special kind of interaction between the learner and his environment, and it is not possible to specify exactly what form of discussion will be taken at any given moment by stimulation from the environment. The process is usually initiated, however, by verbally stated questions of the "problem-solving" variety. An important alternative method is to more or less directly place the individual within a problem situation, without the use of words to describe it. A science demonstration may be used to serve this function. Also, videos can be used with considerable effectiveness to initiate problem-solving discussion by "getting the students into the situation" in a highly realistic manner.

7. *Assessing learning attainments.* The environment of the learner also acts to assess the extent to which the individual has attained a specific learning objective or subobjective. It does this by delib-

erately placing the learner in representative problem situations that concretely reflect the capability the individual is expected to have learned. Most frequently, this is done by asking questions. Although it is conceivable for the learner to formulate for himself or herself the questions to be asked, this is difficult for even the experienced adult learner. Preferably, the questions must come from an independent source, to ensure that they will be uninfluenced by the learner's wishes, but will accurately represent the objective.

8. *Providing feedback.* Feedback concerning the correctness of the learner's responses is closely related to assessment of learning outcomes. The questions that are asked of the learner, followed by his/her answers, must in turn be followed by information that lets the learner know whether he or she is right or wrong. Sometimes, this feedback from the learner's environment is very simple to arrange: a foreign word pronounced by the student may sound like one heard on a tape; the color of a chemical solution may indicate the presence of an element being sought. At other times, it may be considerably more complex, as, for example, when the adequacy of a constructed prose paragraph describing an observed event is assessed, and the results fed back to the learner.

These eight functions, then, represent the ways in which the learner's environment acts on the individual. These are the external conditions of learning that, when combined with certain prerequisite capabilities within the learner, bring about the desired change in performance. Obviously, there are many ways to establish these conditions in the learning environment, and many combinations of objects, devices, and verbal communications may be employed in doing so. Probably the most important consideration for the design of the learning environment, however, is not that several alternative ways of accomplishing the same function are usually available. Rather, the important point is that for a given function, certain means of interacting with the learner are quite ineffective. Accordingly, the characteristics of various media of instruction in performing these functions need to be considered carefully in making a choice (Gagne, 1965, pp. 268–271).

The learning theorists described above are the ones Hilgard believed would agree with his twenty principles (with the exception of the motivation and personality theorists, whom Hilgard didn't identify, so we can't check with them directly). Obviously these theorists are unanimous in seeing teaching as the management of procedures that will assure specified behavioral changes as prescribed learning products. The role of the teacher, therefore, is that of a behavior shaper. Stated this baldly, it smacks of what contemporary critics of education see as a God-playing role (Bereiter, 1972, p. 25; Illich, 1970, p. 30).

TEACHING CONCEPTS DERIVED FROM LEARNING THEORIES OF ADULTS

When we look at the concepts of teaching of those theorists who derived their theories of learning primarily from studies of adults, it is obvious that they are very different from those discussed in the previous section. Carl Rogers makes one of the sharpest breaks in his lead statement:

Teaching, in my estimation, is a vastly over-rated function. Having made such a statement, I scurry to the dictionary to see if I really mean what I say. Teaching means "to instruct." Personally I am not much interested in instructing another in what he should know or think. "To impart knowledge or skill." My reaction is, why not be more efficient, using a book or programmed learning? "To make to know." Here my hackles rise. I have no wish to make anyone know something. "To show, guide, direct." As I see it, too many people have been shown, guided, directed. So I come to the conclusion that I do mean what I said. Teaching is, for me, a relatively unimportant and vastly overvalued activity (1969, p. 103).

Rogers goes on to explain that in his view teaching and the imparting of knowledge make sense in an unchanging environment, which is why it has been an unquestioned function for centuries. "But if there is one truth about modern man, it is that he lives in an environment which is continually changing," and therefore, the aim of education must be the facilitation of learning (pp. 104–105). He defines the role of the teacher as that of a facilitator of learning. The critical element in performing this role is the personal relationship between the facilitator and the learner, which in turn is dependent on the facilitator's possessing three attitudinal qualities: (1) realness or genuineness, (2) nonpossessive caring, prizing, trust, and respect, and (3) empathic understanding and sensitive and accurate listening (pp. 106–126).

He provides the following guidelines for a facilitator of learning:

1. The facilitator has much to do with setting the initial mood or climate of the group or class experience. If his own basic philosophy is one of trust in the group and in the individuals who compose the group, then this point of view will be communicated in many subtle ways.

2. The facilitator helps to elicit and clarify the purposes of the individuals in the class as well as the more general purposes of the group. If he is not fearful of accepting contradictory purposes and conflicting aims, if he is able to permit the individuals a sense of freedom in stating what they would like to do, then he is helping to create a climate for learning.

3. He relies upon the desire of each student to implement those purposes which have meaning for him as the motivational force behind significant learning. Even if the desire of the student is to be guided and led by someone else, the facilitator can accept such a need and motive and can either serve as a guide when this is desired or can provide some other means, such as a set course of study, for the student whose major desire is to be dependent. And, for the majority of students, he can help to use a particular individual's own drives and purposes as the moving force behind his learning.

4. He endeavors to organize and make easily available the widest possible range of resources for learning. He endeavors to make available writings, materials, psychological aids, persons, equipment, trips, audio-visual aids—every conceivable resource which his students may wish to use for their own enhancement and for the fulfillment of their own purposes.

5. He regards himself as a flexible resource to be used by the group. He does not downgrade himself as a resource. He

makes himself available as a counselor, lecturer, and advisor, a person with experience in the field. He wishes to be used by individual students and by the group in ways which seem most meaningful to them insofar as he can be comfortable in operating in the ways they wish.

6. In responding to expressions in the classroom group, he accepts both intellectual content and the emotionalized attitudes, endeavoring to give each aspect the approximate degree of emphasis which it has for the individual or the group. Insofar as he can be genuine in doing so, he accepts rationalizations and intellectualizing, as well as deep and real personal feelings.

7. As the acceptant classroom climate becomes established, the facilitator is able increasingly to become a participant learner, a member of the group, expressing his views as those of one individual only.

8. He takes the initiative in sharing himself with the group—his feelings as well as his thoughts—in ways which do not demand or impose but represent simply the personal sharing which students may take or leave. Thus, he is free to express his own feelings in giving feedback to students, in his reaction to them as individuals, and in sharing his own satisfactions or disappointments. In such expressions it is his "owned" attitudes which are shared, not judgments of evaluations of others.

9. Throughout the classroom experience, he remains alert to the expressions indicative of deep or strong feelings. These may be feelings of conflict, pain, and the like, which exist primarily within the individual. Here he endeavors to understand these from the person's point of view and to communicate his empathic understanding. On the other hand, the feelings may be those of anger, scorn, affection, rivalry, and the like—interpersonal attitudes among members of the group. Again he is as alert to these as to the ideas being expressed and by his acceptance of such tensions or bonds he helps to bring them into the open for constructive understanding and use by the group.

10. In his functioning as a facilitator of learning, the leader endeavors to recognize and accept his own limitations. He realizes that he can only grant freedom to his students to the extent that he is comfortable in giving such freedom. He can only be under-

standing to the extent that he actually desires to enter the inner world of his students. He can only share himself to the extent that he is reasonably comfortable in taking that risk. He can only participate as a member of the group when he actually feels that he and his students have an equality as learners. He can only exhibit trust of the students' desire to learn insofar as he feels that trust. There will be many times when his attitudes are not facilitative of learning. He will find himself being suspicious of his students. He will find it impossible to accept attitudes which differ strongly from his own. He will be unable to understand some of the student feelings which are markedly different from his own. He may find himself feeling strongly judgmental and evaluative. When he experiences attitudes which are nonfacilitative, he will endeavor to get close to them, to be clearly aware of them, and to state them just as they are within himself. Once he has expressed these angers, these judgments, these mistrusts, these doubts of others and doubts of himself, as something coming from within himself, not as objective facts in outward reality, he will find the air cleared for a significant interchange between himself and his students. Such an interchange can go a long way toward resolving the very attitudes which he has been experiencing, and thus make it possible for him to be more of a facilitator of learning (Rogers, 1969, pp. 164–166).

Although Maslow does not spell out his conception of the role of teacher, he no doubt would subscribe to Rogers' guidelines, with perhaps a bit more emphasis on the teacher's responsibility for providing safety. Several followers of Rogers and Maslow have experimented with translating their theories into classroom behavior. George Brown, for example, describes the development of confluent education ("the term for the integration or flowing together of the affective and cognitive elements in individual and group learning") in the Ford-Esalen Project in Affective Education in California in the late 1960s in his *Human Teaching for Human Learning,* 1971. Elizabeth Drews describes an experiment to test a new program designed to foster self-initiated learning and self-actualization in ninth graders in Michigan in which the teachers defined their roles as facilitators of learning (Drews, 1966).

Flowing in the same stream of thought, Goodwin Watson provides the following summary of "what is known about learning," which is easily read as "guidelines for the facilitation of learning":

1. Behavior which is rewarded—from the learner's point of view—is more likely to recur.

2. Sheer repetition without reward is a poor way to learn.

3. Threat and punishment have variable effects upon learning, but they can and do commonly produce avoidance behavior in which the reward is the diminution of punishment possibilities.

4. How "ready" we are to learn something new is contingent upon the confluence of diverse—and changing—factors, some of which include:

   a. adequate existing experience to permit the new to be learned (we can learn only in relation to what we already know);

   b. adequate significance and relevance for the learner to engage in learning activity (we learn only what is appropriate to our purposes);

   c. freedom from discouragement, the expectation of failure, or threats to physical, emotional, or intellectual well-being.

5. Whatever is to be learned will remain unlearnable if we believe that we cannot learn it or if we perceive it as irrelevant or if the learning situation is perceived as threatening.

6. Novelty (per 4 and 5 above) is generally rewarding.

7. We learn best that which we participate in selecting and planning ourselves.

8. Genuine participation (as compared with feigned participation intended to avoid punishment) intensifies motivation, flexibility, and rate of learning.

9. An autocratic atmosphere (produced by a dominating teacher who controls direction via intricate punishments) produces in learners apathetic conformity, various—and frequently devious—kinds of defiance, scapegoating (venting hostility generated by the repressive atmosphere on colleagues), or escape. . . . An autocratic atmosphere also produces increasing dependence upon the authority, with consequent obsequiousness, anxiety, shyness, and acquiescence.

10. "Closed," authoritarian environments (such as are characteristic of most conventional schools and classrooms) condemn most learners to continuing criticism, sarcasm, discouragement, and failure so that self-confidence, aspiration (for anything but escape), and a healthy self-concept are destroyed.

11. The best time to learn anything is when whatever is to be learned is immediately useful to us.

12. An "open," nonauthoritarian atmosphere can, then, be seen as conducive to learner initiative and creativity, encouraging the learning of attitudes of self-confidence, originality, self-reliance, enterprise, and independence. All of which is equivalent to learning how to learn (Watson, 1960–1961).

Houle has proposed a "fundamental system" of educational design that rests on seven assumptions:

1. Any episode of learning occurs in a specific situation and is profoundly influenced by that fact.

2. The analysis or planning of educational activities must be based on the realities of human experience and upon their constant change.

3. Education is a practical art (like architecture), which draws on many theoretical disciplines in the humanities and the social and biological sciences.

4. Education is a cooperative rather than an operative art. ("An operative art is one in which the creation of a product or performance is essentially controlled by the person using the art. . . . A cooperative art . . . works in a facilitative way by guiding and directing a natural entity or process. The farmer, physician, and educator are three classic examples of cooperative artists.")

5. The planning or analysis of an educational activity is usually undertaken in terms of some period that the mind abstracts for analytical purposes from the complicated reality.

6. The planning or analysis of an educational activity may be undertaken by an educator, a learner, an independent analyst, or some combination of the three.

7. Any design of education can best be understood as a complex of interacting elements, not as a sequence of events (Houle, 1972, pp. 32–39).

He then identifies the following components in his fundamental system, which it is the task of the educator to manage:

1. A possible educational activity is identified.

2. A decision is made to proceed.

3. Objectives are identified and refined.

4. A suitable format is designed.

   a. Learning resources are selected.

   b. A leader or group of leaders is chosen.

   c. Methods are selected and used.

   d. A time schedule is made.

   e. A sequence of events is devised.

   f. Social reinforcement of learning is provided.

   g. The nature of each individual learner is taken into account.

   h. Roles and relationships are made clear.

   i. Criteria for evaluating progress are identified.

   j. The design is made clear to all concerned.

5. The format is fitted into larger patterns of life.

   a. Learners are guided into or out of the activity both at the beginning and subsequently.

   b. Life styles are modified to allow time and resources for the new activity.

   c. Financing is arranged.

   d. The activity is interpreted to related publics.

6. The program is carried out.

7. The results of the activity are measured and appraised.

8. The situation is examined in terms of the possibility of a new educational activity (pp. 48–56).

Because Tough's studies have been concerned with the self-initiated learning projects of adults, he has focused on the "helping role" of the teacher or other resource person. His investigations have produced the following "fairly consistent composite picture of the ideal helper":

One cluster of characteristics might be summarized by saying that the ideal helper is warm and loving. He accepts and cares about the learner and about his project or problem, and takes it seriously. He is willing to spend time helping. He is approving, supportive, encouraging, and friendly. He regards the learner as an equal. As a result of these characteristics, the learner feels free to approach this ideal helper, and can talk freely and easily with him in a warm and relaxed atmosphere.

A second cluster of characteristics involves the helper's perceptions of the person's capacity as a self-planner. The ideal helper has confidence in the learner's ability to make appropriate plans and arrangements for this learning. The helper has a high regard for his skill as a self-planner, and does not want to take the decision-making control away from him.

Third, the ideal helper views his interaction with the learner as a dialogue, a true encounter in which he listens as well as talks. His help will be tailored to the needs, goals, and requests of this unique learner. The helper listens, accepts, understands, responds, helps. These perceptions of the interaction are in sharp contrast to those of "helpers" who want to control, command, manipulate, persuade, influence, and change the learner. Such helpers seem to view communication as "an inexhaustible monologue, addressed to everyone and no one in the form of 'mass communication'. . . . Such a helper perceives the learner as an object, and expects to do something to that object. He is not primarily interested in the other person as a person, and in his needs, wishes, and welfare."

Another cluster of internal characteristics involves the helper's reasons for helping. He may help because of his affection and concern for the learner. Or the helper may, in an open and positive way, expect to gain as much as he gives. Other sorts of motivation, too, are possible pleasure for knowing he was helpful, satisfaction from seeing progress or from the learner's gratitude. . . .

Finally, the ideal helper is probably an open and growing person, not a closed, negative, static, defensive, fearful, or suspicious sort of person. He himself is frequently a learner, and seeks growth and new experiences. He probably tends to be spontaneous and authentic, and to feel free to behave as a unique person rather than in some stereotyped way (Tough, 1979, pp. 195–197).

These characteristics fit well into an integrated conception of the role of the andragogical teacher. An operational set of principles for that conception of the andragogical teacher is shown in Table 5-3.

CONCEPTS OF TEACHING DERIVED FROM THEORIES OF TEACHING

Some teaching theories, especially the mechanistic models, have evolved directly from learning theories. Others have evolved from analyses of teacher behavior and its consequences and from experimenting with manipulation of the variables in the teaching-learning situation. The previous section presented teaching theories derived from learning theories; this section discusses concepts derived from theories of teaching.

Dewey's Concepts

Perhaps the system of ideas about effective teaching propounded by John Dewey during the first half of this century has had the greatest impact in the field. Dewey contrasted his basic principles with those of traditional education:

To imposition from above is opposed expression and cultivation of individuality; to external discipline is opposed free activity; to learning from texts and teacher, learning through experience; to acquisition of isolated skills and techniques by drill, is opposed acquisition of them as means of attaining ends which make direct vital appeal; to preparation for a more or less remote future is opposed making the most of the opportunities of present life; to static aims and materials is opposed acquaintance with a changing world (Dewey, 1938, pp. 5–6).

Table 5-3
The Role of the Teacher

Conditions of Learning	Principles of Teaching
The learners feel a need to learn.	1. The teacher exposes students to new possibilities of self-fulfillment. 2. The teacher helps each student clarify his own aspirations for improved behavior. 3. The teacher helps each student diagnose the gap between his aspiration and his present level of performance. 4. The teacher helps the students identify the life problems they experience because of the gaps in their personal equipment.
The learning environment is characterized by physical comfort, mutual trust and respect, mutual helpfulness, freedom of expression, and acceptance of differences.	5. The teacher provides physical conditions that are comfortable (as to seating, smoking, temperature, ventilation, lighting, decoration) and conducive to interaction (preferably, no person sitting behind another person). 6. The teacher accepts each student as a person of worth and respects his feelings and ideas. 7. The teacher seeks to build relationships of mutual trust and helpfulness among the students by encouraging cooperative activities and refraining from inducing competitiveness and judgmentalness. 8. The teacher exposes his own feelings and contributes his resources as a colearner in the spirit of mutual inquiry.
The learners perceive the goals of a learning experience to be their goals.	9. The teacher involves the students in a mutual process of formulating learning objectives in which the needs of the students, of the institution, of the teacher, of the subject matter, and of the society are taken into account.

(table continued on next page)

Table 5-3 (Continued)

Conditions of Learning	Principles of Teaching
The learners accept a share of the responsibility for planning and operating a learning experience, and therefore have a feeling of commitment toward it.	10. The teacher shares his thinking about options available in the designing of learning experiences and the selection of materials and methods and involves the students in deciding among these options jointly.
The learners participate actively in the learning process.	11. The teacher helps the students to organize themselves (project groups, learning-teaching teams, independent study, etc.) to share responsibility in the process of mutual inquiry.
The learning process is related to and makes use of the experience of the learners.	12. The teacher helps the students exploit their own experiences as resources for learning through the use of such techniques as discussion, role playing case method, etc.
	13. The teacher gears the presentation of his own resources to the levels of experience of his particular students.
	14. The teacher helps the students to apply new learning to their experience, and thus to make the learning more meaningful and integrated.
The learners have a sense of progress toward their goals.	15. The teacher involves the students in developing mutually acceptable criteria and methods for measuring progress toward the learning objectives.
	16. The teacher helps the students develop and apply procedures for self-evaluation according to these criteria.

(Knowles, 1980, pp. 57–58).

Dewey's system is organized around several key concepts. The central concept is experience. In Dewey's system, experience is always the starting point of an educational process; it is never the result.

All genuine education comes about through *experience* (p. 13).

The central problem of an education based upon *experience* is to select the kind of present experiences that live fruitfully and creatively in subsequent experiences (pp. 16-17).

A second key concept is *democracy*.

The question I would raise concerns why we prefer democratic and humane arrangements to those which are autocratic and harsh. . . . Can we find any reason that does not ultimately come down to the belief that democratic social arrangements promote a better quality of human experience, one which is more widely accessible and enjoyed, than do nondemocratic and antidemocratic forms of social life? (pp. 24–25).

Another key concept is *continuity*.

The principle of continuity of experience means that every experience both takes up something from those which have gone before and modifies in some way the quality of those which come after. . . . Growth, or growing and developing, not only physically but intellectually and morally, is one exemplification of the principle of continuity (pp. 27–28).

A primary responsibility of educators is that they not only be aware of the general principle of the shaping of actual experience by environing conditions, but that they also recognize in the concrete what surroundings are conducive to having experiences that lead to growth. Above all, they should know how to utilize the surroundings, physical and social, that exist so as to extract from them all that they have to contribute to building up experiences that are worth while (p. 35).

Another key concept is *interaction*.

The word "interaction" expresses the second chief principle for interpreting an experience in its educational function and force. It assigns equal rights to both factors in experience—objective and internal conditions. Any normal experience is an interplay of these two sets of conditions. Taken together, or in their interaction, they form what we call a situation. The trouble with traditional education was not that it emphasized the external conditions that enter into the control of the experiences, but that it paid so little attention to the internal factors which also decide what kind of experience is had [the powers and purposes of those taught] (pp. 38–44).

It is not the subject per se that is educative or that is conducive to growth. There is no subject that is in and of itself, or without regard to the stage of growth attained by the learner, [an end] such that inherent educational value may be attributed to it. Failure to take into account adaptation to the needs and capacities of individuals was the source of the idea that certain subjects and certain methods are intrinsically cultural or intrinsically good for mental discipline. . . . In a certain sense every experience should do something to prepare a person for later experiences of a deeper and more expansive quality. That is the very meaning of growth, continuity, reconstruction of experience (pp. 46–47).

The educator is responsible for a knowledge of individuals and for a knowledge of subject matter that will enable activities to be selected which lend themselves to social organization, an organization in which all individuals have an opportunity to contribute something, and in which the activities in which all participate are the chief carrier of control. . . . The principle that development of experience comes about through interaction means that education is essentially a social process. . . . The teacher loses the position of external boss or dictator but takes on that of leader of group activities (pp. 61–66).

Many of Dewey's ideas were distorted, misinterpreted, and exaggerated during the heyday of the progressive school movement a few generations ago, which is why it is important to quote him directly. In light of contemporary thinking about teaching, though, don't these ideas seem fresh and useful?

Teaching through Inquiry

A second set of concepts about teaching with roots both in Dewey's ideas—especially his formulation of scientific thinking—and in those of the cognitive theorists is referred to as the discovery method, the inquiry method, self-directed learning or problem-solving learning.

Jerome Bruner, perhaps the most notable proponent of this approach to teaching, offers the cognitive theorists' perspective of inquiry teaching and learning (1961, 1966). In an extensive series of essays, he identifies three roles of teachers as communicators of knowledge, models who inspire, and symbols of "education."

Bruner contends that a theory of instruction or inquiry teaching must meet the following four criteria:

1. A theory of instruction should specify the experiences that most effectively implant in the individual a predisposition toward learning.
2. A theory of instruction must specify the ways in which a body of knowledge should be structured so that it can be most readily grasped by the learner.
3. A theory of instruction should specify the most effective sequences in which to present the materials to be learned.
4. A theory of instruction should specify the nature and pacing of rewards and punishments in the process of learning and teaching (1966, pp. 40–41).

Any attempts to determine whether a theory of instruction meets Bruner's four criteria should include considerations of the following types of questions:

- Are there materials that will increase a student's desire to learn? If so, what are they?
- How can I, as a teacher, enhance the students' will to learn? What can be done to make students eager to learn the material?
- What is the most effective method of presentation for this material? Is an interactive or representative presentation best suited for this material? Bruner identifies modes of presentation in a hierarchical system involving an *enactive mode, iconic mode,* and *symbolic mode* (1966, pp. 10–14). The first level, the enactive mode requires action on the part of the learner; the second level, the iconic mode refers to the process of mentally organizing material; and, the third level, the symbolic mode, involves use of symbols such as language.

- Are the learning materials, tools, and even material appropriate for the level of the students?
- What is the optimal presentation sequence? Is the holistic approach most effective, or should the teacher teach the foundations of the material and then supply the details?
- What and when are rewards to be administered? How will the instruction handle students' successes and errors?

He predicates his system on the will to learn, a trait he believes to exist in all people. The will to learn is an intrinsic motive, one that finds both its source and its reward in its own exercise. The will to learn becomes a "problem" only under specialized circumstances such as those of a school, where a curriculum is set, students confined, and a path fixed. The problem exists not so much in learning itself, but in the fact that what the school imposes often fails to enlist the natural energies that sustain spontaneous learning—curiosity, a desire for competence, aspiration to emulate a model, and a deep-sensed commitment to the web of social reciprocity (the human need to respond to others and to operate jointly with them toward an objective (pp. 125–127).

Bruner further distinguishes teaching in the *expository mode* and teaching in the *hypothetical mode*.

In the former, the decisions concerning the mode and pace and style of exposition are principally determined by the teacher as expositor; the student is the listener. . . . In the hypothetical mode, the teacher and the student are in a more cooperative position. . . . The student is not a bench-bound listener, but takes a part in the formulation and at times may play the principal role in it (1961, p. 126).

The hypothetical mode leads to students' engaging in acts of discovery, a process which Bruner sees as having four benefits: (1) increasing intellectual powers, (2) shifting from extrinsic to intrinsic rewards, (3) learning the heuristics of discovering, and (4) making material more readily accessible in memory. This mode is more congruent with and more likely to nurture the will to learn.

Bruner conveys the operational aspects of discovery teaching by describing it in action in case studies of actual courses. But Postman and Weingartner provide the following list of behaviors observable in teachers using the inquiry method:

- The teacher rarely tells students what he thinks they ought to know. He believes that telling, when used as a basic teaching strategy, deprives students of the excitement of doing their own finding and of the opportunity for increasing their power as learners.

- His basic mode of discourse with students is questioning. While he uses both convergent and divergent questions, he regards the latter as the more important tool. He emphatically does not view questions as a means of seducing students into parroting the text or syllabus; rather, he sees questions as instruments to open engaged minds to unsuspected possibilities.

- Generally, he does not accept a single statement as an answer to a question. In fact, he has a persisting aversion to anyone, any syllabus, any text that offers The Right Answer. Not because answers and solutions are unwelcome—indeed, he is trying to help students be more efficient problem solvers—but because he knows how often The Right Answer serves only to terminate further thought. He knows the power of pluralizing. He does not ask for the reason, but for the reasons. Not for the cause, but the causes. Never the meaning, the meanings. He knows, too, the power of contingent thinking. He is the most "It depends" learner in his class.

- He encourages student-student interaction as opposed to student-teacher interaction. And generally he avoids acting as a mediator or judge of the quality of ideas expressed. If each person could have with him at all times a full roster of authorities, perhaps it would not be necessary for individuals to make independent judgments. But so long as this is not possible, the individual must learn to depend on himself as a thinker. The inquiry teacher is interested in students developing their own criteria or standards for judging the quality, precision, and relevance of ideas. He permits such development to occur by minimizing his role as arbiter of what is acceptable and what is not.

- He rarely summarizes the positions taken by students on the learnings that occur. He recognizes that the act of summary, of "closure," tends to have the effect of ending further thought. Because he regards learning as a process, not a terminal event, his "summaries" are apt to be stated as hypotheses, tendencies, and directions. He assumes that no one ever learns once and for all how to write, or how to read, or what were the causes of the Civil War. Rather, he assumes that one is always in the process of acquiring skills, assimilating new information, formulating or refining generalizations. Thus, he is always cautious about defining the limits of learning, about saying, "This is what you will learn between now and the Christmas holidays," or even (especially), "This is what you will learn in the ninth grade." The only significant terminal behavior he recognizes is death, and he suspects that those who talk of learning as some kind of "terminal point" are either compulsive travelers or have simply not observed children closely enough. Moreover, he recognizes that learning does not occur with the same intensity in any two people, and he regards verbal attempts to disregard this fact as a semantic fiction. If a student has arrived at a particular conclusion, then little is gained by the teacher's restating it. If the student has not arrived at a conclusion, then it is presumptuous and dishonest for the teacher to contend that he has. (Any teacher who tells you precisely what his students learned during any lesson, unit, or semester quite literally does not know what he is talking about.)

• His lessons develop from the responses of students and not from a previously determined "logical" structure. The only kind of lesson plan, or syllabus, that makes sense to him is one that tries to predict, account for, and deal with the authentic responses of learners to a particular problem: the kinds of questions they will ask, the obstacles they will face, their attitudes, the possible solutions they will offer, etc. Thus, he is rarely frustrated or inconvenienced by "wrong answers," false starts, irrelevant directions. These are the stuff of which his best lessons and opportunities are made. In short, the "content" of his lessons are the responses of his students. Since he is concerned with the processes of thought rather than the end results of thought (The Answer!), he does not feel compelled to "cover ground" (There's the traveler again), or to insure that his students embrace a particular doctrine, or to exclude a student's idea because it is not germane. (Not germane to what? Obviously, it is germane to the student's thinking about the problem.) He is engaged in exploring the way students think, not what they should think (before the Christmas holidays). That is why he spends more of his time listening to students than talking to or at them.

- Generally, each of his lessons poses a problem for students. Almost all of his questions, proposed activities, and assignments are aimed at having his students clarify a problem, make observations relevant to the solution of the problem, and make generalizations based on their observations. His goal is to engage students in those activities which produce knowledge: defining, questioning, observing, classifying, generalizing, verifying, applying. As we have said, all knowledge is a result of these activities. Whatever we think we "know" about astronomy, sociology, chemistry, biology, linguistics, etc., was discovered or invented by someone who was more or less an expert in using inductive methods of inquiry. Thus, our inquiry, or "inductive," teacher is largely interested in helping his students to become more proficient as users of these methods. He measures his success in terms of behavioral changes in students: the frequency with which they ask questions; the increase in the relevance and cogency of their questions; the frequency and conviction of their challenges to assertions made by other students or teachers or textbooks; the relevance and clarity of the standards on which they base their challenges; their willingness to suspend judgments when they have insufficient data; their willingness to modify or otherwise change their position when data warrant such change; the increase in their tolerance for diverse answers; their ability to apply generalizations, attitudes, and information to novel situations.

These behaviors and attitudes amount to a definition of a different role for the teacher from that which he has traditionally assumed. The inquiry environment, like any other school environment, is a series of human encounters, the nature of which is largely determined by the "teacher." "Teacher" is here placed in quotation marks to call attention to the fact that most of the word's conventional meanings are inimical to inquiry methods. It is not uncommon, for example, to hear "teachers" make statements such as, "Oh, I taught them that, but they didn't learn it." There is no utterance made in the Teachers' Room more extraordinary than this. From our point of view, it is on the same level as a salesman's remarking, "I sold it to him, but he didn't buy it," which is to say, it makes no sense. It seems to mean that "teaching" is what a "teacher" does, which, in turn, may or may not bear any relationship to what those being "taught" do (Postman and Weingartner, 1969, pp. 34–37).

Suchman has described vividly the success of the Inquiry Training Project at the University of Illinois in developing inquiry skills in elementary school children. As a result of this experience, he feels confident in the feasibility of "an inquiry-centered curriculum."

> . . . in which the children would find themselves launched into areas of study by first being confronted by concrete problem-focused episodes for which they would attempt to build explanatory systems. Part of their data gathering might well be in the question-asking mode and certainly along the way time would have to be spent in building inquiry skills through critiques and other such procedures. Yet there would also be room for helping the children enlarge their conceptual systems through more teacher-directed means (Suchman, 1972, p. 158).

Crutchfield counts four sets of skills involved in productive thinking, his synonym for problem-solving or inquiry learning.

1. Skills of problem discovery and formulation
2. Skills in organizing and processing problem information
3. Skills in idea generation, and
4. Skills in the evaluation of ideas (1972, pp. 192–195)

The notion that the development of skills of inquiry should be a primary goal of youth education is the cornerstone of the concept of education as a lifelong process. This makes it especially significant that the Governing Board of the UNESCO Institute for Education in Hamburg, Germany, decided in March 1972 to focus on research and experimental projects in an exploratory study, "The Concept of Lifelong Education and Its Implications for School Curriculum."

Teaching through Modeling

Albert Bandura, at Stanford University, has developed the most elaborate system of thought on imitation, identification, or modeling as concepts of teaching. Labeling the system *social learning,* Bandura regards reinforcement theories of instrumental conditioning, such as Skinner's, as able to account for the control of previously learned matching responses, but unable to account for the way new response patterns are acquired through observation and imitation.

In teaching by modeling, the teacher behaves in ways that he or she wants the learner to imitate. The teacher's basic technique is role modeling. Bandura and Walters (1963) identified three kinds of effects from exposing the learner to a model: (1) a *modeling effect,* whereby the learner acquires new kinds of response patterns; (2) an *inhibitory or disinhibitory effect,* whereby the learner decreases or increases the frequency, latency, or intensity of previously acquired responses; and (3) *an eliciting effect,* whereby the learner merely receives from the model a cue for releasing a response that is neither new nor inhibited. For example, the modeling effect occurs when the teacher shows learners how to listen empathically to one another by listening empathically to them himself. The inhibiting or disinhibiting effect occurs when the teacher lets the learners know, through modeling, that it is or is not approved behavior to express their feelings openly. Thus, the teacher inhibits or disinhibits an old response. The eliciting effect occurs when, through modeling, the teacher teaches the art of giving and receiving feedback by inviting the learners to constructively criticize his/her own performance. Accordingly, the teacher is providing a cue eliciting a response neither new nor inhibited.

Gage remarks that "Learning through imitation seems to be especially appropriate for tasks that have little cognitive structure" (1972, p. 47). This observation seems to be borne out by the fact that social learning has been applied principally to behavioral modification in therapeutic settings to correct deviant or antisocial behavior, but its application to such positive educational purposes as the development of attitudes, beliefs, and performance skills has also been demonstrated (Bandura, 1969, pp. 599–624). No doubt every teacher employs modeling as one of his techniques, whether consciously or unconsciously. His potency as a model will be influenced by such characteristics as age, sex, socio-economic status, social power, ethnic background, and intellectual and vocational status (IBM, p. 195).

Although social learning has been employed chiefly to achieve behavioral changes through external management of reinforcement contingencies, in recent years there has been a growing interest in self-control processes in which individuals regulate their own behavior by arranging appropriate contingencies for themselves. These self-directed endeavors comprise a variety of strategies, about which Bandura makes the following observations.

> The selection of well-defined objectives, both intermediate and ultimate, is an essential aspect of any self-directed program of change. The goals that individuals choose for themselves must be specified in sufficiently detailed behavioral terms to provide adequate guidance for the actions that must be taken daily to attain desired outcomes.
>
> To further increase goal commitment, participants are asked to make contractual agreements to practice self-controlling behaviors in their daily activities. . . . Under conditions where individuals voluntarily commit themselves to given courses of action, subsequent tendencies to deviate are likely to be counteracted by negative self-evaluations. Through this mechanism, and anticipated social reactions of others, contractual commitments reinforce adherence to corrective practices.
>
> Satisfactions derived from evident changes help to sustain successful endeavors, therefore, utilize objective records of behavioral changes as an additional source of reinforcement for their self-controlling behavior. . . .
>
> Since behavior is extensively under external stimulus control, persons can regulate the frequency with which they engage in certain activities by altering stimulus conditions under which the behavior customarily occurs. Overeating, for example, will arise more often when appetizing foods are prominently displayed in frequented places in the household than if they are stored out of sight and made less accessible. . . .
>
> Behavior that provides immediate positive reinforcement, such as eating, smoking, and drinking, tends to be performed in diverse situations and at varied times. Therefore, another important aspect of self-managed change involves progressive narrowing of stimulus control over behavior. Continuing with the obesity illustration, individuals are encouraged gradually to delimit the circumstances under which they eat until eventually their eating behavior is brought under control of a specific set of stimulus conditions. This outcome is achieved by having the clients commit themselves to a graduated program in which they

refrain from eating in non-dining settings, between regular meal-times, and while engaging in other activities such as watching television, reading, or listening to the radio. . . .

The foregoing procedures are primarily aimed at instituting self-controlling behavior, but unless positive consequences are also arranged the well-intentioned practices are likely to be short-lived. . . . Self-control measures usually produce immediate unpleasant effects while the personal benefits are considerably delayed. Self-reinforcing operations are, therefore, employed to provide immediate support for self-controlling behavior until the benefits that eventually accrue take over the reinforcing function.

As a final feature of self-directed change programs, increases in desired behavior and reductions in undesired behavior are attempted gradually. In this way the incidence of experienced discomforts is kept low, and steady progress toward the eventual goal can be achieved (Bandura, 1969, pp. 254–257).

PERSPECTIVE TRANSFORMATION/ CRITICAL REFLECTIVITY

A recent new thrust in theorizing about the purpose of teaching/learning is the notion that it is not sufficient for adult education programs to satisfy the identified learning needs of individuals, organizations, and society. Rather, they should seek to help adult learners transform their very way of thinking about themselves and their world—what Mezirow calls "perspective transformation" (Mezirow, 1985). Brookfield (1986) proposes that this can be achieved through the development of competence in "critical reflectivity." He states his case in these words:

It will be the case, then, that the most significant personal learning adults undertake cannot be specified in advance in terms of objectives to be obtained or behaviors (of whatever kind) to be performed. Thus, significant personal learning might be defined as that learning in which adults come to reflect on their self-images, change their self-concepts, question their previously internalized norms (behavioral and moral), and reinterpret their current and past behaviors from a new perspective. . . .

Significant personal learning entails fundamental change in learners and leads them to redefine and reinterpret their personal, social, and occupational worlds. In the process, adults may come to explore affective, cognitive, and psychomotor domains that they previously had not perceived as relevant to themselves (Brookfield, 1986, pp. 213–214).

He points out that the addition of this "analytic component" to the role of the facilitator of learning. . . . requires that the facilitators and practitioners prompt learners to consider alternative perspectives on their personal political, work, and social lives. Hence, effective facilitation means that learners will be challenged to examine their previously held values, beliefs, and behaviors and will be confronted with ones that they may not want to consider. Such challenges and confrontations need not be done in an adversarial, combative, or threatening manner; indeed, the most effective facilitator is one who can encourage adults to consider rationally and carefully perspectives and interpretations of the world that diverge from those they already hold, without making these adults feel they are being cajoled or threatened. This experience may produce anxiety, but such anxiety should be accepted as a normal component of learning and not something to be avoided at all costs for fear that learners will leave the group. There are forms of fulfillment that are quite unlike those produced by a wholly joyful encounter with a new form of knowledge or a new skill area. It is this dimension of increased insight through critical reflection on current assumptions and past beliefs and behaviors that is sometimes ignored in treatments of adult learning (pp. 285–286).

CHANGE THEORY

Another system of thought that has great implications for educational practice has to do with influencing the educative quality of total environments. Concepts and strategies in this system are drawn from field theory, systems theory, organizational development and consultation theories, and ecological psychology.

The systems theorists have provided conceptual frameworks for analyzing organizations of all types as complex social systems with interacting subsystems (Cleland, 1969; Kast and Rosenzweig, 1970;

Parsons, 1951; Seiler, 1967; Von Bertalanffy, 1968; Zadeh, 1969, Knowles, 1980). Knowles presents an interpretation of some of the applications of their work for human resources development in one of his earlier works (Knowles, 1980, pp. 66–68):

> One of the misconceptions in our cultural heritage is the notion that organizations exist purely to get things done. This is only one of their purposes; it is their work purpose. But every organization is also a social system that serves as an instrumentality for helping people meet human needs and achieve human goals. In fact, this is the primary purpose for which people take part in organizations—to meet their needs and achieve their goals—and when an organization does not serve this purpose for them they tend to withdraw from it. So organizations also have a human purpose.
>
> Adult education is a means available to organizations for furthering both purposes. Their work purpose is furthered to the extent that they use adult education to develop the competencies of their personnel to do the work required to accomplish the goals of the organizations. Their human purpose is furthered to the extent that they use adult education to help their personnel develop the competencies that will enable them to work up the ladder of Maslow's hierarchy of needs for survival through safety, affection, and esteem to self-actualization.
>
> As if by some law of reciprocity, therefore, organization provides an environment for adult education. In the spirit of Marshall McLuhan's *The Medium Is the Message,* the quality of learning that takes place in an organization is affected by the kind of organization it is. This is to say that an organization is not simply an instrumentality for providing organized learning activities to adults; it also provides an environment that either facilitates or inhibits learning.
>
> For example, if a young executive is being taught in his corporation's management-development program to involve his subordinates in decision making within his department, but his own superiors never involve him in making decisions, which management practice is he likely to adopt? Or if an adult church member is being taught to "love thy neighbor," but the total church

life is characterized by discrimination, jealousy, and intolerance, which value is more likely to be learned? Or if an adult student in a course on "The Meaning of Democratic Behavior" is taught that the clearest point of differentiation between democracy and other forms of government is the citizen's sharing in the process of public policy formulation, but the teacher has never given him a chance to share responsibility for conducting the course and the institution has never asked his advice on what courses should be offered, what is he likely to learn about the meaning of democracy?

No educational institution teaches just through its courses, workshops, and institutes; no corporation teaches just through its in-service education programs; and no voluntary organization teaches just through its meetings and study groups. They all teach by everything they do, and often they teach opposite lessons in their organizational operation from what they teach in their educational program.

This line of reasoning has led modern adult-education theorists to place increasing emphasis on the importance of building an educative environment in all institutions and organizations that undertake to help people learn. What are the characteristics of an educative environment? They are essentially the manifestations of the conditions of learning listed at the end of the last chapter. But they can probably be boiled down to four basic characteristics: 1) respect for personality, 2) participation in decision making, 3) freedom of expression and availability of information, and 4) mutuality of responsibility in defining goals, planning and conducting activities, and evaluating.

In effect, an educative environment—at least in a democratic culture—is one that exemplifies democratic values, that practices a democratic philosophy.

A democratic philosophy is characterized by a concern for the development of persons, a deep conviction as to the worth of every individual, and faith that people will make the right decisions for themselves if given the necessary information and support. It gives precedence to the growth of people over the accomplishment of things when these two values are in conflict.

It emphasizes the release of human potential over the control of human behavior. In a truly democratic organization there is a spirit of mutual trust, an openness of communications, a general attitude of helpfulness and cooperation, and a willingness to accept responsibility, in contrast to paternalism, regimentation, restriction of information, suspicion, and enforced dependency on authority.

When applied to the organization of adult education, a democratic philosophy means that the learning activities will be based on the real needs and interests of the participants; that the policies will be determined by a group that is a representative of all participants; and that there will be a maximum of participation by all members of the organization in sharing responsibility for making and carrying out decisions. The intimate relationship between democratic philosophy and adult education is eloquently expressed in these words of Eduard Lindeman:

One of the chief distinctions between conventional and adult education is to be found in the learning process itself. None but the humble become good teachers of adults. In an adult class the student's experience counts for as much as the teacher's knowledge. Both are exchangeable at par. Indeed, in some of the best adult classes it is sometimes difficult to discover who is learning most, the teacher or the students. This two-way learning is also reflected in the management of adult-education enterprises. Shared learning is duplicated by shared authority. In conventional education the pupils adapt themselves to the curriculum offered, but in adult education the pupils aid in formulating the curricula. . . . Under democratic conditions authority is of the group. This is not an easy lesson to learn, but until it is learned democracy cannot succeed (Gessner, 1956, p. 166).

I have a suspicion that for an organization to foster adult learning to the fullest possible degree it must go even farther than merely practicing a democratic philosophy, that it will really stimulate individual self-renewal to the extent that it consciously engages in continuous self-renewal for itself. Just as a teacher's most potent tool is the example of his own behavior, so I believe an organization's most effective instrument of influence is its own behavior.

This proposition is based on the premise that an organization tends to serve as a role model for those it influences. So if its purpose is to encourage its personnel, members, or constituents to engage in a process of continuous change and growth, it is likely to succeed to the extent that it models the role of organizational change and growth. This proposition suggests, therefore, that an organization must be innovative as well as democratic if it is to provide an environment conducive to learning. Table 5-4 provides some illustrative characteristics that seem to distinguish innovative from static organizations, as I interpret the insights from recent research on this fascinating subject. The right-hand column might well serve as a beginning checklist of desirable organizational goals in the dimensions of structure, atmosphere, management philosophy, decision making, and communication (Knowles, 1980, pp. 66–68).

An increasing number of systems theory applicators are developing sophisticated procedures and tools to assess organizational health, diagnose needs for change, feed data back into the system for continued renewal and use the data for precision in planning (Baughart, 1969; Bushnell and Rappaport, 1972; Davis, 1966; Handy and Hussain, 1968; Hare, 1967; Hartley, 1968; Kaufman, 1972; Rudwick, 1969; Schuttenberg, 1972).

The change theorists, building largely on the field-theoretical concepts of Kurt Lewin, have been concerned with the planning of change, the choice and use of strategies of change, organizational development, the role of the consultant and change agent, management of conflict, intervention theory, resistance to change, human relations training and the ethics of change agentry (Argyris, 1962, 1970; Bennis, 1966; Bennis, Benne, and Chin, 1968; Blake and Mouton, 1964; Eiben and Milliren, 1976; Greiner, 1971; Lewin, 1951; Lippitt, 1969; Schein, 1969; Watson, 1967; Zurcher, 1977).

Table 5-4
Some Characteristics of Static Versus Innovative Organizations

DIMENSIONS	CHARACTERISTICS	
	Static Organizations	Innovative Organizations
Structure	Rigid—much energy given to maintaining permanent departments, committees; reverence for tradition, constitution and by-laws.	Flexible—much use of temporary task forces; easy shifting of deparmental lines; readiness to change constitution; depart from tradition.
	Hierarchical—adherence to chain of command.	Multiple linkages based on functional collaboration.
	Roles defined narrowly.	Roles defined broadly.
	Property-bound.	Property-mobile.
Atmosphere	Task-centered, impersonal.	People-centered, caring.
	Cold, formal, reserved.	Warm, informal, intimate.
	Suspicious.	Trusting.
Management Philosophy and Attitudes	Function of management is to control personnel through coercive power.	Function of management is to release the energy of personnel; power is used supportively.
	Cautious—low risk-taking.	Experimental—high risk-taking.
	Attitude toward errors: to be avoided.	Attitude toward errors: to be learned from.
	Emphasis on personnel selection.	Emphasis on personnel development.
	Self-sufficiency—closed system regarding sharing resources.	Interdependency—open system regarding sharing resources.
	Emphasis on conserving resources.	Emphasis on developing and using resources.
	Low tolerance for ambiguity.	High tolerance for ambiguity.
Decision making and Policy making	High participation at top, low at bottom.	Relevant participation by all those affected.
	Clear distinction between policy making and policy execution.	Collaborative policy making and policy execution.
	Decision making by legal mechanisms.	Decision making by problem solving.
	Decisions treated as final.	Decisions treated as hypotheses to be tested.
Communication	Flow restricted.	Open flow—easy access.
	One-way—downward.	Multidirectional—up, down, sideways.
	Feelings repressed or hidden.	Feelings expressed.

(Knowles, 1980, p. 69)

SUMMARY

Theories of learning differ from theories of teaching. Various researchers have studied the topics of learning and teaching theories and the teaching-learning interaction. Consequently, a variety of theories exist about the nature of teaching and the teacher's role. Gage recognizes the distinction between the two theoretical frameworks, and asserts that learning theories address methods of learning while teaching theories address the methods employed to influence learning. Understandably, there is a strong correlation between learning and teaching theories: the learning theory(ies) adopted by the teacher affect the teaching theory(ies) employed. Both learning theories and teaching theories have played a prominent role in the research efforts, providing both principles of teaching and teaching concepts.

Hilgard's contribution is the identification of a schema of twenty learning principles from stimulus-response, cognitive, and motivation and personality theories. He used prominent theorists with similar notions about the roles of teachers to validate his premise. These included Thorndike, Guthrie, Skinner, Hull, Tolman, and Gagne, each an important contributor to the field.

Other theorists, including Rogers and Maslow, have focused on studies of adults in their research efforts. Their findings differ vastly from researchers who focused on animals and children. For instance, Rogers emphasizes the concepts of environment and facilitation in his explication of teaching—a sentiment with which Maslow would undoubtedly agree. The only exception is that Maslow would place an even greater emphasis on the teacher's responsibility for providing safety. Watson, Houle, and Tough have also provided insight in this area of study.

Of the concepts derived from theories of teaching, Dewey's are perhaps the most influential. His work resulted in the development of a system established on the concepts of experience, democracy, continuity, and interaction. It is Dewey's conceptualization of scientific thinking, in conjunction with those of cognitive theorists, that spawned the discovery or inquiry method. Other contributors in this area include Bruner, Suchman, and Crutchfield.

Identification or modeling as concepts of teaching, the most elaborate system of thought or imitation, was developed by Bandura. In this system, role modeling is the teacher's fundamental technique. Gage, analyzing the usefulness of the technique, states, "learning through imitation seems to be especially appropriate for tasks that have little cognitive structure."

Continued research efforts have resulted in new systems of thought. The value of teaching/learning as a tool to invoke critical thinking on the part of adults is an emerging concept: Mezirow calls this perspective transformation, and Brookfield calls it critical reflectivity. Another system of thought, drawing from field theory, systems theory, organizational development and consultation theories and ecological psychology, encompasses the ramifications of influencing the educative quality of total environments.

PART 2

Advancements in Adult Learning

Contemporary Perspectives on Effective Adult Learning

CHAPTER 6

Adult Learning Within Human Resource Development

The disciplines of human resource development (HRD) and adult education (AE) both view the process of adult learning as being central to their theory and practice. Even so, the purposes of HRD and AE differ, and their perspective on adult learning differs. The core difference is related to control of the goals and purposes for which adult learning is employed—organizational versus individual control. This chapter looks closely at HRD, the role of adult learning within HRD, and the issue of control.

HUMAN RESOURCE DEVELOPMENT GOALS

Human resource development (HRD) professionals are in general agreement as to their goals. Most take the position that HRD should focus on increasing the performance requirements of its host organizations through the development of the organization's work force (ASTD-USDL, 1990; Knowles, 1990; McLagan 1989; Swanson, 1995).

Others believe HRD should focus on individual development and personal fulfillment without using organizational performance as the measure of worth (Dirkx, 1996). Yet, it is the increase in performance resulting from HRD that justifies its existence. From either perspective, the question of contribution always comes into play. Holton

(1998) provides a very useful taxonomy of "performance outcomes" and "performance drivers" that accommodates the gap between those focused on the organization first and then the individual versus those focused on the individual first and then the organization. He informs HRD professionals to pay attention to both *performance outcomes* and *performance drivers*. Thus, organization *performance,* such as high quality services delivered to external customers, can be logically connected to *performance drivers,* such as learning and process improvement (see Chapter 17 for a more complete explanation).

HRD, when practiced within productive organizations, should strive to contribute directly to the host organization's goals. The host organization is a purposeful system that must attain effective and efficient survival goals. Consequently, it is the responsibility of HRD to focus on those goals as well as individual employee goals.

HRD can be thought of as a sub-system that functions within the larger organizational system. An organization is defined as a productive enterprise having a mission and goals (Holton, 1997). Additionally, an organization is a system, with definable inputs, processes, outputs, parts and purposes (Rummler and Brache, 1995). Contemporary HRD literature consistently talks of linking HRD to the strategic goals of the organization (for example, Gill, 1995). If HRD is to be respected and useful in organizations, it must position itself as a strategic partner and achieve the same level of importance as traditional core organizational processes such as finance, production, and marketing (Torraco and Swanson, 1995). To gain an understanding of the purpose of the HRD sub-system, the goals of the larger system in which it operates should be considered.

Of the scarce resources that organizations must procure and allocate, perhaps none is more important to the success of the firm than human resources (Edvinsson and Malone, 1997). A major expenditure for most organizations is tied directly to workers, including wages, benefits, and HRD (Becker, 1993; Noe, *et al.,* 1994). And while human resources are unique in that people have feelings, make plans, support families, and develop communities, they are in some ways similar to other resources: Firms expect a return on the money invested in their employees (Cascio, 1987). Unless workers contribute to the profitability and viability of an organization, it would make economic sense to invest the money elsewhere. Even in nonprofit organizations, employees must contribute meaningfully to organizational goals that are essential to survival, even though those goals are not stated in dollars of profit.

The purpose of reviewing this basic reality of organizational survival is not to paint an unfeeling picture of the workplace in which people are merely cogs in a mechanistic machine. There are numerous examples of companies that meet their organizational goals that are also among the most progressive in terms of employee treatment and relations (Levering and Moskowitz, 1994). Nowhere has it been shown that organizational success should be in direct conflict with employee happiness and well-being.

Performance then is defined as the *organizational system outputs that have value to the customer in the form of productivity attributable to the organization, work process, and/or individual contributor levels.* Using this definition, performance is the means by which organizations measure their goals. Performance can be measured in many ways: rate of return, cycle time, and quality of output are three such possibilities. Additionally, it is important to make the distinction between levels of performance. Performance takes place and can be measured at the organizational, process, and individual levels.

If HRD is to be aligned with the goals and strategies of the organization, and performance is the primary means by which the goals and strategies of organizations are realized, then it follows that HRD should be first and foremost concerned with maintaining and/or improving performance at the organizational, process, and individual levels. If HRD is to be a value-added activity of the firm (instead of a line item of cost that is to be controlled and minimized), then HRD practitioners must be concerned about performance and how it enables organizations to achieve their goals.

HRD AND PERFORMANCE IMPROVEMENT

How can HRD improve performance? There are many possibilities at the individual, process, and organizational levels. Figure 6-1 is a matrix of performance levels and variables that can aid in the diagnosis of performance problems (Swanson, 1996, p. 52). Within each cell are enabling questions that permit diagnosis of performance, but each cell can also serve as a conceptual framework for classifying performance interventions.

PERFORMANCE LEVELS

PERFORMANCE VARIABLES	Organization Level	Process Level	Individual Level
Mission/Goal	Does the organization's mission/goal fit the reality of the economic, political, and cultural forces?	Do the process goals enable the organization to meet organizational and individual missions/goals?	Are the professional and personal mission/goals of individuals congruent with the organization's?
System Design	Does the organizational system provide structure and policies supporting the desired performance?	Are processes designed in such a way to work as a system?	Do individuals face obstacles that impede their job performance?
Capacity	Does the organization have the leadership, capital, and infrastructure to achieve its mission/goals?	Does the process have the capacity to perform (quantity, quality, and timeliness)?	Does the individual have the mental, physical, and emotional capacity to perform?
Motivation	Do the policies, culture, and reward systems support the desired performance?	Does the process provide the information and human factors required to maintain it?	Does the individual want to perform no matter what?
Expertise	Does the organization establish and maintain selection and training policies and resources?	Does the process of developing expertise meet the changing demands of changing processes?	Does the individual have the knowledge, skills, and experience to perform?

© *Richard A. Swanson 1996*

Figure 6-1. *Performance diagnosis matrix of enabling questions.*

As an example, the mission/goal variable at the organizational level asks whether the organization's mission and goals fit various internal and external realities. If they do not, then most likely performance is being impeded. Assume that an organization's mission and goals do not fit the reality of its culture and this is resulting in suboptimized performance. HRD could attempt to solve this performance problem through structured intervention in a couple of ways, depending on the outcomes of detailed analysis. A process could be put in place to formulate mission and goals that accommodate the organizational culture. On the other hand, a cultural change process could be implemented to modify the culture so that it is better aligned with the mission and goals of the organization. This example and the performance diagnosis matrix show that numerous impediments to performance, and consequently numerous challenges and opportunities for HRD to improve performance, exist.

When business and industry leaders talk about the high value of core competence to the life of their companies, they are talking primarily about knowledge and expertise that fits within and between the fifteen cells in the performance diagnosis matrix. This learning can also be categorized as public knowledge, industry-specific knowledge, or firm-specific knowledge that is critical to sustaining organizational performance (Leonard-Barton, 1995, p. 21).

Notice that *adult learning* plays an important role in most, if not all, of the matrix cells. Just getting to the point of doing the work in each diagnostic cell of the organizational system requires much to be learned in order to understand and operate within and between these cells. For example, if HRD is to change culture, then certainly the principles and practices of adult learning will play an important role as employees develop and learn new norms. Most process improvement strategies embrace some form of self-directed teams that examine their work processes and learn better ways to perform them. Building leadership capacity is a learning process. In organizations where innovation is a key performance driver, learning becomes central to survival (Senge, 1990; Watkins and Marsick, 1993). It is not difficult to see that there are potential needs for adult learning within every cell of the performance diagnosis matrix.

One important strategic role for HRD is to build the organization's strategic capability— the knowledge and expertise required to figure out the present and to develop rational scenarios of the future and ways to connect them (Torraco and Swanson, 1995). Adult learning, from this perspective, is critical in order to maintain the performance of an existing system and to improve upon that system. Increasingly, it is an organization's intellectual capital that leads to sustained competitive advantage (Edvinsson and Malone, 1997; Stewart, 1997). Adult learning becomes a powerful organizational improvement strategy when it is embedded in a holistic performance improvement system framework.

HRD AND ADULT LEARNING

The issue of control—organizational versus individual—is useful in exploring the role of adult learning in HRD. Cervero and Wilson help in their book, *Planning Responsibly for Adult Education: A Guide to Negotiating Power and Interests* (1994), by noting that the AE (adult education) literature has been "focused on technical, 'how to' skills, while presupposing some ideally neutral staging area in which these skills will be exercised, and have remained surprisingly silent on the troublesome issues of 'what for' and 'for whom.'" They go on to speak more forcefully, "Which people get to decide the purpose, content, and format of the program? Is it always the people with the most power? Is it the adults who will participate in the program, the leadership of the institution sponsoring the program, or the planners themselves?" (Cervero and Wilson, 1994, p. xii).

So what is the relationship between HRD and adult learning? Swanson (1996) defines HRD as a process of developing and/or unleashing human expertise through organizational development and personnel training and development for the purpose of improving performance at the organizational, work process, and individual levels. McLagan (1989) offers an earlier definition of HRD along similar lines: the integrated use of training and development, organizational development and career development to improve individual, group, and organizational effectiveness. In both definitions, it is apparent that the outcome of HRD is *performance improvement*. It should be equally apparent that *learning*—knowledge and expertise—is a core component of HRD but not the whole of HRD.

HRD is broader than training or adult learning. There are HRD interventions that involve much more than training or learning activities, and some can have no planned educational component. This aspect of HRD falls in the "unleashing" element of the definition. For example, HRD might be involved in improving a business process intended to result in a newly engineered business process and minor work method modifications that are transparent to the worker. They could require no formal learning effort to implement. If training were required, it would be a relatively small part of the entire intervention. One could attempt to argue that the HRD work to improve the process involves acts of learning and is therefore adult learning. The rebuttal is that the desired outcome is to improve the process rather than the learning in individuals working in the business process.

These remarks should not be construed as an argument that the discipline of AE is a subset of HRD. It is not. While adult learning takes places in both HRD and AE and both are deeply committed to *adult learning*, HRD and AE are discrete disciplines. Their area of intersection occurs within adult learning. When adult learning outcomes and learning process decisions about individuals are bounded by rules and requirements of the organization, adult learning is HRD. When the adult learning outcomes and learning process rules and requirements are located in the individual, it is AE. The core difference is in the idea of control. If the organization retains the authority to approve or disapprove learning interventions, the control is with the organization, and therefore it is HRD. To the point that control is overtly and formally shared, the learning process is both AE and HRD (Swanson and Arnold, 1997). For example, Robinson and Stern (1997) offer vivid illustrations of two essential elements that foster corporate creativity and encourage employees to control their learning journey. They speak of "self-initiated activity" (an activity performed by an individual who is not asked to do it) and "unofficial activity" (an activity performed by an individual over a period of time in which he continues to work on his learning journey without direct official recognition and/or support) and the benefits organizations gain by allowing these to take place among workers.

Thus, some HRD processes and interventions do not focus on adult learning. By the same token, AE does not always take place in the context of organizations for the purpose of performance improvement. The outcome of AE can be personal growth, general knowledge, or even amusement.

For HRD, adult learning focuses on development interventions that have two attributes: First, the context is organizational, and second, the desired outcome is learning—knowledge and expertise—that will impact the performance goals of the host organization.

Facilitating adult learning in performance-oriented organizations often creates a tension between the assumptions underlying andragogical practice and the organization's performance requirements. For many, best adult education practices allow maximum individual control and appeal directly to the needs most meaningful to the individual (Hiemstra and Sisco, 1990). When the individual's needs are consistent with the organization's, there is no tension. When the individual's needs and goals are not congruent with the organization's performance requirements, and the organization is providing the required learning experience, a tension exists and inevitably results in some degree of organizational control.

For this reason, learning professionals in HRD must balance practices that lead to the most effective adult learning with those that will lead to performance outcomes. When learning is required, performance will be compromised if effective adult learning principles are not incorporated. However, learning will also be compromised without an emphasis on performance principles because the learning opportunities will likely be discontinued if performance outcomes are not achieved.

Effective HRD professionals have the ability to find the optimum balance in each situation. Fortunately, the majority of learning situations present no problem. In many cases, the best interests of the employee and the organization can be met at the same time. This is especially true in organizations that link employee career advancement to performance so that employees' lives are enhanced as the organization's performance improves.

But there are other instances where adult learning principles can not be wholly implemented. Consider organizational change for example. Can a large organization in a survival mode allow individuals the freedom to choose whether they want to learn a new way to run the organization? Hardly. Can an organization continue to invest in learning programs for its employees that do not lead to performance improvement over the long run? No.

In summary, HRD has a great concern to create more humane organizations. However, by definition, HRD must ensure that the organization's performance improvement needs are met. At certain points, this is likely to lead to some adaptation and compromise of the core andragogical principles. Effective application of adult learning principles in HRD requires practitioners to become comfortable with, and even embrace, the tension between adult learning and performance principles.

THE PREMISE OF INDIVIDUALS CONTROLLING THEIR OWN LEARNING

One of the most popular ideas in AE is that individuals want to have control over their learning based on their personal goals and that learning will increase as a result. The idea is that better outcomes result when the learner retains control throughout the learning phases. There is controversy related to this idea of how much control individual learners want and can handle.

During the 1980s there was considerable discussion about embracing self-directed learning as a unifying theory and goal for the discipline of AE. Even one of the leading proponents, Stephen Brookfield (1988) acknowledged that self-directed learning is far more complex than first proposed, and that the push in AE to embrace self-directed learning was motivated in part by the discipline's search for an identity and unifying theory.

The point of this discussion is not to enter the AE debate about self-directed learning. It must be recognized that the core assumptions of andragogy do not raise learner self-directedness to the same high level as has been proposed by many AE theorists and practitioners. Andragogy suggests that adults have a *self-concept* of being responsible for their own lives and expect others to treat them as being capable of self-direction (see Chapter 4). AE suggests that the purpose of learning should be to develop self-directed learning capacity in adults (Brookfield, 1986). The self-concept principle in adult learning theory has consistently been confused with the democratic humanism goals of AE that all adults become self-directing. The first is a *characteristic of adults*, the latter a *purpose for learning*. This should not be interpreted to say that the AE goals are wrong, but rather that the core learning principle of independent self-concept must be considered separately from the goals and purposes of AE. It is the latter that has falsely made HRD look inconsistent with adult learning principles. HRD practice is generally in harmony with the andragogical notion of independent "self-concept," but clearly does not share the goals and purposes of AE.

Because HRD focuses on performance outcomes, the significance of learner control is viewed as secondary by most professionals in HRD. AE reaction to the performance focus rests with the concern that the feelings and worth of human beings as individuals are ignored by too much emphasis on bottom-line results. And, there is evidence that learning or enhancing the capacity to learn, is a valuable outcome in and of itself and that sponsoring organizations logically benefit (Robinson and Stern, 1997). Thus, the line is sometimes falsely drawn between those who view HRD as tied to business goals and focused on the bottom line and those who would like to take a more humanistic stance in the matter. In fact, HRD shares concerns for a humanistic workplace, has *adult learning* as one of its core components, but also embraces organizational performance theory. The gap is not as wide as some would portray it to be.

THE PHASES OF THE ADULT LEARNING PLANNING PROCESS

Adult learning is defined as *the process of adults gaining knowledge and expertise*. Additionally, the ideas that (1) learners universally want to have control over their learning process and (2) that learning increases as a result comes from AE. Adult learning theory takes a more situational stance on shared control.

Just what are the issues surrounding this core idea of learners controlling their own learning process? A contradiction exists between the AE ideal of individuals taking control of their learning and the reality of adult limitations in taking control of their own decision-making. The following sections discuss the practical issues facing HRD as it relates to adults directing their own learning at the needs, creation, implementation, and evaluation planning phases.

Figure 6-2, titled "Adult Learners Controlling their Learning Process," provides the framework for this discussion. It shows the four phases of the adult learning planning process and an outer ring of theory.

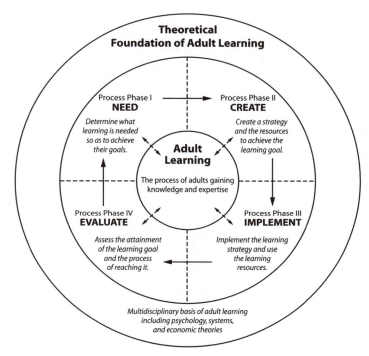

Figure 6-2. *Adult learners controlling their learning process.*

The four phases of the adult learning planning process are:

- **Need.** Determine what learning is needed so as to achieve goals.
- **Create.** Create a strategy and resources to achieve the learning goal(s).
- **Implement.** Implement the learning strategy and use the learning resources.
- **Evaluate.** Assess the attainment of the learning goal and the process of reaching it.

These four phases serve as the categories or lenses used to search for what is known about learners controlling their own learning process.

Adults Determine their own Learning Needs

"Who needs what, as defined by whom?" is a wonderful way to sum up the issues of needs assessment in relation to the issue of control. At the *need* phase, adults who exhibit control will fully determine the learning needs required to achieve their personal goal(s). The idea of control at the need determination phase can better be examined through the perspective of four types of learning:

Type of Learning	Locus of Control
Unintended Learning	No control
Self-directed Learning	Learner controlled
Mediated Learning	Shared control between learner and external authority
Authority-directed Learning	Authority controlled (organization or individual)

Even though there are limitations to learner control, Pentland (1977) found that the top four reasons why adults chose to learn on their own were all related to wanting to retain control of the learning process. In this vein, the determination of learning *needs*, the up-front commitment to learning, is the phase with the greatest amount of attention in the literature.

The determination of learning *needs* perspective in the AE literature is primarily reactive in nature rather than strategic or even tactical. Learning professionals are portrayed as reacting to the needs expressed by adult learners. The control resides with the learner, and the learning professional responds to those felt needs. This assumes that the learner is a) fully aware of his or her needs, b) can accurately assess the specific learning required, and c) is motivated enough to engage in any learning needed, even if threatening. Brookfield (1986, p. 97) reacts to this notion in saying that "to take learner's definitions of need as always determining appropriate practice is to cast the facilitator as a technician within the consumer mode. It is to remove from the facilitator all professional judgment and to turn him or her into a 'knee-jerk' satisfier of consumer needs. Education becomes one giant department store in which facilitators are providers of whatever learners (consumers) believe will make them happy."

The extension of this idea into HRD is to conduct a learning/training *wants* analysis among employees and to call it a training *needs* analysis. Employees are surveyed as to what training they would like to have and then the training options gaining the most votes are used as a basis for the course offerings. Recent developments in conducting these low-level surveys through computers and electronic data-gather systems have provided an air of sophistication to this incomplete and/or incompetent practice. Surveys of this nature can be one important element in a sound *needs* analysis process, but not the process itself.

The fundamental flaw with this approach is that there is no substantial attention given to individuals, work process, or the organization. It does nothing well. This popular vote strategy requires almost no professional expertise on the part of those running the process and allows them to hide behind the cloak of democracy. On the positive side, the fundamental strength of this approach is that it provides the opportunity to participate, even if at a minimum level. Given such opportunity, objections are minimized and motivation is increased even when unpopular alternatives are put forward.

The reality is that this approach is not effective for improving performance (Swanson, 1996). Employee *wants* are only sometimes related to real performance improvement *needs*. Frequently, this is not due to employee ignorance, but simply the fact that they do not have the expertise, information, or time to properly analyze their needs. Their wants are their best guess, but are not accurate. Performance improvement often requires joint planning, and occasionally, an external analyst. While this may create some tension initially as control is shifted to the organization, adults frequently become quite comfortable with it when they realize that giving up some control will ultimately enable them to do their jobs better and thus gain another form of control.

Adults Create and Implement their own Learning

The second phase of the adult learning planning process is *creating* a strategy and the resources to achieve the learning goal. The third phase is *implementing* the learning strategy and using the learning resources.

Rosenblum and Darkenwald (1983) concluded from their experimental research that high motivation could lead to high satisfaction and achievement *without* participant planning involvement. If this was the case, one interpretation could be that involvement at the *need* phase is critical for the purpose of motivation and that similar learner involvement in the other phases is not as important. This could also be the reason why there is so little planning literature related to the *create* and *implement* phases other than in-process instructional techniques for engaging the learner. Without the issue of control, it is easy to see that these techniques at the *create* and *implement* phases use the core assumptions of andragogy while avoiding the fundamental question of control.

The relevant AE literature focused on learner control of the creation and implementation planning phase is scant. Most inferences must be made from related studies and from the *mediated learning*— the shared control between the learner and an external authority (usually the instructor).

For example, the effect of adult learners' self-concepts and their opinions about the content at the time they are directly engaged in the learning process has been studied. The classic Spelman and Levy (1966) study related to adults' self-concept of powerlessness and the distorting impact it had on their learning. In this study, heavy smokers learned as much general medical knowledge as the nonsmokers, but learned significantly less about the relation to lung cancer than the nonsmokers. Smokers, feeling relatively powerless in context of their smoking addiction and its consequences, ended up learning less about lung cancer. The "liberating knowledge" was ineffectual.

In a more hopeful vein, part of Tolman's (1959) theory of purposive behaviorism explains *expectancies* in context of experience. Tolman suggests that adults learn where the goal is and how to get to it. Thus, it is reasonable to think that there is a melding of purposes between the organization and the individual contributor and that the means (creation and implementation) of achieving those purposes becomes relatively easy.

It could be that self-directed learning decisions at the *create* and *implement* phases result in high motivation, minimum growth, and high satisfaction. Thus, a counter theory to self-directed learning is that pursuing the opinions of adults to create and implement learning leads to low-risk decisions—comfort rather than growth. The control dilemma concerns HRD professionals as they struggle to meet organizational goals, determine the content and method of programs, and seek to fully engage learners.

Brookfield sheds light on this dilemma: "For a facilitator to completely ignore learners' needs and expressions of preference is arrogant and unrealistic. But it is just as misguided for a facilitator to completely repress his or her own ideas concerning worthwhile curricula or effective methods and to allow learners complete control over these (1982, p. 97). When it comes to the *create* and *implement* phases of planning learning theory and practice—the shared control between the external authority or instructor and the learner is the primary focus rather than learner self-direction. Within this model, professional educators engage learners and potential learners in the *create* phase so as to establish motivation and community and to promote validity of the experience and materials. At the *implementation* phase, shared control can take a variety of forms including formative evaluation, team learning, and peer instruction.

Adults Evaluate their own Learning

The fourth phase of the adult learning planning process is evaluation which is defined as "a systematic collection of evidence to determine if desired changes are taking place (Swanson, 1996, p. 26)." Before discussing adult learners controlling the *evaluation* of their own learning, it is critical to separate learning that they have controlled up to this phase from learning that has been controlled by others up to this point.

Assuming the learner has retained and executed control to this stage, the learner should be asking the evaluation question, "What systematic collection of evidence needs to be carried out to determine whether my desired changes took place?" The follow-up question is, "Based on the evidence collected, to what degree did the desired changes take place?" The questions are focused on learning outcomes or summative evaluation, not the process of working toward the learning outcomes or formative evaluation.

The learning evaluation literature is careful about noting direct measures of outcomes versus proxy, or related, measures. For example, a direct measure of a desired knowledge and/or expertise learning outcome would require instruments to directly measure the change.

An indirect measure of knowledge might be to ask oneself or participants if they thought they learned a lot or whether they were satisfied with their learning. Indirect measures have highly questionable validity. Research has shown that participant self-ratings of learning are not related to actual learning (Alliger and Janak, 1989; Alliger, et al, 1997; Dixon, 1991). While self-ratings are generally reliable (consistent), they are generally not trusted as being accurate (valid). Furthermore, participant ratings can be easily inflated by influential techniques by the instructor (Swanson and Fentress, 1976).

Thus, if adult learners rely on proxy measures—*self-assessment* of anticipated outcomes— they will most likely make false conclusions based on invalid data. Worse yet, if the learning professional, serving as a resource to the adult learning process, relies on learner perceptions and feelings about desired changes having taken place (even more indirect measures), the problem is compounded. Examples of such highly questionable evaluation practices relying on secondary sources of perception data are reported in the literature (see Cervero and Wilson, 1994, p. 60–61, 86–87, 111–113).

The adult learner, wanting to retain control over the evaluation process while gaining valid data, will, in most instances, have to reach outside his or her internal reference to gain rational evaluation data. Obtaining direct measures of learning—knowledge and expertise—from formal tests or expert judges would be the most likely alternative. In many avocational realms of personal development, interest groups provide external measures of skill through competitive judging (for example, car shows, stamp shows, dance competition). At a less threatening level, experts serving as mentors can provide similar evaluation.

The humanistic side of the evaluation literature has had a resistance to summative, outcome evaluation. The formative evaluation view is that evaluation should be diagnostic and have the purpose of improving learning, rather than simply determining if the desired changes took place. Formative evaluation is seen as feedback and feed-forward between the various phases of learning. Again, the purpose of formative evaluation is to be a part of the learning process, not to assess the drive toward organization performance and the demands for adult competence in the workplace. Furthermore, it is controlled by the organization, not the individual. HRD functions in an organizational world and demands results and the assessing of results. If not management, work teams will likely be full partners in the *evaluation* phase of learning outcomes rather than the individual learners.

In summary, adult learning theory provides sound advice to HRD at each phase of the planning process:

Phase	Sound Practice
Need	Engage learners in this phase to gain higher motivation. Do not expect self-reported needs to be accurate for either the individual or the organization.
Create	Engage learners in this phase to gain higher validity in the selected learning strategies.
Implement	Engage learners in this phase to better mediate the actual learning.
Evaluate	Engage learners in this phase to gain higher self-reflection and integration of the knowledge and expertise being sought.

CONCLUSION

Exploring the gaps between research and practice is a primary role for the reflective practitioner in HRD (Swanson and Holton, 1997). The call to action is to implement best known practices *and* to conduct more research related to the methods to assess valid learning needs, create and implement valid strategies for achieving learning goals, and conduct valid assessment of learning. This effort should be directed at organization needs as well as those of individual performers.

The idea that the goal of HRD is or should be performance improvement is by no means universally accepted by practitioners or researchers in the field. Some hold that fostering learning or the capacity to learn is a valuable outcome in and of itself and assume that sponsoring organizations will logically benefit. Thus, the line is sometimes drawn between those who view HRD as tied to business goals and focused on performance and those who would like to take a more humanistic stance in the matter. This dichotomy can be termed the performance-versus-learning debate as a matter of convenience (see Swanson, 1995; Watkins and Marsick, 1995).

This debate, like many others, is fueled by an often misconstrued delineation of the opposing sides. Upon closer examination, the two sides may have more in common than first proposed. On the one hand, those who adhere to the performance orientation of HRD do not do so in an attempt to deny the dignity and worth of employees. Neither do they deny that learning is a necessary component of performance. The goal of performance-focused HRD is simply to ensure that the HRD process within organizations contributes to the goals of the organizational system within which it operates. This does not necessarily imply an authoritarian management style. Some might argue that to *ignore* performance issues is itself inhumane and inconsiderate of the workforce. While organizational performance does not guarantee job security, poor organizational performance puts jobs at serious risk. On the other hand, those on the learning side of the debate are not so naive to think that organizational goals and performance are irrelevant to HRD. Quite to the contrary, they *are* seen as core, but that learning is not always directly tied to the bottom line of an organization.

From the HRD perspective, adult learning, when practiced within productive organizations, should strive to contribute directly to the advancement of the host organization's goals. The host organization is a purposeful system that must pursue effective and efficient survival goals. Consequently, it is the responsibility of HRD to focus on organizational goals as well as individual goals.

CHAPTER 7

New Perspectives on Andragogy

This chapter discusses new perspectives on andragogy that have emerged from research and theory in a variety of disciplines. The chapter is organized by the core andragogical principles and examines new thinking that refines and elaborates on each principle. These core principles are 1) the learner's need to know, 2) self-directed learning, 3) prior experiences of the learner, 4) readiness to learn, 5) orientation to learning and problem solving, and 6) motivation to learn.

LEARNER'S NEED TO KNOW

The core principle that adults "need to know" why before they engage in learning has led to the now generally accepted premise that adults should be engaged in a collaborative planning process for their learning. Indeed, one of the distinguishing characteristics of many adult learning programs is the shared control of program planning and facilitation. Even in learning situations in which the learning content is prescribed, sharing control over the learning strategies is believed to make learning more effective. Engaging adults as collaborative partners for learning satisfies their "need to know" as well as appeals to their self-concept as independent learners.

Because mutual planning is so widely accepted and generally found to be effective by most practitioners, few researchers have been motivated to test this assumption. Training researchers have conducted research related to this premise that suggests three dimensions to the need to know: the need to know *how* learning will be conducted, *what* learning will occur, and *why* learning is important.

How learning is conducted. Tannenbaum, Mathieu, Salas and Cannon-Bowers (1991) studied a group of new employees to examine the extent to which training fulfillment predicted post-training attitudes. Training fulfillment was defined as the extent to which training met or fulfilled the group's expectations and desires. The study focused mostly on how the training was conducted and was somewhat consistent with adult learning principles. Their study showed that training fulfillment was related to post-training organizational commitment, academic self-efficacy, physical self-efficacy, and motivation to use the training. The positive results were strongest for commitment and motivation to use training. These findings clearly point to the importance of understanding trainees' expectations and desires through needs assessment and mutual planning.

What is learned. Hicks and Klimoski (1987) studied a group of managers attending training on performance appraisals. The group that received a more realistic preview of what topics would be covered and the expected outcomes and were given a choice about whether to attend the training were more likely to believe the workshop was appropriate for them, believed they were better able to profit from the workshop, showed more commitment to their decision to attend the training, and were more satisfied with the learning. Students with a high degree of choice also were more motivated to learn and learned more.

Baldwin, Magjuka, and Loher (1991) directly tested the proposition that trainee involvement in planning about learning would enhance the learning process. Their findings reinforce the importance of choice about learning. Trainees who had a choice about attending training, and received their choice, had higher pretraining motivation and learning. The worst results were found for those offered a choice, but did not get their choice.

Why they should learn. Clark, Dobbins, and Ladd (1993) explored a third dimension of the learner's need to know in their study of fifteen training groups across twelve different organizations representing a wide variety of organizational types and training topics. Their findings showed that job and career utility were significant predictors of training motivation. Furthermore, when employees had the chance to provide input into the training decision, they were more likely to perceive job and career utility.

Reber and Wallin's (1984) work took this a step further. They investigated the effect of trainees receiving knowledge of results from previous trainees' successful application of training. Trainees with knowledge of results achieved post-training goals, while others did not.

Implications. These studies all focused on adult learning in one setting (organizational training), so some caution is appropriate in generalizing about all adult learning situations. Nonetheless, these are strong studies that directly support this andragogical assumption. The message to adult learning professionals is that the common prescription to involve adults in mutual planning and as learning partners is a sound one. However, the exact means by which this effect works cannot be determined from this research. That is, engaging adults in planning the learning process could enable people to decide not to participate in low-value learning, or could actually change their attitude toward the learning. Regardless, the research seems to point to three areas in which adults need information and involvement before learning: the how, what, and why of learning.

SELF-DIRECTED LEARNING

Perhaps no aspect of andragogy has received so much attention and debate as the premise that adults are self-directed learners. That adults can and do engage in self-directed learning (SDL) is now a foregone conclusion in adult learning research. Questions remain as to whether self-directed learning is a characteristic of adult learners, and whether it should be a goal of adult educators to help all adult learners become self-directed. Much of the confusion surrounding the self-directed learning assumption stems from conceptual confusion about the meaning of self-directed learning (SDL).

There are two conceptions of self-directed learning prevalent in the literature (Brookfield, 1986; Candy, 1991). First, self-directed learning is seen as self-teaching, whereby learners are capable of taking control of the mechanics and techniques of teaching themselves in a particular subject. For example, a person who completes an independent study course would clearly engage in self-teaching. Second, self-directed learning is conceived of as personal autonomy, which Candy (1991) calls autodidaxy. Autonomy means taking control of the goals and purposes of learning and assuming ownership of learning. This leads to an internal change of consciousness in which the learner sees knowledge as contextual and freely questions what is learned.

These two dimensions of self-directed learning are relatively independent, though they may overlap. A person may have a high degree of personal autonomy, but choose to learn in a highly teacher-directed instructional setting because of convenience, speed, or learning style. For example, a person may decide to learn more about personal financial planning, and, after weighing different strategies, decide that attending courses at a university is his or her preferred approach. In fact, many adults decide that traditional instruction is the best approach when they know little about a subject. Choosing traditional instruction over self-teaching does not mean a person has given up ownership or control just because he or she chooses to access learning in this manner. Conversely, just because an adult engages in self-teaching does not mean that the person is autonomous. Continuing the earlier example, the student in the independent study course may have little ownership if the supervising teacher sets all the requirements. Thus, the presence or absence of activities associated with self-teaching is not an accurate indicator of personal autonomy. For most learning professionals, the most important dimension of self-directed learning is building personal autonomy.

The assumption that all adults have full capacity for self-teaching and personal autonomy in every learning situation is generally not accepted. Any particular learner in a particular learning situation is likely to exhibit different capabilities and preferences. Grow (1991) suggested that self-directed learning is situational and that the "teacher's" job is to match styles with the student. Grow (1991) proposed four stages, and corresponding teaching styles as presented in Table 7-1.

It is important to note that mismatches can occur in either direction. That is, too much self-directedness can be as big a problem as too little, depending upon the learner. For example, a learner who is experienced with the subject matter and has strong learning skills will likely be frustrated in highly controlled learning situations. Conversely, a learner who is inexperienced with the subject and has poorly developed self-directed learning skills will likely be intimidated, at least initially, in highly self-directed learning situations. Because learners in any given learning situation are likely to vary widely as to what stage they are in, the teacher has to structure the learning situation to accommodate all stages.

Table 7-1
Grow's Stages in Learning Autonomy

Stage	Student	Teacher	Examples
Stage 1	Dependent	Authority, coach	Coaching with immediate feedback, drill. Informational lecture. Overcoming deficiencies and resistance
Stage 2	Interested	Motivator, guide	Inspiring lecture plus guided discussion. Goal-setting and learning strategies
Stage 3	Involved	Facilitator	Discussion facilitated by teacher who participates as equal. Seminar. Group projects
Stage 4	Self-directed	Consultant, delegator	Internship, dissertation, individual work or self-directed study group

It is also important to note that the reason a learner is in a particular stage may be related to self-teaching skills, or personal autonomy, or both. Suppose a learner exhibits stage one behaviors. That person could be highly autonomous, but does not know how to learn particular material. Or, the person could have strong self-teaching skills, but little autonomy. Or, the person could be highly autonomous and a good self-teacher, but simply chooses not to learn individually.

Garrison (1997) more formally captured this multidimensional view of self-directed learning. He proposed a comprehensive model of self-directed learning based on three core components: 1) self-management (control), 2) motivation (entering and task), and 3) self-monitoring (responsibility). According to Garrison, AE has traditionally focused on the first component, the control of learning, and paid less attention to the learning processes. He suggests that equal attention should be focused on motivation issues, including the motivation to engage in self-directed learning and to complete self-directed learning tasks. His third component, self-monitoring, is the cognitive learning processes as well as metacognitive skills a person needs to engage in self-directed learning. Adult learning professionals need to pay attention to all three components.

A related stream of research comes from psychology and the concept referred to as locus of control (Rotter, 1966; Rotter, 1990). Locus of control occurs when "people attribute the cause or control of events to themselves or to an external environment. Those who ascribe control of events to themselves are said to have internal locus of control and are referred to as *internals*. People who attribute control to outside forces are said to have an external locus of control and are termed *externals*" (Spector, 1982).

Internals perceive greater control and actually seek situations in which control is possible (Kabanoff and O'Brien, 1980). When it comes to successfully performing a task that requires luck or skill, *externals* are more likely to choose luck and *internals* choose skill (Kahle, 1980). There appears to be a relationship between locus of control and experience. Phares (1976) notes that *internals* exert greater control of their environment, exhibit better learning, seek new information more actively, and seem more concerned with information than with social demands of situations. Externals tend to be more nervous than internals (Archer, 1979). Thus, internals do not need as much help when it comes to learning and externals, even after given help, tend to not take control.

"Locus of control is considered an important personality variable in organizational research and theory" (Spector, 1982, p. 493). As such, it is believed to be a stable trait, not easily changed. Thus, research suggests that freeing those who have not taken charge of their learning in the past to now take charge of their learning must be tempered by realities of the limits of the individual's personality. Some individuals will naturally prefer and seek more independence (internals), while others will prefer and may seek more direction (externals).

As a practical matter, the contingency model of self-directedness seems most appropriate for facilitators of adult learning because it more closely matches the reality of most learning situations. There are many factors that individuals weigh in choosing whether to behave in a self-directed way at a particular point. These may include:

- Learning style
- Previous experience with the subject matter
- Social orientation
- Efficiency

- Previous learning socialization
- Locus of control

That an adult learner may choose not to be self-directed, for whatever reason, does not invalidate the core principle that adults, and adults in the United States in particular, have a self-concept of being independent. In fact, it is having the freedom to choose their learning strategy that is critical. It is the sense of personal autonomy, not self-teaching, that seems to be most important for adults. The biggest problems arise when adult learners want to have more independence in their learning but are denied that opportunity.

Some adult educators insist that all learning should have as its goal increasing personal autonomy in a learner. We agree that there are many learning situations in which this is true, but we must also be careful to avoid imposing a set of goals and purposes on each learning event. While it can be argued that any learning has the effect of building autonomy in a person, there may be learning events in which there is not a core aim to build autonomy in a learner. For example, a CPR class taught by a hospital may help people be more self-sufficient, but may not enhance self-directed learning ability. Grow's model does not necessarily presume a goal of building self-directedness.

PRIOR EXPERIENCE OF THE LEARNER

The role of the adult learner's experience has become an increasingly important area of focus, particularly in the professional development arena. Chapter 4 noted four means by which adults' experiences impact learning. These are:

1. Create a wider range of individual differences.
2. Provide a rich resource for learning.
3. Create biases that can inhibit or shape new learning.
4. Provide grounding for adults' self-identity.

Traditionally, adult learning professionals have focused on items 1, 2, and 4 by emphasizing experiential learning techniques. However, much of the recent emphasis has been on item 3, focusing on how an adult's experience serves to shape or inhibit new learning. Several lines of research are connected to this central premise that adults' experience plays a major role in shaping their learning. Though they are largely separate streams of research, and none are specifically anchored in the andragogical model, collectively they reinforce this core principle. The remainder of this section summarizes these different lines of research.

Chris Argyris (1982) and Donald Schon (1987) have written extensively about the difficulties, and importance of, overcoming the natural tendency to resist new learning that challenges existing mental schema from prior experience. Argyris labels learning as either "single-loop" or "double-loop" learning. Single-loop learning is learning that fits prior experiences and existing values, which enables the learner to respond in an automatic way. Double-loop learning is learning that does not fit the learner's prior experiences or schema. Generally it requires learners to change their mental schema in a fundamental way.

Similarly, Schon (1987) talks about "knowing-in-action" and "reflection-in-action." Knowing-in-action is the somewhat automatic responses based on our existing mental schema that enable us to perform efficiently in daily actions. Reflection-in-action is the process of reflecting while performing to discover when existing schema are no longer appropriate, and changing those schema when appropriate. The most effective practitioners, and learners, are those who are good at reflection-in-action and double-loop learning.

Three streams of closely related cognitive psychological research help explain how prior experience influences learning: schema theory, information processing, and memory research (Jonassen and Grabowski, 1993). Schema are the cognitive structures that are built as learning and experiences accumulate and are packaged in memory. Merriam and Cafarella (1991) point out that we all carry around a set of schemata that reflect our experiences and in turn become a basis for assimilating new information. Rummelhart and Norman (1978) proposed three different modes of learning in relation to schema: *accretion, tuning,* and *restructuring.* Accretion is typically equated with learning of facts and involves little change in schema. Tuning involves a slow and incremental change to a person's schemata. Restructuring involves the creation of new schema and is the hardest learning for most adults.

Schema theory is closely related to mental models. Senge (1990), building on schema theory and Argyris' work, identifies "mental models" as one of the five core characteristics of the learning organization. The learning organization, a relatively new strategy that many organizations embrace, is defined by Marquardt as "organization that learns powerfully and collectively and is continually transforming itself to better collect, manage, and use knowledge for corporate success" (1996, p.19). It is a complex strategy that positions learning as a core asset of the organization to cope with the rapid pace of change in a global economy.

Senge (1990) defines mental models as "deeply held internal images of how the world works, images that limit us to familiar ways of thinking and acting" (p. 174). In other words, mental models are the cognitive structures that arise from an individual's experiences. They enable employees to function efficiently on a day-to-day basis. However, they also impede change because many people resist changes that do not fit their mental model, particularly if change involves restructuring long or deeply held schema. To become more effective learners, adults have to identify their mental models, test them, and then learn how to change them. In Argyris' terms, they have to become better double-loop learners, which Schon would label as reflection in action. The result can be powerful improvement in individual and organizational learning, and perhaps performance, if employees understand that their mental models are assumptions, not facts, which filter their view of the world and events.

Information processing theory suggests that prior knowledge acts as a filter to learning through attentional processes. That is, learners are likely to pay more attention to learning that fits with prior knowledge schema and, conversely, less attention to learning that does not fit.

The predominant model of human memory divides memory into three components: sensory, short-term and long-term memory (Huber, 1993). Experience affects sensory memory through the process of attention and selecting what information to process. Selection depends in part on what information is already stored in long-term memory from prior learning and experience.

For long-term memory, prior experience has a major effect on how information is retained and stored. Ormrod (1990) offers the following principles of long-term memory storage:

1. Some pieces of information are selected and others are excluded.
2. Underlying meanings are more likely to be stored than verbatim input.
3. Existing knowledge about the world is used to understand new information.
4. Some existing knowledge may be added to the new information, so what is learned may be more than, or different from, the information actually learned.

These cognitive processes explain in part the emergence of constructivism as a new perspective on learning (Duffy and Jonassen, 1992). While controversial, especially in its more radical versions, constructivism is emerging as a useful perspective for some adult learning situations (Wiswell and Ward, 1987). Constructivism stresses that all knowledge is context bound, and that individuals make personal meaning of their learning experiences. Thus, learning can not be separated from the context in which it is used. They also stress the cumulative nature of learning. That means new information must be related to other existing information in order for learners to retain and use it. For adults, experience might be conceptualized as a giant funnel of previous knowledge, and new information that enters the top of the funnel cascades downward and eventually falls out unless it "sticks" to some element of prior knowledge.

Constructivists advocate a different approach to leading learning. Savery and Duffy (1996) suggest eight constructivist instructional principles:

1. Anchor all learning activities to a larger task or problem.
2. Support the learner in developing ownership for the overall problem or task.
3. Design an authentic task.
4. Design the task and the learning environment to reflect the complexity of the environment in which learners should be able to function at the end of learning.
5. Give the learner ownership of the process used to develop a situation.

6. Design the learning environment to support and challenge the learner's thinking.

7. Encourage testing ideas against alternative views and alternative contexts.

8. Provide opportunity for and support reflection on both the content learned and the learning process.

The parallels between moderate views of constructivism and andragogy are rather striking. Both stress ownership of the learning process by learners, experiential learning and problem-solving approaches to learning. However, andragogy and the more extreme views of constructivism are not compatible.

Traditional instructional design theory is also evolving to emphasize the importance of mental models (Merrill, 1992). While at sharp odds with many aspects of constructivism, this is one area of clear agreement. Richey and Tessmer (1997) point out that there has been a rediscovery of contextual analysis in instructional design. Although it has always been a part of instructional systems design models, it has been neglected over the years. Traditional front-end environmental analysis emphasized the importance of analyzing elements in the external environment that might affect learning, but largely ignored learner characteristics. *Systemic training design* extends environmental analysis to include learner characteristics such as attitudes and accumulated knowledge from prior experiences (Richey, 1995). One of the core directions for change in instructional design is a commitment to the belief that mental structures do exist and shape the way people learn (Kember and Murphy, 1995). Tessmer and Richey (1997) propose a general model of contextual factors that influence learning, one level of which is the *orienting context*. The orienting context consists of all the pre-learning factors that affect the learning event. The elements of a person's background and experiences are among the critical factors they say shape learning.

In summary, there is growing recognition from multiple disciplines that adults' experience has a very important impact on the learning process. While adult learning leaders have long capitalized on adult learners' experiences as a resource for learning, they have not adequately recognized its role as a gatekeeper for learning. On the one hand, experience can aid in learning new knowledge if the new knowledge is presented in such a way that it can be related to existing knowledge and mental models. On the other hand, those same mental models can become giant barriers to new learning when the new learning challenges them.

Thus, the unlearning process becomes as important as the learning process when new learning significantly challenges existing schema. Kurt Lewin recognized this when he talked about the first stage of change being the "unfreezing" stage (the other two being change and refreezing). From this perspective, individuals cannot be expected to change unless attention is first paid to unfreezing them from their existing beliefs and perspectives. Said differently, people will not engage in double-loop learning until they are unfrozen from existing mental models. Kolb (1984) points out that learning is a continuous process grounded in experience, which means that all learning can be seen as relearning. This is particularly true for adults who have such a large reservoir of experiences.

READINESS TO LEARN

Adults generally become ready to learn when their life situation creates a need to know. It then follows that the more adult learning professionals can anticipate and understand adults' life situations and readiness for learning, the more effective they can be. The challenge has been to develop models to explain typical variability in adult readiness to learn.

Pratt (1988) proposed a useful model of how adults' life situations not only affect their readiness to learn, but also their readiness for andragogical-type learning experiences. He recognizes that most learning experiences are highly situational, and that a learner may exhibit very different behaviors in different learning situations. For example, it is entirely likely that a learner may be highly confident and self-directed in one realm of learning, but very dependent and unsure in another.

Pratt illustrated this by identifying two core dimensions within which adults vary in each learning situation: *direction* and *support*. Pratt's model recognizes that learners may have fundamentally different needs for assistance from an adult learning professional. Some may need direction in the mechanics or logistics of learning while others need emotional support. Learning professionals who notice learners who do not seem ready for learning in an andragogical manner must understand within which dimension the need exists.

Direction refers to the learner's need for assistance from other persons in the learning process and is a function of an adult's competence in the subject matter and general need for dependence. Adults who have high *competence* in the subject matter and low general need for *dependence* will be much more independent as learners than those who have little competence and prefer dependency. Even adults who have low general dependence may need direction in the early stages of learning new subject matter in which they have little competence.

Support refers to the affective encouragement the learner needs from others. It is also the product of two factors: the learner's *commitment* to the learning process and the learner's *confidence* about his/her learning ability. Thus, learners who are very highly committed and confident will need less support. Conversely, those who have low commitment and low confidence will need more support.

Pratt proposes a four quadrant model (see Figure 7-1) to reflect combinations of high and low direction or support. Learners in quadrants 1 and 2 need a more highly teacher-directed approach to learning, while those in quadrants 3 and 4 are more capable of self-direction. It is important to note, however, that learners in quadrant 3 still need a high level of involvement with another person in the learning process, but for support, not direction.

Pratt's model, though untested, provides a conceptual explanation for some of the variability that adult learning facilitators encounter in any group of adult learners. Assemble a group of adults for learning and you will likely find some that need lots of direction and emotional support (quadrant 1), some that need direction, but not much support (quadrant 2), some more who may act like they need direction by being in the group, but are really there to get support (quadrant 3), and finally some who like a true andragogical approach (quadrant 4). To further complicate the picture, those same people may switch quadrants when learning different subject matter. By recognizing situational influences on adult learning behavior, Pratt helps explain why the core assumptions are not always a perfect fit, at least initially in learning situations. It seems reasonable to expect that learners in quadrants 1, 2, and 3 may move toward quadrant 4 as their competence and confidence grows. The challenges for adult learning leaders are to a) recognize where individual learners are at the beginning of a

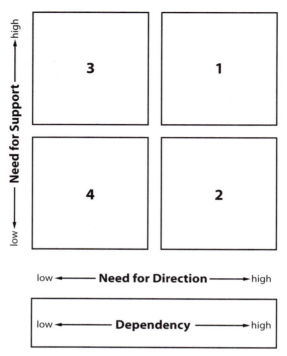

Figure 7-1. Pratt's model of high and low direction and support.

learning experience and b) be attentive to changes in needs for direction and support during the learning experience.

ORIENTATION TO LEARNING: PROBLEM SOLVING

Closely related to the role of prior experience in shaping learning is the role of current experiences in shaping the need to learn. We said earlier that adults generally prefer a problem solving orientation to learning, rather than subject-centered learning. Furthermore, they learn best when new information is presented in real-life context. As a result, the experiential approach to learning has become firmly rooted in adult learning practice.

David Kolb (1984) has been a leader in advancing the practice of experiential learning. He defines learning as "The process whereby knowledge is created through transformation of experience" (p. 38).

For Kolb, learning is not so much the acquisition or transmission of content as the interaction between content and experience, whereby each transforms the other. The educator's job, he says, is not only to transmit or implant new ideas, but also to modify old ones that may get in the way of new ones.

Kolb bases his model of experiential learning on Lewin's problem-solving model of action research, which is widely used in organization development (Cummings and Worley, 1997). He argues that it is very similar to Dewey's and Piaget's as well. Kolb suggests that there are four steps in the experiential learning cycle (see Figure 7-2):

1. *Concrete experience*—full involvement in new here-and-now experiences.

2. *Observations and reflection*—reflection on and observation of the learner's experiences from many perspectives.

3. *Formation of abstract concepts and generalization*—creation of concepts that integrate the learners' observations into logically sound theories.

4. *Testing implications of new concepts in new situations*—using these theories to make decisions and solve problems.

Kolb goes on to suggest that these four modes combine to create four distinct learning styles (see Chapter 8 for more information on learning styles).

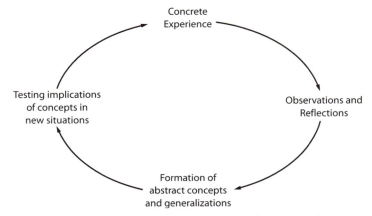

Figure 7-2. Kolb's experiential learning model.

Kolb's model has made a major contribution to the experiential learning literature by a) providing a theoretical basis for experiential learning research and b) providing a practical model for experiential learning practice. The four steps in his model are an invaluable framework for designing learning experiences for adults. At a macro level, programs and classes can be structured to include all four components, and at the micro level these components can be included as units or lessons. Table 7-2 provides examples of learning strategies that may be useful in each step.

Table 7-2
Kolb's Model with Suggested Learning Strategies

Kolb's Stage	Example Learning/Teaching Strategy
Concrete Experience	Simulation, Case Study, Field trip, Real Experience, Demonstrations
Observe and Reflect	Discussion, Small Groups, Buzz Groups, Designated Observers
Abstract Conceptualization	Sharing Content
Active Experimentation	Laboratory Experiences, On-the-Job Experience, Internships, Practice Sessions

Research on Kolb's model has focused mostly on the learning styles he proposed. Unfortunately, research has done little to validate his theory, due in large part to methodological concerns about his instrument (Cornwell and Manfredo, 1994; Freedman and Stumpf, 1980; Kolb, 1981; Stumpf and Freedman, 1981).

Human resource development practitioners, while always valuing experience, increasingly emphasize experiential learning as a means to improve performance (Swanson, 1996). Action reflection learning is one technique developed to focus on learner's experiences and integrate experience into the learning process (*ARL Inquiry*, 1996). Transfer of learning researchers also focus on experiential learning as a means to enhance transfer of learning into performance (Holton, Bates, Seyler and Carvalho, 1997; Bates, Holton and Seyler, 1997) and to increase motivation to learn (Seyler, Holton and Bates, 1997). Structured on-the-job training (Jacobs and Jones, 1995) has emerged as a core method to more systematically capitalize on the value of experiential learning in organizations and as a tool to more effectively develop new employees through the use of experienced co-workers (Holton, 1996). Experiential learning approaches have the dual benefit of appealing to the adult learner's experience base as well as increasing the likelihood of performance change after training. It seems that many domains of adult learning would benefit in the same manner.

MOTIVATION TO LEARN

The andragogical model of adult learning makes some fundamentally different assumptions about what motivates adults to learn. Adults tend to be more motivated toward learning that helps them solve problems in their lives or results in internal payoffs. This does not mean that external payoffs (for example, salary increase) have no relevance, but rather that the internal need satisfaction is the more potent motivator.

Wlodowski (1985) provides a partial explanation for this difference. He suggests that adult motivation to learn is the sum of four factors:

1. *Success*—adults want to be successful learners.
2. *Volition*—adults want to feel a sense of choice in their learning.
3. *Value*—adults want to learn something they value.
4. *Enjoyment*—adults want to experience the learning as pleasurable.

The first principle of andragogy states that "adults need to know why they need to learn something before undertaking to learn it." Knowing why they need to learn something is the key to giving adults a sense of volition about their learning. Principle 6 states that the most potent motivators for adults are internal ones: for example, quality of life, satisfaction, and self-esteem. Said differently, the learning that adults value the most will be that which has personal value to them.

This position is also quite consistent with expectancy theory (Vroom, 1995), a classic theory of adult motivation in the workplace. Expectancy theory posits that an individual's motivation is the sum of three factors:

- *Valence*—the value a person places on the outcome.
- *Instrumentality*—the probability that the valued outcomes will be received given that certain outcomes have occurred.
- *Expectancy*—the belief a person has that certain effort will lead to outcomes that get rewarded.

Put into learning terms, adult learners will be most motivated when they believe that they can learn the new material (expectancy) and that the learning will help them with a problem or issue (instrumentality) that is important in their life (valence).

Wlodowski (1985) suggests a model of characteristics and skills for instructors who are good motivators of adults. They are grouped into four categories: *expertise, empathy, enthusiasm, clarity* (see Table 7-3). Adult learning facilitators who develop these characteristics are likely to be highly motivating.

Table 7-3
Characteristics and Skills of Motivating Instructors
(Wlodowski, 1985)

1. Expertise: The power of knowledge and preparation
   - Knows something beneficial to adults
   - Knows it well
   - Is prepared to convey it through an instructional process

2. Empathy: The power of understanding and consideration
   - Has a realistic understanding of learner's needs and expectations
   - Has adapted instruction to the learner's level of experience and skill development
   - Continuously considers learners' perspectives

3. Enthusiasm: The power of commitment and animation
   - Cares about and values what is being taught
   - Expresses commitment with appropriate degrees of emotion, animation, and energy

4. Clarity: The power of language and organization
   - Can be understood and followed by most learners
   - Provide for learners a way to comprehend what has been taught if it is not clear in the initial presentation

*Wlodowski, 1985

SUMMARY

That adults have a need to know prior to learning is now axiomatic for learning professionals. Research in organizational training suggests there are three aspects to the need to know: the need to know how the learning will be conducted, what will be learned, and why it will be valuable. Research indicates that the need to know affects motivation to learn, learning outcomes, and post-training motivation to use learning.

The concept of self-directedness has perhaps been the most debated aspect of andragogy. There are two prevalent and relatively independent dimensions of self-direction: self-teaching and personal autonomy. The assumption that all adults have full capacity or both dimensions in every possible learning situation is generally not accepted. Grow, addressing this issue, postulates four stages and corresponding teaching styles: Stage 1—dependent student/authority, coach/teacher; Stage 2—interested student/motivator, guide/teacher; Stage 3—involved student/facilitator teacher; and, Stage 4—self-directed student/consultant, delegator teacher.

The role of the adult learner's experience has become an increasingly important focus area as well. Much of the recent emphasis has revolved around the notion that experience creates biases that can greatly impact new learning. Prominent researchers in this area include Argyris, Schon, and Senge. Labeling learning as either single- or double-loop learning, Argyris writes about the difficulties and importance of overcoming the natural tendency to resist new learning that challenges existing mental schema resulting from prior experience. Schon concentrates on knowing-in-action and reflection-in-action, concluding that the most effective practitioners and learners are those who are successful at knowing-in-action and double-loop learning. And, Senge identifies mental models as one of the five core characteristics of learning organization. Other researchers, particularly cognitive psychologists, have conducted extensive research in this field resulting in a generally held belief that adults' prior experiences can both help and hinder the learning process and outcome.

The level of readiness of an adult is closely associated to the need to know. Recognizing that most learning experiences are situational and that the behavior of the learner varies with the learning situation, Pratt proposes a model of how life situation affects both readiness to learn and readiness for andragogical-style learning experiences. He identifies direction and support as core dimensions of variance and proposes a four-quadrant model reflecting combinations of direction and/or support.

Closely related to the role of prior experience in shaping learning is the role of current experiences in shaping the orientation to learning. Adults seem to learn best when new information is present in real-life context. As a result, the experiential approach to learning, most effectively advanced by Kolb, has become firmly rooted in adult learning practice. His four-stage model provides a theoretical basis and a practical model for experiential learning.

It is evident that adults are more motivated toward learning that helps them solve problems or results in internal payoffs. Wlodowski, in a theory closely related to Vroom's expectancy theory, explains the difference between adult and non-adult learners with four factors: success, volition, value, and enjoyment. Vroom uses three factors—valence, instrumentality, and expectancy—in his explanation.

Over the years, a variety of refinements to the core adult learning principles of the andragogical model have emerged. While some might view the refinements as weakening the model, our view is that they strengthen it. Learning is a complex phenomenon that defies description by any one model. The challenge has been, and continues to be, to define what is most characteristic of adult learners, to establish core principles, and to define how to adapt those core principles to varying circumstances. The more researchers identify factors that moderate and mediate adult learning, the stronger the core principles become.

CHAPTER 8

Beyond Andragogy

One aspect of the andragogical model that disturbs many people is that not all adults seem to fit the assumptions. Any facilitator of adult learning will tell you that adult learners are not as homogenous as the andragogical model implies. Research has shown that there are many individual differences among learners that interact with the core adult learning principles to shape adults' learning behaviors. As noted earlier, the andragogical principles are powerful but incomplete descriptors of adults' learning behavior. Experienced adult learning professionals have learned that, like most models, the andragogical learning principles are tempered by an array of other factors that affect learning behavior. Knowles (1984) reinforced this when examining lessons learned from andragogy in practice:

> The andragogical model is a system of elements that can be adopted or adapted in whole or in part. It is not an ideology that must be applied totally and without modification. In fact, an essential feature of andragogy is flexibility (p. 418).

This chapter introduces more new perspectives on adult learning that help explain and refine the core learning principles of andragogy. Included are introductions to the individual difference perspective of psychology, new thinking about learning how to learn, and developmental perspectives. These new understandings are important for developing effective andragogical adult learning in practice.

Individual Differences
in Adult Learners

The major premise of research on individual difference is that instructors should adapt instruction to accommodate differences in individual abilities, styles, and preferences (Jonassen and Grabowski, 1993). By doing so, it is expected that learning outcomes will improve. Instructors are encouraged to either capitalize on learner strengths or help learners develop a broader range of capabilities.

Researchers call this an aptitude-by-treatment interaction, which simply means that the treatment (instruction in this case) interacts with individual "aptitudes" (including abilities, styles, and traits) in producing learning outcomes. Unfortunately, research has not provided consistent support for aptitude-treatment interactions, though it has shown many instances in which the interactions do occur (Jonassen and Grabowski, 1993; Snow, 1989). Methodological issues have limited researchers from generalizing about this premise. At the same time, most practitioners find high face validity in the notion that different learners require different instructional strategies based on their individual differences. It is the anecdotal evidence, case studies, and promising research studies that keep the individual differences hypotheses alive. The safe conclusion at this point is that individual differences do indeed affect learning, but researchers simply do not have the tools and methodologies to adequately measure or study them. In addition, learning may be so highly context specific, and the interactions so complex, that consistent relationships will never emerge, at least not with the degree of generalization we might desire.

Jonassen and Grabowski (1993) present a typology of individual differences that impact learning (see Table 8-1). Table 8-1 incorporates three broad categories of individual differences: *cognitive, personality,* and *prior knowledge*. While there is no generally agreed upon schema for categorizing individual differences, this one is quite useful for adult learning purposes. Prior knowledge was considered in Chapter 7 in our discussion of experience. This section will be devoted primarily to the cognitive group of differences because they seem to have a large impact on adult learners.

Table 8-1
Individual Learner Differences

COGNITIVE

---

1. General Mental Abilities
   - Hierarchical abilities (fluid, crystallized, and spatial)
2. Primary Mental Abilities
   - Products
   - Operations
   - Content
3. Cognitive Controls
   - Field dependence/independence
   - Field articulation
   - Cognitive tempo
   - Focal attention
   - Category width
   - Cognitive complexity/simplicity
   - Strong vs. weak automatization
4. Cognitive Styles: Information Gathering
   - Visual/haptic
   - Visualizer/verbalizer
   - Leveling/sharpening
5. Cognitive Styles: Information Organizing
   - Serialist/holist
   - Conceptual style
6. Learning Styles
   - Hill's cognitive style mapping
   - Kolb's learning styles
   - Dunn and Dunn learning styles
   - Grasha-Reichman learning styles
   - Gregorc learning styles

PERSONALITY

---

7. Personality: Attentional and Engagement Styles
   - Anxiety
   - Tolerance for unrealistic expectations
   - Ambiguity tolerance
   - Frustration tolerance

(table continued on next page)

Table 8-1 (Continued)

---

8. Personality: Expectancy and Incentive Styles
   - Locus of control
   - Introversion/extroversion
   - Achievement motivation
   - Risk taking vs. cautiousness

PRIOR KNOWLEDGE

---

9. Prior Knowledge
   - Prior knowledge and achievement
   - Structural knowledge

Jonassen and Grabowski, 1993

Jonassen and Grabowski (1993) conceptually divide cognitive differences into four levels:

1. *Cognitive abilities*—psychometric models of intelligence, including primary and secondary abilities (categories 1 and 2 in Table 8-1).

2. *Cognitive controls*—patterns of thinking that control the ways individuals process and reason about information. These are the psychometric entities that regulate perception, and are direct descendants from cognitive abilities (category 3 in Table 8-1).

3. *Cognitive styles*—as defined by Messick (1984), they are "characteristic self-consistencies in information processing that develop in congenial ways around underlying personality trends." They reflect ways in which learners process information to make sense out of their world (categories 4 and 5 in Table 8-1).

4. *Learning styles*—general tendencies to *prefer* to process information in different ways. They are less specific than cognitive styles, and are usually assessed by self-reported preferences (category 6 in Table 8-1).

Level 4, learning styles, is the most visible level and can be thought of as the "outer level" while cognitive abilities is the "inner level" and may be the least visible. Cognitive abilities influence cognitive controls, which influence cognitive styles, which in turn influence learning styles. As Table 8-1 shows, the list of characteristics that could be considered in each category is extensive. We will consider only selected ones that show promise for enhancing the core learning principles.

Cognitive Abilities—New Thinking about Intelligence

Intelligence has traditionally referred to in a unidimensional manner rooted in the psychological conception of intelligence as academic IQ. At one time, cross-sectional studies led to the conclusion that intelligence declined in the adult years. This was inconsistent with the general observation that adults did not seem to become "less smart" and, in fact, usually became quite a bit more successful and competent as they aged. This led researchers to question IQ as a universal measure of intelligence, and to search for conceptions of intelligence that would help explain outcomes of adult life and adult learning. This section reviews thinking about alternate forms of intelligence, most of which tends to support the andragogical notions of adult learning.

One of the earlier attempts to explicate multiple intelligences was Horn and Cattell's theory of *fluid* and *crystallized* intelligence (Cattell, 1963; Horn and Cattell, 1966). Fluid intelligence is similar to the traditional notions of IQ, and refers to the ability to solve novel problems. It was believed to peak in teen years and remain stable in adult years, largely because it is most closely linked to physiological factors such as memory. Crystallized intelligence, on the other hand, is a function of experience and education, and increases in adult years. The presumption was that any loss in fluid abilities was compensated for by crystallized intelligence in stable environments. In fact, adults do show some loss of fluid abilities, particularly on speeded tasks. But, they also become better at using the knowledge they have.

The research on the relationship between aging and adult intelligence is somewhat controversial. The pioneering work of Schaie (1994) and the Seattle Longitudinal Study, suggests that earlier conclusions about decline in IQ may not be correct. In this study, Schaie and his colleagues have followed a set of subjects since 1956 and used the Primary Mental Abilities test to assess IQ. When the data on IQ is analyzed cross-sectionally, a decline in IQ with age is shown. When analyzed longitudinally, no decline is indicated. In fact, IQ shows a slight rise during middle age, and only declines below the 25-year-old level after reaching age 67. The conclusion from these studies is that there is no decline in fluid or crystallized intelligence until late in life.

Kaufman (1990) disputes these findings based on his analysis of data from the Wechsler Adult Intelligence Scale (WAIS and WAIS-R). He argues that the WAIS-R is the most valid assessment instrument for adult intelligence, particularly in clinical settings. Longitudinal analyses from WAIS-R data support Horn and Cattell's (1966) theory that fluid abilities decline substantially throughout life, starting as early as the late 20s, but that crystallized intelligence remains relatively stable until old age.

There are complex research methodology issues underlying these studies that are beyond the scope of this book but also affect conclusions about adult intelligence. These two lines of research not only use different instruments but different research methods as well. The conclusions at this point are that a) crystallized intelligence does NOT decline until old age but b) fluid intelligence may. The implication of this research is that adult learning professionals must be alert to the possibility that adult learners, particularly older ones, may not respond as quickly to totally new material or situations. Adjustments may need to be made to allow additional time for learning. On the other hand, when learning depends on prior experience and education, no adjustments should be needed.

Others have also proposed models of multiple intelligences, but they have not been fully researched. Guilford (1967) also observed that IQ tests were inadequate for assessing adult intelligence and this led him to propose a three-factor structure of intellect. He suggested three types of mental abilities:

- *Intellectual abilities*—classified according to operation (cognition, memory, production, and evaluation)
- *Intellect*—classified according to content (verbal, numeric, behavioral)
- *Intelligence*—classified according to product (simple to complex)

Because the product is the result of the interaction between mental abilities and learning content, adults might develop better mental abilities compensating for any loss of learning content.

Another perspective was offered by Gardner's (1983) theory of multiple intelligences. He suggests there are seven types of intelligence: academic, linguistic, logical-mathematical, spatial, musical, bodily kinesthetic, understanding oneself, and understanding others.

He suggests that a person might exhibit high intelligence in one or more of these, and low intelligence in others. Critics classify Gardner's multiple intelligences as *talents,* not intelligence.

Sternberg (1988) regards most theories of intelligence as incomplete. He argues for a broader view of intelligence that leads to educational systems that more fully promote lifelong learning and success (Sternberg, 1997). His theory outlines three components of intelligence:

- *Meta-components*—"the executive processes used to plan, monitor, and evaluate problem solving"
- *Performance components*—"the lower-order processes used to implement the commands of the meta-components"
- *Knowledge-acquisition components*—"processes used to learn how to solve problems in the first place" (p. 59)

Unlike Gardner, these three are not independent, but rather work together to define intellect. And, as adults age, continued learning makes all three components stronger, allowing intellect to continue to increase, despite any age-related decline in memory or sensory capacity.

All theories of intellectual development point to the importance of adult experience. The recurring theme in all these conceptions is that adults grow as learners because of their life experiences. It is likely that experience enables adults to apply their learning more effectively as it strengthens their ability to manage learning processes. Conversely, as they become better at applying their learning and managing their learning processes, they expect opportunities to do just that. In andragogical terms, they seek more control over their learning process. A multidimensional view of intelligence also reinforces the notion that there are certain learning situations in which adults may not be ready for a pure andragogical approach. If certain types of intelligence do decline as adults age (for example, fluid intelligence) and they become increasingly reliant on experience to compensate, then learning totally new material unrelated to prior learning will be more challenging.

Cognitive Controls

The cognitive control that has been the most extensively researched and has received the most attention in adult learning literature is field *dependence/independence* (Joughin, 1992; Smith, 1982). It refers to "the degree to which the learner's perception or comprehension of information is affected by the surrounding perceptual or contextual field (Jonassen and Grabowski, 1993, p. 87). Field dependents tend to see and rely on the cues in the environment to aid in understanding information, whereas field independents tend to learn independent of external cues.

There are many implications that arise from this difference that affect learning. Research-based findings on learning and instruction include (Jonassen and Grabowski, 1993):

Field dependent learners:

- Like group-oriented and collaborative learning
- Prefer clear structure and organization of material
- Attend to the social components of the environment
- Respond well to external reinforcers
- Prefer external guidance
- Field independent learners:
- Like problem solving
- Prefer situations in which they have to figure out the underlying organization of information (for example, outlining)
- Like transferring knowledge to novel situations
- Prefer independent, contract-oriented learning environments
- Respond well to inquiry and discovery learning

As Joughin (1992) suggests, field dependence/independence may have its greatest impact on self-directed learning for adults. At first glance, it would appear that field dependents would be more limited in their ability to develop strong self-directed learning skills. Indeed, the behaviors exhibited by field independent types are most often those ascribed to more "mature" adult learners: independent, critical reflection, goal-oriented, self-organizing, etc. (Even, 1982). Joughin (1992) suggests that the capacity for self-directed learning may be more limited in field-dependent types. He goes on to cite others (Chickering, 1976; Even, 1982; Mezoff, 1982) who suggest similar lines of thinking.

We tend to agree with Brookfield (1986) in urging caution about this conclusion. As discussed earlier, we must distinguish between the *behaviors* of self-teaching, with the internal cognitive process of feeling and acting with *autonomy*. It seems possible that a field-dependent person might exhibit self-directed behaviors quite differently than a field-independent person. Brookfield (1986) goes on to suggest that field-dependent persons are more aware of context, which contributes to critical thinking and facilitation skills. He cites his own research that showed that successful independent learners cited networks of learners as their most important resource. Field-dependent persons might be more likely to develop such networks.

Most measures of self-directedness assess behaviors, not internal feelings of autonomy. It seems clear that field independence/dependence could affect the *manner* in which self-directed learning is conducted. If learners are forced into a traditional mode of independent learning, field independent persons may indeed excel. However, we suspect that if internal feelings of autonomy were assessed, both types could be shown to be effective self-directed learners. As Brookfield (1988) and Caffarella and O'Donnell (1988) note, research indicates that the field-independent type self-directed learning is more typical of males, the middle-class, and American culture. It seems possible then that field-dependent persons (as well as other cultures, gender, and socioeconomic status) are likely to choose different styles of independent learning, probably using networks of people and seeking more assistance, but they still feel quite autonomous. Learning professionals will have to allow room for alternate styles to emerge and should avoid forcing all learners into a field-independent style of self-directed learning, which is the traditional definition.

Cognitive Styles

The terms *learning style* and *cognitive style* are often erroneously used interchangeably. Cognitive styles are thought to be more stable traits and refer to a person's typical manner of acquiring and processing information (Messick, 1984). Learning style is a broader concept, embracing more than just cognitive functioning, and refers to more general preferences for types of learning situations. Some learning style taxonomies include cognitive styles as one type of learning style (Flannery, 1993; Hickcox, 1995). While not totally incorrect, we prefer to separate them.

Acquiring information. Learners tend to have characteristic ways in which they prefer to receive information. Traditionally, cognitive pyschologists have divided them into three categories: visual, verbal, and tactile or psychomotor (Jonassen and Grabowski, 1993; Wislock, 1993). Others, such as James and Galbraith (1985), expand the list to seven elements (or more): print, aural (listening), interactive, visual, haptic (touch), kinesthetic (movement), and smell. The implication of this work is that adult learning professionals should design learning experiences that accommodate multisensory preferences.

Processing information. One of the most common distinctions is made between *global* versus *analytical* (or holist versus serial) information processing. Global persons tend to take in the whole picture first, then the details. They focus on multiple elements of the subject at once and look for interconnections among elements. Analytical persons are completely different in that they prefer to process information in a step-by-step linear manner, focusing on one element of the subject at a time. These characteristics are closely related to the intuitive versus sensing scale of the Myers-Briggs Type Indicator.

The implication of this for learning professionals is that information must be presented in multiple approaches so that different learners can understand it. Swanson (see Chapter 10) proposes the "whole-part-whole" approach to learning in which learners are presented with the global picture, the parts of information, and the global perspective is repeated with application.

Learning Styles

Learning styles refer to the broadest range of preferred modes and environments for learning. Though there is little uniformity in the way researchers define them, they tend to differ from cognitive style in two key ways: 1) learning styles include cognitive, affective, and psychomotor/physiological dimensions, and 2) they include characteristics of instruction and instructional settings along with learning. James and Blank (1993) and Smith (1982) provide a useful summary of available instruments. Table 8-2 describes some representative learning-style theories and associated instruments.

Table 8-2
Representative Learning Style Systems

Researcher	Style dimensions	Instrument(s)
Cognitive learning style systems		
Kolb (1984)	Two dimensions (perceptual and processing)proposed: concrete experience vs. abstract generalization, and active experimentation vs. reflective observation. Results in four styles: divergers, assimilators, convergers, and accomodators	Learning Style Inventory (1984)
McCarthy		4MAT system
Gregorc (1984)	Two dimensions (perceptual and processing) proposed: abstract vs. concrete experience, and sequential vs. random ordering of information. Results in four styles, though ranges are allowed: concrete sequential, concrete random, abstract sequential, and abstract random	Gregorc Learning Style (1984)
Cognitive, Affective, and Physiological Systems		
Dunn and Dunn (1974), Dunn, Dunn and Price (1989)	Assesses 20 factors in four groups: environmental, sociological, emotional, and physical preferences.	Learning Style Inventory (1989) (for children) Productivity Environmental Preference Survey (1989) (for adults)
Canfield (1988)	Assesses 20 factors in four groups: conditions of learning, content of learning, mode of learning, and expectations of learning	Canfield's Learning Style Inventory

(*table continued on next page*)

Table 8-2 (Continued)

Personality Systems (with implications for learning)

Briggs and Meyers (1977)	Assesses four scales: extraversion vs. introversion; intuition vs. sensing; thinking vs. feeling; and judging vs. perceiving	Myers-Briggs Type Indicator (MBTI)
Costa and McRae (1992)	Assesses "big five" personality dimensions: neuroticism, extra-version, openness, agreeableness, conscientiousness. Emerging as a strong research-based approach to personality assessment	NEO-PI-R

Learning-style research has shown both great promise and great frustration. On the one hand, learning styles have great face validity for learning professionals. Most know intuitively that there are differences in styles among the adult learners with which they work. By considering various dimensions of style differences, they are often able to improve learning situations and reach more learners.

On the other hand, all of the learning style systems have suffered from limited research, questionable psychometric qualities of the instruments, and mixed research findings. Kolb's theory and accompanying instrument, the Learning Style Inventory (LSI), have come under particularly harsh critique (Kolb, 1981; Stumpf and Freedman, 1981; Reynolds, 1997), perhaps because it is one of the older and better documented theories. However, more recent work suggests that the constructs in Kolb's theory may be valid, but not measured correctly by the LSI (Cornwell and Manfredo, 1994).

There can be little question that the research support for learning styles is mixed at best. One key reason is that there is no unifying theory or generally accepted approach to learning style research and practice. Another flaw in most critiques is that they fail to separate the validity of learning-style theory and constructs from the measurement issues. A theory can not be dismissed simply because we don't yet know how to measure it. Of course, neither can a theory be assumed valid until it can be measured and researched. For example, just because Kolb's LSI has not withstood rigorous instrument validation (Reynolds, 1997) does not mean that his theory is invalid. It could mean that we simply don't know how to measure the constructs yet.

This confusion has led some researchers to appropriately urge caution in using learning styles (Bonham, 1988; James and Blank, 1993). We agree with the cautions, but also urge caution in rejecting them, particularly when the phenomona continues to be regularly observed by researchers and practitioners. We also agree with Merriam and Caffarella (1991) and Hiemstra and Sisco (1990) that learning-style instruments are best used at this point to 1) create awareness among learning leaders and learners that individuals have different preferences, 2) as starting points for learners to explore their preferences, and 3) as catalysts for discussion between leaders and learners about the best learning strategies.

Summary of Individual Differences Perspectives

Research in individual differences has been instrumental in advancing understanding of individual differences in adult learning behaviors. As noted, there remains much uncertainty in the research, but the key point is clear: individuals vary in their approaches, strategies, and preferences during learning activities. Few learning professionals would disagree. At one level, merely being sensitive to those differences should significantly improve learning. Even better, the more that is understood about the exact nature of the differences, the more specific learning theorists can be about the exact nature of adaptations that should be made.

Understanding of individual differences helps make andragogy more effective in practice. Effective adult learning professionals use their understanding of individual differences to tailor adult learning experiences in several ways. First, they tailor the manner in which they apply the core principles to fit adult learners' cognitive abilities and learning-style preferences. Second, they use them to know which of the core principles are applicable to a specific group of learners. For example, if learners do not have strong cognitive controls, they may not initially emphasize self-directed learning. Third, they use them to expand the goals of learning experiences. For example, one goal might be to expand learners' cognitive controls and styles to enhance future learning ability. This flexible approach explains why andragogy is applied in so many different ways (Knowles, 1984).

LEARNING HOW TO LEARN

Much of the emphasis in individual difference research is on how learning professionals should alter their learning facilitation and leadership to make learning more meaningful to learners. A complementary response has been an emphasis on helping learners expand their learning abilities through "learning-how-to-learn" interventions. While almost all the evidence is anecdotal, learning how to learn holds great promise for helping adults expand their learning effectiveness.

Smith (1982) defines learning how to learn as:

Learning how to learn involves possessing, or acquiring, the knowledge and skill to learn effectively in whatever learning situation one encounters (p. 19).

. . . we describe the person who has learned how to learn as capable of learning efficiently, for many purposes, in a variety of situations, no matter what the method . . . (p. 20).

Gibbons (1990) offers a useful model that helps clarify the range and scope of learning-how-to-learn research and practice. First, she suggests that learners need to be effective at learning in three *kinds of learning*:

1. *Natural learning*—learning that occurs as the individual interacts spontaneously with the environment. Skills include learning from interaction with others, the environment, exploration, practice, and the teacher within.

2. *Formal learning*—learning in which the content is chosen by others and presented to the learner. Skills include learning from instruction, assigned learning tasks, basic learning skills, and how to generalize from a learning activity.

3. *Personal learning*—self-directed, intentional learning activities. Skills to be learned include learning to decide what to learn, how to manage the learning process, how to learn from experience, how to be an intentional learner and to take learning action.

The second dimension defines three *aspects of learning*:

1. *Reason*—the executive operation, more concerned with the management of thinking than the thinking itself. Closely related to meta-cognition or cognitive strategies (Weinstein and Mayer, 1986), a key element of reason's role in thinking is learning to improve one's ability in perceiving, analyzing, proposing, imagining, and reflecting.

2. *Emotion*—responding with feeling, developing commitment, and acting with confidence. Key elements in this aspect are experiencing feelings, clarity, developing confidence, developing determination, and trusting intuition.

3. *Action*—using learning to take meaningful action. Key elements include making decisions, taking initiative, practicing, solving problems, and influencing others.

Finally, there are three domains of learning in which adults must be effective:

1. *Technical*—instrumental learning to conduct the practical activities of work and life.

2. *Social*—learning how to relate to others for mutual benefit.

3. *Developmental*—learning how to develop oneself as a person and a learner.

Smith (1982) suggests that there are three interrelated components to learning how to learn that are useful to help learners become more effective: needs, learning styles, and training.

Needs

Learners have a variety of needs if they are to grow as learners. Smith divides them into four groups (see Figure 8-1). First, learners need general understandings about learning and its importance to develop a positive attitude and motivation to learn. Then, they need basic skills such as reading, writing, math, and listening to be able to perform in learning situations. Third, they need to understand their personal strengths and weaknesses as learners, as well as their person-

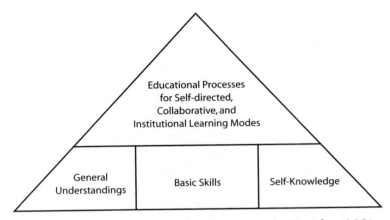

Figure 8-1. Learning how-to-learn needs (Smith, 1982).

al preferences for learning situations and environments. Finally, they need the skills to perform in three learning processes: self-directed, collaborative, and institutional. Self-directed learning requires highly developed skills for planning, directing, and monitoring one's own learning. Collaborative learning requires strength in teamwork and interpersonal skills. Institutional learning requires basic study skills such as taking notes, writing, and test taking.

Learning Style

The core premise of learning style is that individual learner preferences will lead to learners being less effective in learning situations that require them to leave the comfort of their preferred learning strategies and styles. And, because it is completely unrealistic for a person to expect that all learning situations and leaders will accommodate their personal style, they will find themselves in many situations outside their comfort zone. Unless they develop a broader array of learning skills, they will struggle in those situations that don't fit their natural style. Furthermore, learning-how-to-learn theorists believe that learners do not have to be limited to only their natural strengths. That is, people can learn how to learn differently from ways they naturally prefer.

The array of skills and abilities grouped under the learning-how-to-learn label is diverse. Essentially, it involves learning how to function from an "opposite" style on every individual difference discussed so far. If you are a field-independent person, it means learning to learn in a field-dependent manner. If you have strong academic skills, but weak practical intelligence, it means developing practical intelligence. If you are a global learner, it means learning to learn more analytically—and so on.

Training

This third component refers to deliberate efforts to help learners develop the skills they lack. Such training might include workshops, coaching, self-study, and practice. Training topics might range from basic study skills taught in schools to learning-style workshops.

The promise of learning how to learn is becoming more important in a world economy that is increasingly dependent on knowledge and intellectual capital and faced with rapid change. For organizations, it has become increasingly important that employees be highly skilled learners so they can learn new technologies and adapt to changing market demands. For individuals, a person's job security is increasingly dependent on an ability to grow and learn, sometimes in rather radical ways. Adults today are often faced with demands to learn and relearn their jobs multiple times in a career. Those who do not have strong learning skills usually face layoffs.

It is for this reason that the American Society for Training has identified learning how to learn as one of the basic skills workers need (Carnevale, Gainer, and Meltzer, 1990). The U.S. Department of Labor has included it in their SCANS model of skills workers need to develop to be competitive in today's workplace (The Commission on the Skills of the American Workforce, 1990). As more states focus on enhanced workforce development systems, learning how to learn is likely to become more important.

DEVELOPMENTAL PERSPECTIVES ON ADULT LEARNING

Adults do not become adults in an instant—it is a developmental process. In addition, researchers now understand that development does not end when adulthood is reached, but rather continues to progress in a variety of ways. Adult development theories have a profound influence on thinking about adult learning because adults' learning behavior varies considerably due to developmental influences. What is not clear is exactly how it changes, largely because adult development theory is still mostly an array of untested models.

It is impossible to fully capture the full complexity of adult development theory in a chapter. Our purpose in this section is to discuss ways in which adult development theory suggests adult learning behavior might vary from the adult learning core principles. By necessity in an introductory book, our discussion of adult learning theories will be somewhat limited, focusing on a few representative models. Readers seeking a more complete discussion of adult development should consult Bee (1996), Tennant and Pogson (1995), Knox (1977), or Merriam and Caffarella (1991).

Tennant and Pogson (1995) explain why adult development matters:

The identity of adult education as a field of study is largely premised on the identity of the adult. Much of the adult education literature, especially the literature on adult learning, makes reference to the distinct attributes of adults, and builds a rationale for practice based on these distinct attributes. . . . Because adult education necessarily involves some kind of intervention in the lives of participants, it is important for adult educators to recognize the nature and limits of this intervention, and to locate their intervention in some kind of life-span framework (p. 69).

Overview of Adult Development Theories

Adult development theories are generally divided into three types: physical changes, cognitive or intellectual development, or personality and life-span role development (Merriam and Caffarella, 1991; Tennant, 1995). Cognitive development theory's primary contributions are twofold. First, they help to explain some differences in the way adults learn at different stages in their life. Second, they help explain why the core learning principles are exhibited in different ways at different stages of life. Role development theory's primary contributions are to help explain when adults are most ready for and most need learning and to explain when they may be most motivated to learn.

Bee (1996) characterizes development theories as varying along two dimensions. First, some theories focus on *development,* while some focus on *change* during adult life. *Development theories* imply a hierarchical ordering of developmental sequences, with higher levels being better than lower levels. They include a normative component, which suggests that adults should progress to higher levels of development. Many of the cognitive development theories fit into this category. Consider, for example, about how your thinking and perspectives on issues has matured during your life. As you have aged, you have probably developed a more balanced perspective on life and began to recognize that there are many diverse and valid opinions. This change represents a maturation and development process to what is generally considered a preferred level of thinking.

Change Theories

These theories are merely descriptive of typical changes experienced by adults. There is no normative hierarchy intended, so one phase is not better than another. The theories seek merely to describe typical or expected changes. Many of the life-span role development theories fit into this category. Think about your life and the many changes you may have experienced that are typical of many adults— going to school, setting up a home, getting married, having children, death of a parent, etc. There is no developmental order implied here, simply a sequence of events.

The second dimension along which these theories vary is whether they include defined *stages,* or *no stages.* Stage theories imply fixed sequences of sequentially occurring stages over time. Stage theories are quite common, and are best represented by Levinson's (1978) theory of adult development. Others offer no such fixed sequence of events. According to Bee (1996), Pearlin's (1980) theory of sources of adult distress over the life span is a good example.

We tend to agree with the prevailing thinking today that there is no one theory that is "best." Rather, adult development should be viewed as consisting of multiple pathways—multidimensional (Daloz, 1986; Merriam and Caffarella, 1991). This position is not intended to be an easy way out, but rather acknowledges the complexity of adult development. Adults develop along multiple dimensions simultaneously. The challenge for adult educators is to understand development well enough to recognize which dimensions are most relevant to a particular group of learners in a particular learning situation. That is our emphasis in this chapter.

Life-Span Role Development Perspectives

The core contribution that life-span development theories make to working with andragogical principles of adult learning is in clarifying and refining adult readiness to learn. The premise of all these theories is that there are certain predictable types of changes that occur throughout an adult's life. Life change is often an adult's primary driving force for learning. As the core principles of andragogy state, adults are most ready to learn when the learning meets an immediate life need, and are most motivated when it fills an internal need. Understanding the changes and transitions in adults' lives enable adult educators to:

- Anticipate learning needs that arise at various life points
- Understand how life events facilitate or inhibit learning in a particular situation
- Prepare adults for life changes
- Capitalize on "teachable moments" (Havigurst, 1972) to accelerate learning
- Plan learning experiences that are more meaningful

Think about your own life course for a moment. How have the events of your life led you to or away from learning? How have your learning needs changed as you progressed through life? How have life events affected your motivation to engage in learning? How has learning changed your life course? I suspect that most readers will immediately feel the importance of life-span development to adult learning.

Life-span theories. Perhaps the best known of this group of theories are those describing the life course, and the best known of those is Levinson (1978, 1986) because it was popularized by Gail Sheehy's book *Passages.* Levinson divides adult life into three eras: early adulthood (17–45), middle adulthood (40–60), and late adulthood (60+). Life then consists of alternating periods of stability and transitions. Each era brings with it certain predictable tasks, and each transition between eras certain predictable challenges. It was Levinson's work that made midlife crisis a part of American culture. While Levinson's model has drawn much criticism, primarily for its highly structured view of adult life, it has persisted as a core development theory.

Table 8-3
Levinson's Life Task Developmental Model

Developmental Period	Age Group	Task
Early adult transition	17–22	Explore possibilities and make tentative commitments
Entering the adult world	22–29	Create first major life structure
Age 30 transition	29–33	Reassess life structure
Settling down	33–40	Create second life structure
Midlife transition	40–45	Ask "what have I done with my life?"
Entering middle adulthood	45–50	Create new life structure
Age 50 transition	50–55	Minor adjustments to middle life structure
Culmination of middle adulthood	55–60	Build second middle life structure
Late life transition	60–65	Prepare for retirement and old age
Late adulthood	65+	Create late life structure and deal with declines of old age

Identity development. Another widely known and influential theory is Erikson's theory of identity development. Erikson proposed that an adult's identity develops through resolution of eight crisis or dilemmas (see Table 8-4).

Table 8-4
Erikson's Stages of Identity Development

Approximate Age	Stage	Potential Strength to be Gained
0–1 years	basic trust versus mistrust	Hope
1–3 years	autonomy vs. shame and doubt	Will
4–5 years	initiative vs. guilt	Purpose
6–12 years	industry vs. inferiority	Competence
13–18 years	identity vs. role confusion	Fidelity
19–25 years	intimacy vs. isolation	Love
25–65 years	generativity vs. self-absorption and stagnation	Care
65+ years	ego integrity vs. despair	Wisdom

If successfully resolved, each dilemma gives a person a certain strength. Erikson also believes that these dilemmas present themselves at certain predictable ages.

Ego development. Loevinger (1976) proposed a ten-stage model of ego development progressing from infancy to adulthood (see Table 8-5). Unlike Erikson or Levinson, she does not presume that adults progress through all stages. In fact, many get stuck in the middle stages. For adults, the developmental tasks are generally to move from a conformist stage to a more individualistic or autonomous stage. This theory has important implications for the andragogical assumption of self-directedness, because the ego development stage may affect an adult's self-directedness.

Impact of Life-Span Theories. Regardless of whether one views the life course through Levinson's life stages, Erikson's developmental task, or Loevinger's ego development, or some other life-span perspective, the impact on learning is similar. First, all three researchers say that adult life is a series of stages and transitions, each of which pushes the adult into unfamiliar territory. Second, each transition to a new stage creates a motivation to learn. If adult learning professionals listen closely to the motivations of their learners, they will often hear some form of life transition pushing the adult to learn. By under-

Table 8-5
Loevinger's Stages of Ego Development

Stage	Description
Presocial stage	Baby differentiates himself from his surroundings
Symbiotic stage	Baby retains symbiotic relationship with mother
Impulsive stage	Child asserts separate identity
Self-protective stage	Child learns self-control of impulses
Conformist state	Child or adult models behavior after the group
Self-aware stage	Self-awareness increases as does acceptance of individual differences
Conscientious stage	Person lives by individually created rules and ideals
Individualistic stage	Person focused on independence vs. dependence
Autonomous stage	Adults are fully independent and can cope with inner conflict

standing the developmental life span, practitioners can be more attuned to adults' motivations to learn.

Cognitive Development Perspectives

Like life-span developmental perspectives, cognitive development theories also help to clarify and refine the andragogical principles. The core premise of cognitive development theories is that changes occur in a person's thinking process over time. These changes may affect adult learners by:

- Changing the way they interpret new information
- Altering readiness for different learning experiences
- Creating differing views and interpretations of material
- Creating different degrees of meaningfulness for different people
- Creating different developmental learning tasks

Clearly, the more one knows about cognitive development, the more likely adult learning can be tailored to meet the needs of specific learners.

Consider how your personal views have changed during your adult life. Do you think about issues the same way you used to? Do you approach new information in the same manner? Do you find certain types of issues and learning more meaningful to you now than before? Most adults can chart progressions in their thinking that match at least some of the cognitive development theories.

The foundation of most adult cognitive development theories is the work of Piaget (Merriam and Caffarella, 1991). Piaget hypothesized that children move through four stages of thinking: *sensory motor, preoperational, concrete operational,* and *formal operations.* Formal operations, at which a person reaches the ability to reason hypothetically and abstractly, is considered the stage at which mature adult thought begins, though many adults never reach it. Because he was a child development specialist, Piaget's model implies that cognitive development stops upon reaching adulthood. Adult development theorists dispute that idea and have focused on various ways that cognitive development continues beyond *formal operations.* The following are some selected examples.

Dialectic thinking. Dialectic thinking is a level of thinking at which a person comes to see, understand, and accept alternate views and truths about the world, and the inherent contradictions in adult life. At this stage, the search for single truths and approaches to life is abandoned. A number of theorists have proposed dialectic thinking stages. Kramer (1989) and Riegel (1976) both suggested stage models of dialectic thinking that directly parallel the four stages of thought proposed by Piaget. In their view, dialectic thought develops along with formal operations and occurs in children at a low level. Others have looked at dialectical thinking as some type of extension to Piaget's four stages. Pascual-Leone (1983) proposed four stages of dialectic thought that occur after formal operations. Benack and Basseches (1989) also proposed four stages of post-formal thought that result in dialectic thinking.

Though the exact nature of its development is unclear, it does seem clear that dialectic thinking is an important developmental task for adults. Dialectic thinking enables adults to make peace with the complexity of life in which few truths exist and in which numerous contradictions and compromises are confronted daily. At some point, adults begin to realize that these are not wrong, but inherent in life.

Other post-formal operations. Other theorists have recognized that thinking develops beyond formal operations, but propose different types of post-formal operations. For example, Arlin (1984) proposed a fifth stage of development, the problem-finding stage. Labouvie-Vief (1990) suggested that the hallmark of mature adult thought was the ability to make a commitment to a position or life course, despite recognizing the many different possibilities. That is, once one realizes the dialectic nature of life, a person must still must make choices and commitments.

Relativistic thinking. Closely related to dialectic thinking is relativistic thinking. Perry (1970) proposed a nine-stage model of cognitive development based on his research with college students. These stages describe change from dualistic, right-wrong, black and white type thinking to more complex relativistic thinking. Relativism indicates that knowledge is contextual, and there are few truths. In that sense, Perry's work is similar to dialectic thinking, but different in that he does not describe it as a post-formal operation.

Impact of Cognitive Development Theories

Cognitive development theories are particularly useful in helping adult learning professionals understand why some adults struggle with highly complex issues that require dialectical or relativistic thinking. For example, some adult educators stress helping adults develop critical thinking skills (Brookfield, 1986). Critical thinking requires adults to be able to challenge assumptions that guide their lives, which also requires a higher level of cognitive development to recognize that there are multiple "correct" ways to live. Critical thinking may be a significant development step for a learner who has not reached that stage.

Implications From Developmental Theories

Though few of the theories about adult development have been thoroughly tested, they have persisted because most adults intuitively recognize that development continues throughout adult life. These theories provide the best framework available for understanding that development. A close examination of the development literature suggests these implications for adult learning:

- Adult learning is inextricably intertwined with adult development.
- Adult development occurs along multiple paths and multiple dimensions.
- Adult learning will vary primarily with stages of cognitive development.
- Motivation and readiness to learn will vary primarily according to stage of life-span development.
- Adult learning facilitators must be attentive to learners' stage of development, and tailor learning experiences to fit that developmental stage.

SUMMARY

This chapter focuses on individual difference perspective of psychology, developmental perspectives, and life-span development perspectives that enhance the core learning principles of andragogy. Individual difference perspective advocates that instructors adapt their teaching methodologies to accommodate differences in individual abilities, styles, and preferences. Theoretically, the result of such accommodation is increased learning outcomes. The research to support this contention is, however, mired in methodological problems. Thus, there is relatively little empirical evidence to support this premise. Yet, individual case studies, anecdotes, and current research efforts continue to sustain the individual difference perspectives.

Individual differences can be classified into broad categories of cognitive, personality, and prior knowledge. Cognitive differences can be further classified into the subcategories of cognitive abilities, cognitive controls, cognitive styles, and learning styles. While there is an extensive list of characteristics that could be included in each category, the individual differences that most directly impact adults' learning behavior described in the andragogical model are intelligence, field dependence/independence, learning style, locus of control, and prior knowledge.

Teaching learners how to learn serves as the complement to adjusting the instructional methodology. The fundamental precept in this response is that by broadening learning capabilities, learners can more readily adapt to a wide range of learning situations, thereby increasing the learning outcome. Learning how to learn has become increasingly important in the workplace. For employees to successfully obtain and retain their positions, they must be able to learn in a variety of learning environments. Employees are not often afforded the luxury of selecting their own learning situation and methodology and, consequently, must adapt or face the possibility of the loss of a job.

The developmental perspective of adult learning focuses on the progressive aspect of becoming an adult—it is not a status that is achieved instantaneously. Adult development theories are generally divided into three types: physical changes, cognitive or intellectual development, or personality and social role development. And, according to Bee, development theories vary only in two dimensions. The first of these dimensions involves development and change. Development theories imply a hierarchical ordering of developmental sequences, and change theories are descriptive of changes typically experienced by adults. The second variance revolves around the inclusion or exclusion of stages. Stage theories imply fixed, sequentially occurring stages.

Life-span development theories clarify and refine adult learning principles by addressing the readiness to learn aspect of the learning event. Grounded in the premise that certain predictable types of changes occur in an adult's life, these changes often trigger a learning need.

CHAPTER 9

Andragogy in Practice

The adult learner has taken the center stage as the millennium approaches. The first edition of *The Adult Learner* was published a quarter of a century ago and carried a subtitle, "The Neglected Species." You will note that the subtitle has been dropped. The adult learner is no longer a neglected species.

Furthermore, the world has changed radically in the past twenty-five years. Information technology, knowledge work, open systems, and large-scale changes are just a few of the lexicons of the past quarter century. Combine these with increases in medical science and human longevity, and adults have necessarily become viewed as dynamic and growing organisms. Adult development is a focus of concern on many fronts.

From the perspective of learning, adults who are willing and able to learn are prized members of society. For example, universities vie for adult learners and corporations realize their true value lies in the hidden brain power of their employees. This is the good news. The bad news is that many adults are not willing to learn or have difficulty learning. Adults who exhibit these static characteristics are not able to maintain or improve their social and economic status.

Almost all adults can benefit from assistance in their learning journey, and a significant number of adults require help. To meet this challenge, there is a large cadre of adult learning professionals. This book is meant to provide these professionals with the latest in adult learning theory and practice.

ANDRAGOGY IN PRACTICE

The power of andragogy lies in its dynamic application, not in a rigid recipe for action. We offer *Andragogy in Practice* (see Figure 9-1) as a new approach to more systematically apply andragogy across multiple domains of adult learning practice. Figure 9-1 graphically summarizes the core content of this approach.

The three rings of andragogy in practice are: (1) Goals and Purposes for Learning, (2) Individual and Situational Differences, and (3) Andragogy: Core Adult Learning Principles.

"Goals and Purposes for Learning," the outer ring, are portrayed as developmental. The traditional view among scholars and practitioners of learning is to think exclusively of individual growth. To this we have added the realms of institutional and societal growth as critical elements for understanding andragogy in practice. Adult learning is equally powerful in developing better institutions and societies.

"Individual and Situational Differences," the middle ring, are portrayed as variables. We continue to learn about the differences that impact adult learning. These variables are grouped into the categories of individual learner differences, subject matter differences, and situational differences. They also are critical elements for understanding andragogy in practice. They act as filters that shape the practice of andragogy.

The center ring, "Andragogy: Core Adult Learning Principles," summarizes androgogical principles within the context of practice. Each of these six principles: (1) learner's need to know, (2) self-concept of the learner, (3) prior experience of the learner, (4) readiness to learn, (5) orientation to learning, and (6) motivation to learn—are perspectives that come *directly* from the adult learner.

Using this model, we suggest a three-dimensional thinking process for approaching adult learning situations:

1. The core principles of andragogy provide a sound foundation for planning adult learning experiences. Without any other information, they reflect the best approach to effective adult learning.

2. Analysis should be conducted to understand: (a) the particular adult learners and their individual characteristics; (b) the characteristics of the subject matter; and, (c) the characteristics of the

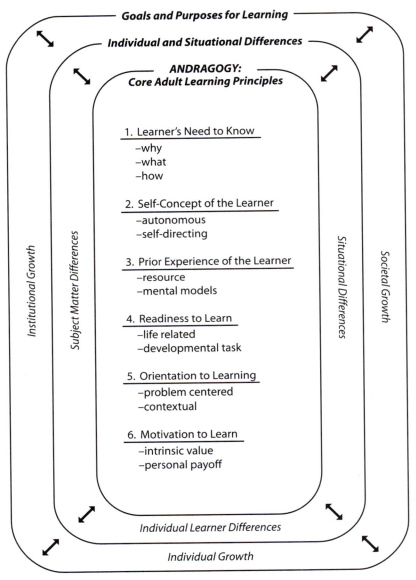

Figure 9-1. *Andragogy in practice (Knowles, Holton, and Swanson, 1998).*

particular situation in which adult learning is being used. Each of these factors will change the extent to which the core principles of andragogy are applicable to specific learners in a specific learning situation. In some cases, they may cause a facilitator to place greater emphasis on a particular principle, in other cases, less emphasis.

3. The goals and purposes for which the adult learning is conducted provide a frame that puts shape to the learning experience. This factor will likely modify emphasis among the core learning principles; that is, learning within organizational human resource development has a different set of goals and purposes than does adult learning conducted for adult basic education. Thus, the core principles will be implemented differently in those situations.

CONCLUSION

Andragogy's core adult learning principles take the learner seriously. They go beyond basic respect for the learner and view the adult learner as a primary source of data for making sound decisions regarding the learning process.

While each principle of andragogy is important, as a set they must be viewed as "a system of elements that can be adopted in whole or in part. It is not an ideology that must be applied totally or without modification. In fact, an essential feature of andragogy is flexibility" (Knowles, 1984, p. 418). It is easy to see direct interactions between the principles of andragogy and the variations derived through the ring of Individual and Situational Differences and the ring of Goals and Purposes for Learner. Together they constitute *Andragogy in Practice*.

PART 3

Practice in Adult Learning

*Insights, Tools, and Research
Supporting Andragogy in Practice*

CHAPTER 10

*Whole-Part-Whole Learning Model**

INTRODUCTION

Human learning is one the most complex subjects of the scientific and scholarly world. While it is easy to demonstrate how little we know about the human mind, we can, on the other hand, acknowledge the sheer volume of research and common sense available to us to better understand the learning phenomena. We are not ignorant about the learning process. In fact, we know quite a bit about how people learn.

The origins of the Whole-Part-Whole Learning Model go back to 1972. At that time, the Johns-Manville Corporation contacted me to talk to the corporate training and education personnel about the psychology of learning. It became apparent that these people had a real need to improve their practice and that they wanted to be theoretically sound. They were not theoreticians, yet, they had an appreciation for the practical potential of sound theory. Two elements from that early presentation remain as key elements of the Whole-Part-Whole Learning Model (WPW Learning Model). The first element was to separate the field of learning psychology into two camps—the behaviorist/connectionist camp and the gestalt/cognitive camp. The second element was to acknowledge the value of each camp and to integrate it through Tolman's concept of "purposive-behaviorism" (1959).

*Richard A. Swanson, Bryan D. Law, *Performance Improvement Quarterly,* vol., no. 1, pp. 43–53. The paper was originally presented to the European Conference on Educational Research, Enschede, The Netherlands, June 24, 1992.

MODEL OVERVIEW

This WPW Learning Model goes beyond the present holistic, behavioristic, whole-part, and part-whole learning models. The WPW Learning Model purports that there is a natural whole-part-whole rhythm to learning. The basic WPW Learning Model is as follows (See Figure 10-1):

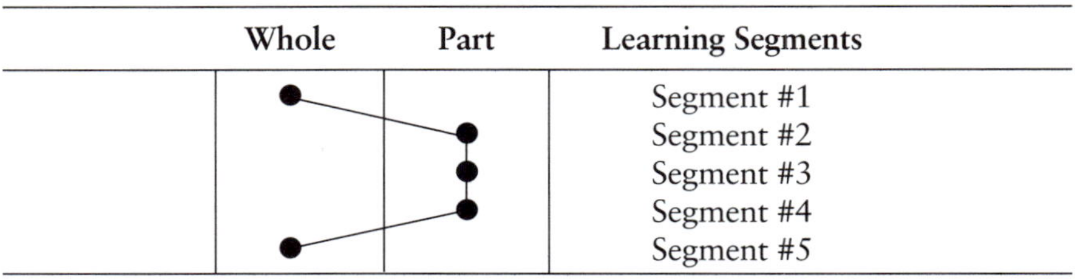

Whole	Part	Learning Segments
		Segment #1
		Segment #2
		Segment #3
		Segment #4
		Segment #5

Figure 10-1. Basic Whole-Part-Whole Learning Model.

Through the "first whole," the model introduces new content to learners by forming in their minds the organizational framework required to effectively and efficiently absorb the forthcoming concepts into their cognitive capabilities. The supporting cognitive capabilities and component behaviors are then developed in the classical behavioristic style of instruction found in the "part," or several parts, aspect of the WPW Learning Model. After the learner has successfully achieved the performance criteria for the individual "parts" or components within the whole, the instructor links these parts together, thus, forming the "second whole." The whole-part-whole learning experience provides the learner with the complete understanding of the content at various levels of performance and even allows for higher order cognitive development to the levels of improvement and invention (Swanson, 1991).

The WPW Learning Model can be considered systematic on several counts. One is that the model can be used all the way from program design to real time instructional adjustments during a live presentation. The following review of the literature supports both the psychological foundations of whole-part-whole instruction and its systemic nature.

Beyond the superficial rhetoric of broad purpose and goals, most education and training thrives on the "parts"—the details of knowledge, expertise, and activity (Skinner, 1954; 1968). Even though this behaviorist perspective on learning has been under intellectual attack, the pragmatic requirements of education and training in our culture see to it that the "parts" and the mastery of the "parts" are as strong as ever. Without diminishing the behavioral stronghold on educational and training practices, it is the Gestalt psychology concept that the whole is greater than the sum of the parts that is being more fully explored through this treatise. The approach is not to attack behaviorism. Behaviorism (the "parts") is seen as a critical aspect of WPW Learning Model. Instead, the focus is on the "first whole" and "second whole" that envelope the "parts."

THE FIRST WHOLE OF THE WHOLE-PART-WHOLE LEARNING MODEL

There are two main purposes of the "first whole." One is to provide a mental scaffolding through advance organizers and schemata alignment to prepare learners for the new instruction they will receive. The "first whole" also provides motivation for the participant to want to learn by making the content meaningful and connecting it to the learner.

Advance Organizers

The concept of an advance organizer was originally introduced by Ausubel (1968) as a technique for helping students learn and retrieve information by making it meaningful and familiar. This is accomplished by introducing the basic concepts of the new material, from which the students are able to organize the more specific information that will follow (Luiten, Ames, and Ackerman, 1980).

The need for advance organizers comes from the psychological principle that previous knowledge and experiences form their own mental structures at a given level of development (Di Vesta, 1982). These individual structures are called schemata. "We have schemata for eating in restaurants, attending hockey games, and visiting our grandmothers. The knowledge associated with each of these activities is our schema for the activity" (Gage and Berliner, 1988, p. 293). The participant's orientations that encompass the previous consequences and their interpretations of experiences represent that person's current world view (Di Vesta, 1982).

Understanding that differences in individuals are present is important for an instructor. For example, an instructor giving a lecture on quality management in industry to thirty students is in the room with thirty different schemata, or mental structures, of what quality management in industry means. A unified concept in the classroom between the instructor and each of the students becomes an essential foundation for the instruction that follows.

A simple and powerful example of a unifying concept can be the editorial cartoon found in most daily newspapers. The effective editorial cartoon presents a clear concept to thousands of readers, each having their own personal schemata regarding that topic. Through the cartoon, readers have a common starting point for which to discuss the concepts with other readers whether they agree with the original cartoon or not. Other examples of creating a unifying concept are video productions, literature (in the forms of essays, articles, or research), pictures or diagrams, and even music. All of these could be used in an instructional setting for the purpose of schemata alignment among students.

The act of creating a basic construct and/or framework for the learner at the beginning of instruction is a way to focus the learner and to introduce the content. These ideas are supported by Hilgard and Bower (1966) and Knowles (1988). The organization of knowledge should be an essential concern of the teacher or educational planner so that the direction from simple to complex is not from arbitrary, meaningless parts to meaningful wholes, but instead from simplified wholes to more complex wholes (Knowles, 1988).

Organization of knowledge in the beginning stages of instruction also serves the even larger purpose of memory retention and retrieval upon completion of instruction. "We have made it appear probable that association depends upon organization, because an association is the after-effect of an organized process. . . . Learning amounts to association, and association is the after-effect of organization" (Kohler, 1947, p.163–164).

Motivating the Learner

Motivation on the part of the learner is an important aspect of the WPW Learning Model due to the fact that without learners valuing the new content that is being taught, there is little hope for retention or transfer to the workplace. However, many instructors leave student motivation in the hands of the students as their own responsibility. Support for the idea that motivation should be incorporated into a structured and systematic form of instruction came first from Lewin (1951). "Learning occurs as a result of change in cognitive structures produced by changes in two types of forces: (1) change in the structure of the cognitive field itself, or (2) change in the internal needs or motivation of the individual" (Knowles, 1988, p.23).

The potential for change in the motivation of an individual is possible due to the fact that human behavior is goal oriented. One of the distinguishable characteristics of human behavior is its purposeful, goal-directed nature (Gage and Berliner, 1988). Lindeman (1926), as cited by Knowles, gives a key assumption about adult learning that has been supported by later research. "Adults are motivated to learn as they experience needs and interests that learning will satisfy" (Knowles, 1988, p.31).

Clearly, the opportunity to motivate the student comes from capitalizing on the learner's own internal desire for goal attainment and personal achievement. "Perseverance can be increased by increasing the expectation of reward and the bad consequences of failure" (Gage and Berliner, 1988, p.334).

Motivation is also attained through clearly stated learning objectives at the beginning of instruction. While much has been written about the value of clear, student-oriented terminal objectives for the purpose of evaluation, they also aid in motivation. Research done by Bandura in 1982 identifies the following two instructional motivational variables: "These two cognitive variables are self-efficacy (one's belief that one can execute a given behavior in a given setting) and outcome expectancies (one's belief that the given outcome will occur if one engages in the behavior)" (Latham, 1987, p. 265).

Clarifying instructional objectives for the component instruction and the overall terminal objective meshes with the first component of motivation. By clarifying the purpose and rationale for instruction as it relates to the learner, then by detailing the how, what, and why of the instruction through clear objectives, the learner is fundamentally prepared for the instruction to follow.

To summarize, the importance of the "first whole" is found in the preparation of the learner for the instructional events to follow. This preparation will prove instrumental in the learners' recognition and recall on which the "second whole" is based (Kohler, 1947).

THE SECOND WHOLE OF THE WHOLE-PART-WHOLE LEARNING MODEL

While it is true of any system that each element within the system is critical to the success of the system, in the Whole-Part-Whole Learning Model, the "second whole" must be considered the major component. Based upon Gestalt psychology that the whole is greater than the sum of the parts, it is here, in the "second whole," that we contend that complete understanding occurs.

The "second whole" links the individual "parts" back together to form the complete whole, for it is not only the mastery of each individual part of instruction that is important, but the relationship between those "parts" through the "second whole" that provides the learner with the complete understanding of the content.

Wolfgang Kohler, in his book *Gestalt Psychology* (1947), provides the basis for the "second whole" in his writings on association and recall. Kohler, using research done with animals, explains that because of the large amount of information that must be processed and stored, a simplification effect occurs. Simplification of large quantities of stimulus is narrowed down to only the outstanding features of the original stimuli. These outstanding features remain only as traces of the original stimulus. "Hence, only some effect of the first process (part) can remain when the process (part) itself has subsided. . . . All sound theories of memory, habit and so forth must contain hypothesis about memory traces as psychological facts" (Kohler, 1947, p. 149).

Knowing this about the cognitive capabilities of an individual, whole-part instruction becomes illogical. Ending instruction upon the completion of the final part leaves the learner with unorganized and vague traces of the preceding parts. The learner is also faced with the difficult task of organizing those parts into a whole on their own in order for the new knowledge to become useful. Kohler (1947) said of the organization of traces that, "They must be organized in a way which resembles the organization of the original process. With this organization they take part in processes of recall" (p.150).

The organization of the traces should be facilitated by the instructor, thus aiding the student in a comprehensive recall of the instructional material. Kohler speaks of the interrelationship between the organized traces (or parts). "When the members of a series are well associated, they prove to have characteristics which depend upon their position in the whole series—just as tones acquire certain characteristics when heard within a melody" (Kohler, 1947, p.158).

To summarize, the interrelationship between the "parts" of the content begins with the realization that only traces from the full amount of instructional material will remain upon completion of instruction. It is essential, therefore, for the instructor to go back and strengthen those traces by forming the instructional whole (for example, whole concept, whole definition). Upon the formation of the instructional whole, the "parts" of instruction take on new meaning *within* the whole just as the tones acquire certain characteristics within the melody.

After the formation of the cognitive whole, the instructor must pursue the transfer of this new knowledge from short-term memory/working memory into the long-term memory. Information that is rehearsed is encoded for storage in the long-term memory (Gage and Berliner, 1988). Instructors can support this rehearsal by incorporating active learning (Gage and Berliner, 1988) into the "second whole." Active learning, in which learners take a participative role rather than a passive role, is incorporated in the "parts" instruction to aid in the mastery of the individual components. Furthermore, using active learning in the "second whole" will allow students to practice all of their skills in one continuous procedure. Production facilitates both learning and retention (Campbell, 1988; Perry and Downs, 1985).

Repetitive practice of the whole procedure not only aids in the transfer to long-term memory, but also provides the learner with a sense of comfort and eventually a relaxation with the procedure as a whole. Just as driving an automobile for the first time was a nervous collection of individual part performance, after a number of times behind the wheel, driving an automobile became a single procedure.

It is at this stage that the next step in the "second whole" may be pursued. The successful attempts by the learner on the complete procedure create in the learner a readiness for further understanding that until now was not available. According to Rosenshine (1986), further cognitive development can take place after automaticity, which he explains as follows.

After substantial practice, students achieve an automatic stage where they are successful, and rapid, and no longer have to think through each step. The advantage of automaticity is that the students who reach it now can give their full attention to comprehension and application (Rosenshine, 1986).

The full attention that the learners are now able to give provides the instructor with the opportunity and the responsibility to develop the instructional whole further through the introduction of a higher level cognition that the learners are now ready for. The learner who has become successful at driving an automobile is now ready for further development with such topics as driving in poor weather, night driving, or the dangers of speeding. Previous to automaticity, this would not have been as effective. As instructors, we become ethically responsible for pursuing this further development of learning. For just as the driving instructor knows that operation of an automobile does not only occur on dry pavement during the daytime, successful practice in the classroom is not an automatic guarantee of success in the workplace.

A pattern will not often be repeated in precisely the environment in which it occurred when the association was formed. Now quite apart from the cruder obstacles that have been considered above, even a slight change of the surrounding field may make a given pattern unable to cause recall of associated items. This is because the change introduces a new organization in which the experiences corresponding to that pattern are no longer present (Kohler, 1947).

Kohler (1947) argues that instructors should prepare the learners for the differing applications through the analysis, synthesis, and evaluation (see Bloom, 1956) procedures or at least to the troubleshooting stage of comprehension (see Swanson, 1991). By developing the learner through to this point, the instructor has not only formed the complete content whole in the learner's mind, but has also provided a deeper understanding of that content whole upon which the learner can keep adding to and refining as experiences dictate. The "second whole" provides the opportunity to the delight both the instructor and the learner by moving from knowledge to wisdom. Dewey (1933) and others see this reflection as a major prerequisite to wisdom.

THE PARTS OF THE WHOLE-PART-WHOLE LEARNING MODEL

The "parts" component of the Whole-Part-Whole Learning Model, relies on the standard systematic and behavioristic approach to instruction. Thousands of books and articles have been written regarding the effectiveness of this approach to teaching specific, structured material. To argue for what has already been established would be redundant. There are, however, some important points that should be addressed regarding this component of the WPW Learning Model. The first is that the learner must attain mastery of each "part" in order for the "second whole" to be effective. If the learner does not understand one of the "parts," there cannot be the full understanding of the whole. Next, each "part" within the WPW Learning Model can (and should) be structured in a whole-part-whole fashion. Thus, within the larger whole-part-whole instructional program design, there are subset whole-part-whole unit designs being created. This provides the learner with the same benefits in the individual lesson that the larger program design provides.

CONCLUSION

The Whole-Part-Whole Learning Model provides a systematic design framework for the instructor to follow. It lends itself to the practical work of designing education and training programs while holding on fiercely to learning theory and research. It provides a general whole-part-whole learning template. This learning template can be used at both the program design and lesson design levels. From a systems perspective, each of the program segments, whether they are classified as a part or a whole, can then constitute a subsystem. In curricular language, each program segment is a lesson. The initial lesson would therefore be focused on establishing the "first whole." Succeeding lessons would then take on the logical "part(s)" and the concluding "second whole" functions. Each of the program lessons (or subsystems) are then designed to use the same whole-part-whole template (see Figure 10-2).

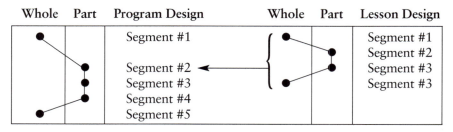

Whole	Part	Program Design	Whole	Part	Lesson Design
		Segment #1			Segment #1
					Segment #2
		Segment #2 ←			Segment #3
		Segment #3			Segment #3
		Segment #4			
		Segment #5			

Figure 10-2. Whole-Part-Whole Learning Model applied to program and lesson design.

The general program design of whole-part-whole lessons have been applied to the practical problem of differentiating between three types of training: management, motivational, and technical training. Through a series of structured observations of good training practices, general WPW program design templates were developed for these three types of training. Figure 10-3 illustrates the general program template of lessons.

It is interesting to note the unique roles of the "first whole" among the three types of training programs. Most technical training is focused on closed systems that are external to the learner. These learners typically understand and accept the fact that work systems get revised and/or replaced. In contrast, most management training is an attempt to alter the personal internal systems that managers operate by and which they often resist changing. Thus, dealing with program objectives and purpose becomes the critical role of the "first whole" for management training, while overviewing the new system is more typical of technical training. In motivational training (efforts at altering basic values and beliefs), the "first whole" addresses the critical need to accept the group and/or individuals. The templates and their proposed elements provide a logical springboard for establishing the specific whole-part-whole lessons that make up a particular learning program.

As noted in the introduction, the Whole-Part-Whole Learning Model goes beyond the present holistic, behavioristic, whole-part, and part-whole learning models. The WPW Learning Model purports that there is a natural whole-part-whole rhythm to learning. The WPW Model is an effort to acknowledge and use theory and best practices to design sound learning programs.

Technical Training Program Template of Lessons

Whole-Part

1.	•	Operation/equipment/system Overview
2.		Start-up
3.		Operation
4.		Shut-down
5.		Defects/faults
6.		Troubleshooting
7.		Solo Performance

Motivational Training Program Template of Lessons

Whole-Part

1.	•	Acceptance of group/individuals
2.		Problem/opportunity
3.		Fear/greed illustrations (with role models)
4.		The solution
5.		Solicit commitment to solution
6.		Vision success

Management Training Program Template of Lessons

Whole-Part

1.	•	Objectives/Purpose of training
2.		Illustration of good/bad performance
3.		Conceptual model
4.		Elements of the model
5.		Techniques
6.		Practice/role playing
7.		Managerial implications discussion

Figure 10-3. General program design templates using the whole-part-whole learning model.

REFERENCES

Ausubel, D.P. (1968). *Educational Psychology: A Cognitive View.* NY: Holt, Reinhart and Winston.

Bandura, (1977). *Social Learning Theory.* Englewood Cliffs, NJ: Prentice-Hall.

Bloom, B. S., Engelhart, M. D., Furst, E. J., Hill, W. H., and Krathwohl, D. R. (1956). *Taxonomy of Educational Objectives. Handbook 1: Cognitive Domain. The Classification of Educational Goals.* New York: Longmans, Green.

Campbell, J. P. (1988). "Training Design for Performance Improvement." *Productivity in Organizations.* San Francisco: Jossey-Bass, pp. 177–215.

Dewey, J. (1933). *How We Think.* Boston, MA: Heath and Company.

Di Vesta, F. J. (1982). "Cognitive Development." *Encyclopedia of Educational Research,* 5th ed. New York: Macmillan and Free Press.

Gage, N. L., and Berliner, D. C. (1988). *Educational Psychology,* 4th ed. Houston, TX: Houghton Mifflin.

Gagne, R., Briggs, L., and Wager, W. (1988). *Principals of Instructional Design,* 3rd ed. New York: Holt, Reinhart and Winston.

Hilgard, E. R. and Bower, G. H. (1966). *Theories of Learning.* NY: Appleton-Century-Crofts.

Knowles, M. S. (1988). *The Adult Learner: A Neglected Species,* 3rd ed. Houston, TX: Gulf Publishing.

Kohler, W. (1947). *Gestalt Psychology.* New York: Meridian.

Latham, G. P. (1989). Behavioral Approaches to the Training and Learning Process. In I.L. Goldstein and Associates (Ed.), *Training and Development in Organizations,* pp. 256–295. San Francisco, CA: Jossey-Bass Publications.

Lewin, K. (1951). *Field Theory in Social Science.* NY: Harper.

Lindeman, E. C. (1926). *The Meaning of Adult Education.* NY: New Republic.

Luiten, J., Ames, W., and Ackerman, G. (1980). A Meta Analysis of the Effects of Advance Organizers on Learning and Retention. *American Educational Research Journal.* Vol. 17, pp. 211–218, 291, 405.

Perry, P., and Downs, S. (1985). Skills, Strategies, and Ways of Learning. *Programmed Learning and Educational Technology,* Vol. 22, pp. 177–181.

Rosenshine, B. V. (1986). Effective Teaching in Industrial Education and Training. *Journal of Industrial Teacher Education,* Vol. 23, pp. 5–19.

Skinner, B. F. (1954). The Science of Learning and the Art of Teaching. *Harvard Educational Review,* Vol. 24, pp. 86–97.

Skinner, B. F. (1968). *The Technology of Teaching.* NY: Appleton-Century-Crofts.

Swanson, R. A. (1991). Ready-Aim-Frame. *Human Resource Development Quarterly,* Vol. 2, pp. 203–205.

Tolman, E. C. (1959). Principles of Purposive Behavior. In S. Koch (Ed.), *Psychology: A Study of Science: Vol 2. General Systematic Formulations, Learning, and Special Processes,* NY: McGraw Hill, pp. 92–157.

CHAPTER 11

From Teacher to Facilitator of Learning *

I was brought up to think of a teacher as one who is responsible (accountable is the current jargon) for what students should learn, how, when, and if they have learned. Teachers are supposed to transmit prescribed content, control the way students receive and use it, and then test if they have received it.

That is how all my teachers had performed. It was the only model of teaching I knew. When I was invited to teach at George Williams College in Chicago shortly after World War II, that is how I taught. At first I was pleased and proud concerning my performance. I was a pretty good transmitter. My content was well organized, with a good logical outline. I illustrated abstract concepts or principles with interesting examples. I spoke clearly and dynamically. I brought forth frequent chuckles. I invited interruptions for questions of clarification. I had lively discussions and practice exercises following my lectures. My tests were fair, and produced a good curve of distribution.

I remember feeling so good when my students did what I told them to do, which was most of the time. Most of the students were preparing for careers as YMCA secretaries, and they were conscientious and well behaved. They took notes, did homework, and were able to feed back on the final exam (most of what I told them), with the A students remembering my very words. I felt psychically rewarded by

---

*Malcom S. Knowles. 1981. *Educational Materials Catalog*. Follett Publishing Co.

being such a good transmitter of content and controller of students. I was really a good teacher.

I had started taking courses toward a master's degree in adult education at the University of Chicago a year earlier, and my first courses were with teachers who did just about the same things I was doing in my course. Toward the end of my course at George Williams College, I enrolled in a seminar in psychological counseling at the University of Chicago under Professor Arthur Shedlin, an associate of Carl Rogers. I was shocked by what happened at the first meeting. Some fifteen students sat around the seminar table for 20 minutes talking small talk. Finally, somebody asked if anyone knew where the teacher was. One of the people responded that his name was Art and that he had been designated by the Psychology Department to meet with us. Somebody else then asked if there was a course outline. Art responded, "You would like a course outline?" Silence for several minutes. Another student broke the silence by saying, "I'd like to know why everybody is here—what did you come to learn?" So we went around the table stating our goals and expectations. When Art's turn came, he said, "I am hoping that you will help me become a better facilitator of learning."

Never Before Worked So Hard

I won't attempt to reconstruct the ensuing events, but I can tell you that during the following week I read all the books Carl Rogers had written, located students who had taken the seminar and asked them what it was all about, and developed a plan for student inquiry teams, which I presented at the second meeting (which was adopted, with some modifications). I never read so many books and articles and worked so hard in any course I had ever taken. I had never before experienced taking that degree of responsibility for my own learning, alone and with other students, as I did in that seminar. It was exhilarating. I began to sense what it means to get turned on to learning. I began to think about what it means to be a facilitator of learning rather than a teacher. Fortunately, my next seminar, with Cyril O. Houle, reinforced this line of inquiry.

After my completion of the seminar with Cyril Houle, George Williams College asked me to teach adult education methods again.

That was the day I decided to switch from being a teacher to being a facilitator of learning. At the opening session I explained to the students that I wanted to experiment with a different approach to teaching, and described my own experience in being exposed to two role models—Shedlin and Houle—of the role of learning facilitator. I confessed that I was not secure about my ability to bring it off, since I had never done it before, that it would only work if they agreed to take a higher level of responsibility for their own learning and that I wouldn't do it if they felt the risk was too high. They unanimously agreed to experiment with me.

I spent the rest of the first meeting having the students introduce themselves and identify their special interests and resources. I distributed a syllabus that listed the objectives the course was intended to help them accomplish and the content units (I called them "inquiry units"), with references to resource materials, that would lead to the accomplishment of the objectives. I asked them which inquiry units they would take responsibility for during the week. In the second session I had them volunteer for the inquiry units they were especially interested in, and we formed "inquiry teams."

The inquiry teams met, with me as a roving consultant and resource person, for the next four weeks, and then the rest of the semester was spent with the teams putting on "show and tell" sessions. I had never seen such creative presentations and pride of accomplishment. By the end of that semester, I was a confirmed facilitator of learning.

Inquiry Units and Teams

When I analyzed what had happened to me, I was able to identify very fundamental changes. My self-concept had changed from teacher to facilitator of learning. I saw my role shifting from content transmitter to process manager and—only secondarily—content resource.

In the second place, I experienced myself as adopting a different system of psychic rewards. I had replaced getting my rewards from controlling students with getting my rewards from releasing students. And I found the latter rewards much more satisfying.

Finally, I found myself performing a different set of functions that required a different set of skills. Instead of performing the function of content planner and transmitter, which required primarily presentation skills, I was performing the function of process designer and manager, which required relationship building, needs assessment, involvement of students in planning, linking students to learning resources, and encouraging student initiative.

I have never been tempted since then to revert to the role of teacher.

CHAPTER 12

Making Things Happen By Releasing the Energy of Others*

Several years ago I began an intellectual adventure that has paid high dividends in terms of understanding the role of leadership and in selecting more effective leadership strategies. The adventure consisted of seeing what would happen if one conceptualized a social system (family, group, organization, agency, corporation, school, college, community, state, nation, or world) as a system of human energy.

All at once a set of questions very different from those typically asked by leaders started coming to mind: What is the sum total of the human energy available in the system? What proportion of this energy is now being used? Where is the unused energy located? Why is it not being tapped? What kinds of energy (physical, intellectual, psychic, moral, artistic, technical, social) are represented? What might be done to release this energy for accomplishing greater goals for the system and the individuals in it?

---

*Malcolm S. Knowles, *Journal of Management Development*, University of Queensland Business School, Australia, September 1983.

By virtue of simply asking these kinds of questions, I began to have to think differently about the role of leadership. Having been raised in the era of Frederick Taylor's "scientific management," I had perceived the role of leadership to consist primarily of controlling followers or subordinates. Effective leaders, I had been taught, were those who were able to get people to follow their orders. The consequence of this doctrine was, of course, that the output of the system was limited to the vision and ability of the leader, and when I realized this fact I started rethinking the function of leadership. It gradually came to me that the highest function of leadership is releasing the energy of the people in the system and managing the processes for giving that energy direction toward mutually beneficial goals. Perhaps a better way of saying this is that creative leadership is that form of leadership that releases the creative energy of the people being led.

In the intervening years since this way of thinking emerged in my mind, I have been trying to understand it—and test its validity—in two ways. First, I have been observing leaders of various sorts (teachers, business executives, educational administrators, and organizational and political leaders) through this frame of reference. I have wanted to see if I could identify characteristics that "releasing leaders" possess that "controlling leaders" don't have. Second, I have reexamined the research literature on human behavior, organizational dynamics, and leadership to find out what support it contains for this way of viewing the concept of leadership. I would like to share with you the results of this bifocal inquiry in the form of the following propositions regarding the behavioral characteristics of creative leaders:

1. Creative leaders make a different set of assumptions (essentially positive) about human nature from the assumptions (essentially negative) made by controlling leaders. It has been my observation that creative leaders have faith in people, offer them challenging opportunities, and delegate responsibility to them. Two of the clearest presentations of these contrasting assumptions in the literature are reproduced in Exhibit 1: by Douglas McGregor in the case of assumptions by managers and by Carl Rogers in the case of assumptions by educators.

Exhibit 1
A Comparison of Assumptions About Human Nature and Behavior by Leaders in Management and Education

Theory X Assumptions about Human Nature (McGregor)* (Controlling)	Assumptions Implicit in Current Education (Rogers)** (Controlling)
The average human being inherently dislikes work and will avoid it if he can.	The student cannot be trusted to pursue his own learning.
Because of this characteristically human dislike of work, most people must be coerced, controlled, threatened in the interest of organizational objectives.	Presentation equals learning. The aim of education is to accumulate brick upon brick of factual knowledge.
The average human being prefers to be directed, wishes to avoid responsibility, has relatively little ambition, wants security above all.	The truth is known. Creative citizens develop from passive learners. Evaluation is education and education is evaluation.

Theory Y Assumptions about Human Nature (Releasing)	Assumptions Relevant to Significant Experiential Learning (Releasing)
The expenditure of physical and mental effort is as natural as play or rest.	Human beings have a natural potentiality for learning.
External control and threat of punishment are not the only means for bringing about effort toward organizational objectives. Man will exercise self-direction and self-control in the service of objectives to which he is committed.	Significant learning takes place when the subject matter is perceived by the student as relevant to his own purposes. Much significant learning is acquired through doing.
Commitment to objectives is a function of the rewards associated with their achievement.	Learning is faciliated by student's responsible participation in the learning process.

The average human being learns, under proper conditions, not only to accept but to seek responsibility.

Self-initiated learning involving the whole person—feelings as well as intellect—is the most pervasive and lasting.

A high capacity for imagination, ingenuity, and creativity in solving organizational problems is widely, not narrowly distributed in the population.

Creativity in learning is best facilitated when self-criticism and self-evaluation are primary, and evaluation by others is of secondary importance.

Under the conditions of modern industrial life, the intellectual potential of the average human being is only partially utilized.

Creativity in learning is best facilitated when self-criticism and self-evaluation are primary, and evaluation by others is of secondary importance.

The most socially useful thing to learning in the modern world is the process of learning, a continuing openness to experience, an incorporation into oneself of the process of change.

*Adapted from McGregor (1960), pp. 33–34 and 47–48 in Knowles (1978), p. 102.
**Adapted from Rogers (1972), pp. 272–279 in Knowles (1978), p. 102.

The validity of the positive set of assumptions is supported by research that indicates that when people perceive the locus of control to reside within themselves, they are more creative and productive (Lefcourt, 1976) and that the more they feel their unique potential is being used, the greater their achievement (Herzberg, 1966; Maslow, 1970).

2. Creative leaders accept as a law of human nature that people feel a commitment to a decision in proportion to the extent that they feel they have participated in making it. Creative leaders, therefore, involve their clients, workers, or students in every step of the planning process, assessing needs, formulating goals, designing lines of action, carrying out activities, and evaluating results (except, perhaps, in emergencies). The validity of this proposition is supported by locus of control studies (Lefcourt, 1976) and by research on organizational change (Bennis, Benne, and

Chin, 1968; Greiner, 1971; Lippitt, 1969; Martorana, 1975), administration (Baldridge, 1978; Dykes, 1968; Getzels, Lipham, and Campbell, 1968; Likert, 1967; McGregor, 1967), decision making (Marrow, Bowers, and Seashore, 1968; Millett, 1968; Simon, 1961), and organizational dynamics (Argyris, 1962; Etzioni, 1961; Schein, 1965; Zander, 1977).

3. Creative leaders believe in and use the power of self-fulfilling prophesy. They understand that people tend to come up to other people's expectations for them. The creative coach conveys to his team that he knows they are capable of winning; the good supervisor's employees know that he or she has faith that they will do superior work; the good teacher's students are convinced that they are the best students in school. The classic study demonstrating this principle, Rosenthal and Jacobson's *Pygmalion in the Classroom* (1968), showed that the students of teachers who were told that they were superior students were superior students; whereas, the students of teachers who were told that they were inferior students were inferior students. And, of course, there was no difference in the natural ability of the two groups of students. The relationship between positive self-concept and superior performance has been demonstrated in studies of students (Chickering, 1976; Felker, 1974; Rogers, 1969; Tough, 1979) and in general life achievement (Adams-Webber, 1979; Coan, 1974; Gale, 1974; Kelly, 1955; Loevinger, 1976; McClelland, 1975).

4. Creative leaders highly value individuality. They sense that people perform at a higher level when they are operating on the basis of their unique strengths, talents, interests, and goals than when they are trying to conform to some imposed stereotype. They are comfortable with a pluralistic culture and tend to be bored with one that is monolithic. As managers, they encourage a team arrangement in which each member works at what he or she does best and enjoys most; as teachers they strive to tailor the learning strategies to fit the individual learning styles, paces, starting points, needs, and interests of all the students. This proposition is widely supported in the research literature (Combs and Snygg, 1959; Czikszentmihalyi, 1975; Erikson,

1974; Goldstein and Blackman, 1978; Gowan, et al., 1967; Kagan, 1967; Maslow, 1970; Messick, et al., 1976; Moustakas, 1974; Tyler, 1978).

I would like to add another dimension to this proposition—more of a philosophical note than a behavioral observation. It is that creative leaders probably have a different sense of the purpose of life from that of the controlling leaders. They see the purpose of all life activities—work, learning, recreation, civic participation, worship—as a way to enable each individual to achieve his or her full and unique potential. They seek to help each person become what Maslow (1970) calls a self-actualizing person, whereas the controlling leader's mission is to produce conforming persons.

5. Creative leaders stimulate and reward creativity. They understand that in a world of accelerating change, creativity is a basic requirement for the survival of individuals, organizations, and societies. They exemplify creativity in their own behavior and provide an environment that encourages and rewards innovation in others. They make it legitimate for people to experiment, and treat failures as opportunities to learn rather than as acts to be punished (Barron, 1963; Bennis, 1966; Cross, 1976; Davis and Scott, 1971; Gardner, 1963; Gowan, et al., 1967; Herzberg, 1966; Ingalls, 1976; Kagan, 1967; Schon, 1971; Toffler, 1974; Zahn, 1966).

6. Creative leaders are committed to a process of continuous change and are skillful in managing change. They understand the difference between static and innovative organizations (as illustrated in Exhibit 2) and aspire to make their organizations the latter. They are well grounded in the theory of change and skillful in selecting the most effective strategies for bringing about change (Arends and Arends, 1977; Baldridge and Deal, 1975; Bennis, Benne, and Chin, 1968; Goodlad, 1975; Greiner, 1971; Hefferlin, 1969; Hornstein, et al., 1971; Lippitt, 1973; Mangham, 1978; Martorana and Kuhns, 1975; Schein and Bennis, 1965; Tedeschi, 1972; Zurcher, 1977).

Exhibit 2
Some Characteristics of Static Vs. Innovative Organizations

DIMENSIONS	CHARACTERISTICS	
	Static Organizations	Innovative Organizations
Structure	Rigid—much energy given to maintaining permanent departments, committees; reverance for tradition, constitution, & by-laws. Hierarchial—adherence to chain of command. Roles defined narrowly. Property-bound.	Flexible—much use of temporary task forces; easy shifting of departmental lines; readiness to change constitution, depart from tradition. Multiple linkages based on functional collaboration. Roles defined broadly. Property-mobile.
Atmosphere	Task-centered, impersonal. Cold, formal, reserved. Suspicious.	People-centered, caring. Warm, informal, intimate. Trusting.
Management Philosophy and Attitudes	Function of management is to control personnel through coercive power. Cautious, low risk-taking. Attitude toward errors: to be avoided. Emphasis on personnel selection. Self-sufficiency—closed system regarding sharing resources. Low tolerance for ambiguity.	Function of management is to release the energy of personnel; power is used supportively. Experimental—high risk-taking. Attitude toward errors: to be learned from. Emphasis on personal development. Interdependency—open system regarding sharing resources. High tolerance for ambiguity.
Decision-making and Policy-making	High participation at top, low at bottom. Clear distinction between policy-making and policy-execution. Decision-making by legal mechanisms. Decisions treated as final.	Relevant participation by all those affected. Collaborative policy-making and policy-execution. Decision-making by problem-solving. Decisions treated as hypotheses to be tested.
Communication	Restricted flow—constipated. One-way—downward. Feelings repressed or hidden.	Open flow—easy access. Multidirectional—up, down, sideways. Feelings expressed.

7. Creative leaders emphasize internal motivators over external motivators. They understand the distinction revealed in Herzberg's (1959) research between satisfiers (motivators), such as achievement, recognition, fulfilling work, responsibility, advancement, and growth, and dissatisfiers (hygienic factors), such as organizational policy and administration, supervision, working conditions, interpersonal relations, salary, status, job security, and personal life. They take steps to minimize the dissatisfiers but concentrate their energy on optimizing the satisfiers. This position is strongly supported by subsequent research (Levinson, Price, et al., 1963; Likert, 1967; Lippitt, 1973).

8. Creative leaders encourage people to be self-directing. They sense intuitively what researchers have been telling us for some time—that a universal characteristic of the maturation process is movement from a state of dependency toward states of increasing self-directedness (Baltes, 1978; Erikson, 1950, 1959, 1964, 1974; Goulet and Baltes, 1970; Gubrium and Buckholdt, 1977; Havighurst, 1970; Kagan and Moss, 1962; Loevinger, 1976; Rogers, 1961). They realize that because of previous conditioning as dependent learners in their school experience, adults need initial help in learning to be self-directing and look to leaders for this kind of help (Kidd, 1973; Knowles, 1975, 1978, 1980; Tough, 1967, 1979). And, to provide this kind of help, they have developed their skills as facilitators and consultants to a high level (Bell and Nadler, 1979; Blake and Mouton, 1976; Bullmer, 1975; Carkhuff, 1969; Combs, et al, 1978; Lippitt and Lippitt, 1978; Laughary and Ripley, 1979; Pollack, 1976; Schein, 1969; Schlossberg, et al, 1978).

No doubt additional propositions and behavioral characteristics could be identified, but these are the ones that stand out in my observation of creative leaders and review of the literature as being most central. And I have seen wonderful things happen when they have been put into practice. I have seen low-achieving students become high-achieving students when they discovered the excitement of self-directed learning under the influence of a creative teacher. I have seen bench workers in a factory increase their productivity and get a new sense of personal pride and fulfillment under a creative supervisor. I have seen an entire college faculty (at Holland College, Prince Edward Island, Canada) become creative facilitators of learning and content resource consultants through the stimulation of a creative administration. And I have observed several instances in which the line managers of major corporations moved from controlling managers to releasing managers when their management-development programs were geared to these propositions.

Perhaps we are on the verge of beginning to understand how to optimize the release of the enormous pent-up energy in our human energy systems.

CHAPTER 13

Some Guidelines for the Use of Learning Contracts*

WHY USE LEARNING CONTRACTS?

One of the most significant findings from research about adult learning (for example, Allen Tough's *The Adult's Learning Projects*) is that when adults go about learning something naturally (as contrasted with being taught something), they are highly self-directing. Evidence is beginning to accumulate, too, that what adults learn on their own initiative, they learn more deeply and permanently than what they learn by being taught.

Those kinds of learning that are engaged in for purely personal development can perhaps be planned and carried out completely by an individual on his own terms and with only a loose structure. But those kinds of learning that have as their purpose improving one's competence to perform in a job or in a profession must take into account the needs and expectations of organizations, professions, and society. Learning contracts provide a means for negotiating a reconciliation between these external needs and expectations and the learner's internal needs and interests.

Furthermore, in traditional education the learning activity is structured by the teacher and the institution. The learner is told what objectives he is to work toward, what resources he is to use and how

---

* Malcolm S. Knowles, 1990.

(and when) he is to use them, and how his accomplishment of the objectives will be evaluated. This imposed structure conflicts with the adult's deep psychological need to be self-directing and may induce resistance, apathy, or withdrawal. Learning contracts provide a vehicle for making the planning of learning experiences a mutual undertaking between a learner and his helper, mentor, teacher, and often, peers. By participating in the process of diagnosing his needs, formulating his objectives, identifying resources, choosing strategies, and evaluating his accomplishments, the learner develops a sense of ownership of (and commitment to) the plan.

Finally, in field-based learning particularly, there is a strong possibility that what is to be learned from the experience will be less clear to both the learner and the field supervisor than what work is to be done. There is a long tradition of field experience learners being exploited for the performance of menial tasks. The learning contract is a means for making the learning objectives of the field experience clear and explicit for both the learner and the field supervisor.

HOW DO YOU DEVELOP A LEARNING CONTRACT?

Step 1—Diagnose Your Learning Needs

A learning need is the gap between where you are now and where you want to be in regard to a particular set of competencies.

You may already be aware of certain learning needs as a result of a personnel appraisal process or the long accumulation of evidence for yourself of the gaps between where you are now and where you would like to be.

If not (or even so), it might be worth your while to go through this process: First, construct a model of the competencies required to perform excellently the role (for example, parent, teacher, civic leader, manager, consumer, professional worker, etc.) you are concerned about. There may be a competency model already in existence that you can use as a thought-starter and checklist; many professions are developing such models. If not, you can build your own, with help from friends, colleagues, supervisors, and expert resource people. A competency can be thought of as the ability to do something at some level of proficiency, and is usually composed of some combination of knowledge, understanding, skill, attitude, and values. For example, "ability to ride a bicycle from my home to the store" is a competency that involves some knowledge of how a bicycle operates and the route to the store; an understanding of some of the dangers inherent in riding a bicycle; skill in mounting, pedaling, steering, and stopping a bicycle; an attitude of desire to ride a bicycle; and a valuing of the exercise it will yield. "Ability to ride a bicycle in cross-country race" would be a higher-level competency that would require greater knowledge, understanding, skill, etc. It is useful to produce a competency model even if it is crude and subjective because of the clearer sense of direction it will give you.

Having constructed a competency model, your next task is to assess the gap between where you are now and where the model says you should be in regard to each competency. You can do this alone or with the help of people who have been observing your performance. The chances are that you will find that you have already developed some competencies to a level of excellence, so that you can concentrate on those you haven't. An example of a model of competencies for the role of adult educator is provided in Chapter 11.

Step 2—Specify Your Learning Objectives

You are now ready to start filling out the first column of the learning contract shown in Figure 13-1, "Learning Objectives." Each of the learning needs diagnosed in Step 1 should be translated into a learning objective. Be sure that your objectives describe what you will learn, not what you will do. State them in terms that are most meaningful to you—content acquisition, terminal behaviors, or directions of growth.

Step 3—Specify Learning Resources and Strategies

When you have finished listing your objectives, move over to the second column of the contract in Figure 13-1, "Learning Resources and Strategies," and describe how you propose to go about accomplishing each objective. Identify the resources (material and human) you plan to use in your field experience and the strategies (techniques, tools) you will employ in making use of them. For example, if in the "Learning Objectives" column you wrote "Improve my ability to organize my work efficiently so that I can accomplish 20 percent

Learning Contract for:			
Name _____			
Activity _____			
Learning Objectives	Learning Resources and Strategies	Evidence of Accomplishment of Objectives	Criteria and Means for Validating Evidence

Figure 13-1. This is a typical learning contract.

more work in a day," you might list the following in the "Learning Resources and Strategies" column:

1. Find books and articles in library on how to organize my work and manage time.
2. Interview three executives on how they organize their work, then observe them for one day each, noting techniques they use.
3. Select the best techniques from each, plan a day's work, and have a colleague observe me for a day, giving me feedback.

Step 4—Specify Evidence of Accomplishment

After completing the second column, move over to the third column, "Evidence of Accomplishment of Objectives," and describe what evidence you will collect to indicate the degree to which you have achieved each objective. Perhaps the following examples of evidence for different types of objectives will stimulate your thinking about what evidence you might accumulate:

Type of Objective	Examples of Evidence
Knowledge	Reports of knowledge acquired, as in essays, examinations, oral presentations, audio-visual presentations, annotated bibliographies.
Understanding	Examples of utilizations of knowledge in solving problems, as in action projects, research projects with conclusions and recommendations, plans for curriculum change, etc.

Type of Objective	Examples of Evidence
Skills	Performance exercises, video-taped performances, etc., with ratings by observers.
Attitudes	Attitudinal rating scales; performance in real situations, role playing, simulation games, critical incident cases, etc., with feedback from participants and/or observers.
Values	Value rating scales; performance in value clarification groups, critical incident cases, simulation exercises, etc., with feedback from participants and/or observers.

Step 5—Specify How the Evidence Will Be Validated

After you have specified what evidence you will gather for each objective in column three, move over to column four, "Criteria and Means for Validating Evidence." For each objective, first specify what criteria you propose the evidence will be judged by. The criteria will vary according to the type of objective. For example, appropriate criteria for knowledge objectives might include comprehensiveness, depth, precision, clarity, authentication usefulness, and scholarliness. For skill objectives, more appropriate criteria may be poise, speed, flexibility, gracefulness, precision, and imaginativeness. After you have specified the criteria, indicate the means you propose to use to have the evidence judged according to these criteria. For example, if you produce a paper or report, who will you have read it and what are their qualifications? Will they express their judgments by rating scales, descriptive reports, evaluative reports, or how? One of the actions that helps to differentiate "distinguished" from "adequate" performance in self-directed learning is the wisdom with which a learner selects his or her validators.

Step 6—Review Your Contract with Consultants

After you have completed the first draft of your contract, you will find it useful to review it with two or three friends, supervisors, or other expert resource people to get their reactions and suggestions. Here are some questions you might have them ask about the contract to get optimal benefit from their help:

1. Are the learning objectives clear, understandable, and realistic; and do they describe what you propose to learn?
2. Can they think of other objectives you might consider?
3. Do the learning strategies and resources seem reasonable, appropriate, and efficient?
4. Can they think of other resources and strategies you might consider?
5. Does the evidence seem relevant to the various objectives, and would it convince them?
6. Can they suggest other evidence you might consider?
7. Are the criteria and means for validating the evidence clear, relevant, and convincing?
8. Can they think of other ways to validate the evidence that you might consider?

Step 7—Carry Out the Contract

You now simply do what the contract calls for. But keep in mind that as you work on it you may find that your notions about what you want to learn and how you want to learn it may change. So don't hesitate to revise your contract as you go along.

Step 8—Evaluation of Your Learning

When you have completed your contract, you will want to get some assurance that you have in fact learned what you set out to learn. Perhaps the simplest way to do this is to ask the consultants you used in Step 6 to examine your evidence and validation data and give you their judgment about their adequacy.

CHAPTER 14

Core Competency Diagnostic and Planning Guide*

SELF-DIAGNOSTIC RATING SCALE COMPETENCIES FOR THE ROLE OF ADULT EDUCATOR/TRAINER

Name _____

Program _____

Indicate on the six-point scale below the level of each competency required for performing the particular role you plan to engage in by placing an "R" at the appropriate point. Then indicate your present level of development of each competency by placing a "P" at the appropriate point. For example, if you plan to make your career in teaching, you might rate required competencies as a learning facilitator as high and as a program developer and administrator as low or moderate; whereas, if you plan a career as a college administrator, you might rate the competencies as a learning facilitator as moderate and as a program developer and administrator as high. (Blanks have been provided at the end of each section for the learners to add competencies of their own.)

---

* Malcolm S. Knowles, 1981. Permission to use this rating scale is granted without limitation.

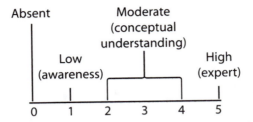

As a Learning Facilitator

A. Regarding the conceptual and theoretical framework of adult learning:

1. Ability to describe and apply modern concepts and research findings regarding the needs, interests, motivations, capacities, and developmental characteristics of adults as learners.

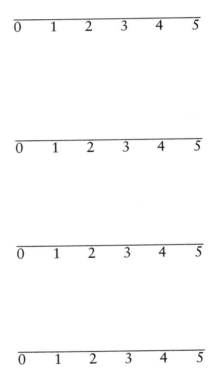

0   1   2   3   4   5

2. Ability to describe the differences in assumptions about youths and adults as learners and the implications of these differences for teaching.

0   1   2   3   4   5

3. Ability to assess the effects of forces impinging on learners from the larger environment (groups, organizations, cultures) and manipulate them constructively.

0   1   2   3   4   5

4. Ability to describe the various theories of learning and assess their relevance to particular adult learning situations.

0   1   2   3   4   5

5. Ability to conceptualize and explain the role of teacher as a facilitator and resource person for self-directed learners.

$$\overline{0 \quad 1 \quad 2 \quad 3 \quad 4 \quad 5}$$

B. Regarding the designing and implementing of learning experiences:

1. Ability to describe the difference between a content plan and a process design.

$$\overline{0 \quad 1 \quad 2 \quad 3 \quad 4 \quad 5}$$

2. Ability to design learning experiences for accomplishing a variety of purposes that take into account individual differences among learners.

$$\overline{0 \quad 1 \quad 2 \quad 3 \quad 4 \quad 5}$$

3. Ability to engineer a physical and psychological climate of mutual respect, trust, openness, supportiveness, and safety.

$$\overline{0 \quad 1 \quad 2 \quad 3 \quad 4 \quad 5}$$

4. Ability to establish a warm, empathic, facilitative relationship with learners of all sorts.

$$\overline{0 \quad 1 \quad 2 \quad 3 \quad 4 \quad 5}$$

5. Ability to engage learners responsibly in self-diagnosis of needs for learning.

$$\overline{0 \quad 1 \quad 2 \quad 3 \quad 4 \quad 5}$$

6. Ability to engage learners in formulating objectives that are meaningful to them.

$$\overline{0 \quad 1 \quad 2 \quad 3 \quad 4 \quad 5}$$

7. Ability to involve learners in the planning, conducting, and evaluating of learning activities appropriately.

$$\overline{0 \quad 1 \quad 2 \quad 3 \quad 4 \quad 5}$$

C. Regarding helping learners become self-directing:

1. Ability to explain the conceptual difference between didactic instruction and self-directed learning.

0   1   2   3   4   5

2. Ability to design and conduct one-hour, three-hour, one-day, and three-day learning experiences to develop the skills of self-directed learning.

0   1   2   3   4   5

3. Ability to model the role of self-directed learning in your own behavior.

0   1   2   3   4   5

D. Regarding the selection of methods, techniques, and materials:

1. Ability to describe the range of methods or formats for organizing learning experiences.

0   1   2   3   4   5

2. Ability to describe the range of techniques available for facilitating learning.

0   1   2   3   4   5

3. Ability to identify the range of materials available as resources for learning.

0   1   2   3   4   5

4. Ability to provide a rationale for selecting a particular method, technique, or material for achieving particular educational objectives.

0   1   2   3   4   5

5. Ability to evaluate various methods, techniques, and

0   1   2   3   4   5

materials as to their effectiveness in achieving particular educational outcomes.

6. Ability to develop and
manage procedures for the
construction of models of
competency.

0   1   2   3   4   5

7. Ability to construct and
use tools and procedures
for assessing competency-
development needs.

0   1   2   3   4   5

8. Ability to use a wide variety of presentation meth-
ods effectively.

0   1   2   3   4   5

9. Ability to use a wide variety of experiential and simulation methods effectively.

0   1   2   3   4   5

10. Ability to use audience-
participation methods
effectively.

0   1   2   3   4   5

11. Ability to use group
dynamics and small-group
discussion techniques
effectively.

0   1   2   3   4   5

12. Ability to invent new techniques to fit new situations.

0   1   2   3   4   5

13. Ability to evaluate learning
outcomes and processes
and select or construct
appropriate instruments
and procedures for this
purpose.

0   1   2   3   4   5

14. Ability to confront new
situations with confidence
and a high tolerance for
ambiguity.

0   1   2   3   4   5

As a Program Developer

A. Regarding the planning process:

1. Ability to describe and implement the basic steps (e.g., climate setting, needs assessment, formulation of program objectives, program design, program execution, and evaluation) that undergird the planning process in adult education.

0	1	2	3	4	5

2. Ability to involve representatives of client systems appropriately in the planning process.

0	1	2	3	4	5

3. Ability to develop and use instruments and procedures for assessing the needs of individuals, organizations, and subpopulations in social systems.

0	1	2	3	4	5

4. Ability to use systems-analysis strategies in program planning.

0	1	2	3	4	5

B. Regarding the designing and operating of programs:

1. Ability to construct a wide variety of program designs to meet the needs of various situations (basic skills training, developmental education, supervisory and management development, organizational development, etc.).

0	1	2	3	4	5

2. Ability to design programs with a creative variety of formats, activities, schedules, resources, and evaluative procedures.

0	1	2	3	4	5

3. Ability to use needs assessments, census data, organizational records, surveys, etc., in adapting programs to specific needs and clienteles.

0	1	2	3	4	5

4. Ability to use planning mechanisms, such as advisory councils, committees, task forces, etc., effectively.

0	1	2	3	4	5

5. Ability to develop and carry out a plan for program evaluation that will satisfy the requirements of institutional accountability and provide for program improvement.

0	1	2	3	4	5

As an Administrator

A. Regarding organizational development and maintenance:

1. Ability to describe and apply theories and research findings about organizational behavior, management, and renewal.

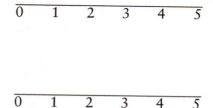

2. Ability to formulate a personal philosophy of administration and adapt it to various organizational situations.

0	1	2	3	4	5

3. Ability to formulate poli- $\overline{0 \quad 1 \quad 2 \quad 3 \quad 4 \quad 5}$
   cies that clearly convey the
   definition of mission,
   social philosophy, educational commitment, etc.,
   of an organization.

4. Ability to evaluate organi- $\overline{0 \quad 1 \quad 2 \quad 3 \quad 4 \quad 5}$
   zational effectiveness and
   guide its continuous self-
   renewal processes.

5. Ability to plan effectively $\overline{0 \quad 1 \quad 2 \quad 3 \quad 4 \quad 5}$
   with and through others,
   sharing responsibilities
   and decision making with
   them as appropriate.

6. Ability to select, supervise, $\overline{0 \quad 1 \quad 2 \quad 3 \quad 4 \quad 5}$
   and provide for inservice
   education of personnel.

7. Ability to evaluate staff $\overline{0 \quad 1 \quad 2 \quad 3 \quad 4 \quad 5}$
   performance.

8. Ability to analyze and $\overline{0 \quad 1 \quad 2 \quad 3 \quad 4 \quad 5}$
   interpret legislation affect-
   ing adult education.

9. Ability to describe finan- $\overline{0 \quad 1 \quad 2 \quad 3 \quad 4 \quad 5}$
   cial policies and practices
   in the field of adult education and to use them as
   guidelines for setting your
   own policies and practices.

10. Ability to perform the role $\overline{0 \quad 1 \quad 2 \quad 3 \quad 4 \quad 5}$
    of change agent vis-a-vis
    organizations and commu-
    nities utilizing educational
    processes.

B. Regarding program administration:

1. Ability to design and operate programs within the framework of a limited budget.

0   1   2   3   4   5

2. Ability to make and monitor financial plans and procedures.

0   1   2   3   4   5

3. Ability to interpret modern approaches to adult education and training to policy-makers convincingly.

0   1   2   3   4   5

4. Ability to design and use promotion, publicity, and public relations strategies appropriately and effectively.

0   1   2   3   4   5

5. Ability to prepare grant proposals and identify potential funding sources for them.

0   1   2   3   4   5

6. Ability to make use of consultants appropriately.

0   1   2   3   4   5

7. Ability and willingness to experiment with programmatic innovations and assess their results objectively.

0   1   2   3   4   5

Training Delivery Problems and Solutions*

The authors surveyed 371 trainers who were asked to recall train-ing delivery problems or difficulties they experienced as novices. The analysis of their 1,098 responses conclude that novice train-ers faced 12 common training delivery problems. Twenty expert trainers were subsequently surveyed and asked to present success-ful strategies for dealing with the 12 training delivery problems. The analysis of their responses concludes with a synthesis of the common training delivery problems experienced by novices and the experts' advice on how to solve these problems.

The training of employees at all levels has taken on a significant role in industry and business. Rapid technological advances in the workplace and the corporation's concern for profit in today's market-place drive the emphasis on training employees. When properly used, training increases both the effectiveness and efficiency of employees (Swanson, 1992). Within this framework and with all the advances in instructional technology, instructor-led training still remains the most popular method of delivering training, year after year, according to Lakewood Research's annual census.

Richard A. Swanson and Sandra K. Falkman. *Human Resource Development Quar-terly,* Vol. 8, no. 4, Winter 1997. Jossey-Bass Publishers.

Most beginning trainers are not graduates of programs specifically designed to train trainers. They are generally subject matter experts in their organizations and have good communication skills. Their preparation to deliver training often follows a "see and do" model. That is, they observe the course in preparation to deliver it and then they teach the course to other employees in a manner similar to what they observed.

Criticism of the training profession has included the lack of research about the processes used to select instructors, the evaluation methods used to rate the instruction, and the evaluation methods used to rate the instructor (Swanson, 1982). As training in industry and business continues to increase, the body of knowledge possessed by expert professional trainers will need to be captured and shared with more employees in organizations (Jacobs, 1992).

Purpose of the Study

Little has been written about the ways in which expert trainers handle specific training delivery problems in the training classroom. Proven and practical techniques for dealing with specific training delivery problems would help novice trainers.

There were three purposes for this research: (a) to determine the difficulties novice trainers experience during the delivery of training, (b) to gather reports from experts on how they handle such situations, and (c) to synthesize this information into a useful aid that defines the training delivery problems and provides specific solutions.

Overview of the Literature

Training and development has grown dramatically during the past three decades. It has become a 30 billion dollar profession. Each year, 15 million employees participate in 17.6 million courses. One out of every eight American workers attends a formal training course every year (Chakiris and Rolander, 1986). Furthermore, more employees each year are finding themselves in the role of trainer without having adequate preparation.

The burden for understanding and mediating the organization's desire for expertise and the learner needs is ultimately left on the trainer's shoulders (Yelon, 1992). The research on training adults in the workplace typically focuses on the needs of the organization (Sleezer, 1992) and the learner (Knowles, 1984). Much less is known and said about the specific problems facing the novice trainers and their role in delivering instruction. Instructor skills are the skills needed by a trainer when using structured learning events, such as group discussions, presentations, role plays, and case studies. These skills also include assessing learners' needs, using media and materials, administering exams or instruments, and providing feedback to participants (McLagan, 1983).

General models of training and learning are important to the profession as are the problems that threaten and discourage practitioners. At the general level, Knowles (1984) suggested that four concepts can be used to think about adult education: (a) the self-concept of the learner, (b) the learner's experience, (c) the learner's readiness to learn, and (d) the learner's perspective of time. Smith's (1983a, 1983b) more specific review and synthesis of the instruction literature identifies those variables that affect training and that the trainer can control. They include: objectives, content structure, instructional sequence, rate of delivery, repetition and practice, knowledge of results, and reinforcement and rewards.

Furthermore, the selection of instructional approaches depends on many criteria, such as conditions of learning, content, and characteristics of the students. Gagne specifically cites nine variables (1987): Gain attention, Inform the learner of the learning objectives, Stimulate the recall of prerequisite learning, Provide learning guidance, Elicit performance, Provide feedback about performance correctness, Assess performance , and Enhance performance and transfer.

Zemke and Zemke (1988) have further defined the specific needs of adult learners. The following are some examples: (1) In a classroom training situation, it is important that the environment be comfortable, both physically and psychologically; (2) Trainers must understand the participants' expectations of the course, because the self-concepts of the participants are involved, and (3) By serving as a facilitator or orchestrator, the effective instructor can manage the classroom by allowing participants to share their experiences and knowledge, can integrate new knowledge, and can provide strategies that will allow transfer of learning back to the job.

Clearly, the job of instructor is complex. And, while general instruction theories abound, the bulk of the practitioner training delivery advice in the literature is not grounded in research (see Pike, 1989). From the literature it is difficult to cull out the common training delivery problems and expert solutions to those problems being faced by novice trainers.

METHODOLOGY

The general methodology of the study involved surveying novice trainers and expert trainers. The novices identified their training delivery problems and the experts provided solutions to those problems. An overview of the general research methodology for this study is: (1) Survey trainers to determine the most frequent training delivery problems that novice trainers experience, (2) Analyze survey data and synthesize results into 10-15 major delivery problems, (3) Identify experts to respond to major training delivery problems experienced by novice trainers, (4) Survey the training experts through a questionnaire as to how they handle the identified training delivery problems, (5) Prepare job aids listing the training delivery problems, general solutions, and specific solutions, and (6) Prepare final report.

SURVEY OF NOVICE TRAINERS

A questionnaire was developed to determine the training delivery problems most frequently encountered by novice trainers. Questions covered basic demographic information and problems the respondents encountered during their first two years on the job. The following open-ended question was used:

As a beginning trainer, what problems or difficulties did you encounter during the delivery phase (or presentation) of training. Please be specific and feel free to use the other side of this questionnaire.

The first draft survey questionnaire was pilot-tested with twenty-five students in a University of Minnesota graduate-level training class and then revised.

The final questionnaire was then sent to the 984 members of the Southern Minnesota Chapter of the American Society for Training and Development. Of the 984 forms that were mailed, 420 (43%) were returned. Some of the returned forms were unusable for various reasons (e. g., blank, problems not listed, returned too late). The 371 (38%) usable questionnaires provide the data for the analysis. A list of 1,098 training delivery problems was derived from the 371 usable questionnaires.

Each of the 1,098 training delivery problems was printed on a note card and sorted into categories. The method used for sorting the data is known as the KJ Method: Affinity Diagrams (Mizuno, 1988). This method, developed by Kawakita Jiro of the Kawakita Research Institute, is used to analyze data that are elusive, confusing, and disorganized. Groupings are made by mutual affinity of the data. The process has seven steps: (1) Choose a theme, (2) Collect the data, (3) Put data onto cards, (4) Sort the cards into categories, (5) Label the cards, (6) Draw the diagrams, and (7) Present the data.

Essentially the technique is a right-brain process (Mizuno, 1988). Those involved in the sorting were directed to use their intuition and creativity to interpret and group the data, as opposed to sorting by rigid analysis and reasoning rules. Nine people were involved in the sorting process—two University professors, six graduate students, and one professional trainer. The four sorting teams worked in three pairs and one triad. Each expert team, A through D, was given one fourth of the cards. In their A, B, C, and D teams the cards were read slowly, once or twice. Cards that contained similar ideas were grouped together on the basis of their affinity or commonality. After the cards had been grouped, the groups were labeled. The label consisted of words written on a blank card that conveyed the meaning of the cards in that group. The labeled groups of cards are then treated as a single card (Mizuno, 1988).

The twelve training delivery problems fell into three basic categories: (a) those pertaining to the trainer, (b) those describing how the trainer relates to the trainees, and (c) those pertaining to presentation techniques.

SELECTION OF EXPERTS

A variety of distinctions can be drawn between novices and experts. The major differences are intellect and experience. Because experts have a broader knowledge base than novices, they solve problems in a different manner. Experts have more focus, recognize cues that allow them to recall "chunks" of information, and are better able to integrate and interconnect knowledge. The knowledge that novices possess may be descriptive at a superficial level. In contrast, experts are able to troubleshoot and make interpretations about information. By using cues to access the stored knowledge they possess, experts are able to assess the situation at hand and devise an action plan that will work effectively (Thomas, 1988).

The goal of this aspect of the project was to establish a list of such experts in the field of training, specifically those who had distinguished themselves through their outstanding delivery skills. Once identified, these experts were presented with a list of the twelve most common training delivery problems faced by novice trainers as identified through the first survey. The experts were asked to respond to the problems with specific techniques they use to overcome similar problems during training presentations.

The potential experts were to be practitioners having a minimum of two years of experience and recognition by either colleagues or academicians as successful trainers. A nomination form was sent to the eight officers of the Southern Minnesota Chapter of the American Society for Training and Development to obtain names of experts. The twelve-member Training and Development Faculty at the University of Minnesota were also asked to nominate experts. Both groups were sent an identical form on which they were asked to nominate up to six people whom they considered to be expert "deliverers" of training. They were asked to provide the company name, address, and telephone number of the nominees. Three association officers responded and provided 15 names. The survey of the university faculty produced six responses and 28 names. The total of 43 names was reduced to 36, because of duplication.

SURVEY OF EXPERTS

Questionnaires were sent to the 36 people who were identified as experts in delivering training. They were asked to respond to the twelve training delivery problems that had been identified as problems for novice trainers in terms of how they handle these problems.

Twenty (56%) surveys were returned. Most of the experts responded in detail to all of the questions. These responses were typed and sorted into categories. Similar responses were grouped using the KJ Method. The three or four solutions that appeared most frequently for each difficult training situation became the basis for the final list of solutions from the experts.

ANALYSIS OF DATA

The primary data analysis revolved around the 1,089 training delivery problems of novice trainers collected through the survey questionnaire. A composite list of 12–15 general training delivery problems had been compiled when the four teams of experts had finished sorting their portion of the problems according to the KJ Method. Enroute, each team wrote its list on a chalkboard, explained the problems to the other teams and defended the rationales behind the problems. A matrix was developed to synthesize the topics into twelve training delivery problems.

The final list that emerged contained the summaries of the training-delivery-problem information collected by the first survey. The purpose of the first survey was to determine the major delivery problems of beginning trainers. The synthesis of this analysis resulted in the "Twelve Most Common Training Delivery Problems of Novice Trainers."

The purpose of the second survey was to have experts propose solutions for handling these problems. It resulted in the "Expert Solutions To The Twelve Most Common Delivery Problems of Beginning Trainers." Essentially, it is a topical outline that synthesizes the solutions from the 20 experts against the 12 training delivery problems that novices experience. The combined data from the two surveys is presented in Figure 1.

Expert Solutions to the Twelve Most Common Training Delivery Problems of Novice Trainers*

1. FEAR

A. *Be well prepared.* Expert trainers have a detailed lesson plan, understand the material, and practice their presentation.

B. *Use ice breakers.* Experts use ice breakers and begin with an activity that relaxes participants and gets them to talk and become involved.

C. *Acknowledge the fear.* Experts understand that fear is normal, confront what makes them afraid, and use positive self-talk or relaxation exercises prior to the presentation.

2. CREDIBILITY

A. *Don't apologize.* Experts are honest about the subject matter and explain that they are either experts or conduits.

B. *Have an attitude of an expert.* Experts are well prepared and well organized. They listen, observe, and apply what they know to what the participants know.

C. *Share personal background.* Experts talk about their areas of expertise and the variety of experiences they have had.

3. PERSONAL EXPERIENCES

A. *Report personal experiences.* Experts tell their personal experiences, sometimes asking themselves probing questions to uncover them.

B. *Report experiences of others.* Experts collect pertinent stories and incidents from other people and/or have participants share their experiences.

C. *Use analogies, movies, or famous people.* Experts use familiar incidents or situations in order to relate to the subject.

4. DIFFICULT LEARNERS

A. *Confront problem learner.* Experts use humor. They may also talk to the individual during a break to determine the problem or to ask the person to leave.

*Based on a survey of 371 novices and 20 experts.

(continued on next page)

B. *Circumvent dominating behavior.* Experts use nonverbal behavior, such as breaking eye contact or standing with their backs to the person and inviting the others to participate.

C. *Small groups for timid behavior.* Experts find that quiet people feel more comfortable talking in small groups or dyads. They structure exercises where a wide range of participation is encouraged.

5. PARTICIPATION

A. *Ask open-ended questions.* Experts incorporate questions into the lesson plans and provide positive feedback when people do participate.

B. *Plan small group activities.* Experts use dyads, case studies, and role plays to allow people to feel comfortable, to reduce fears, and to increase participation.

C. *Invite participation.* Experts structure activities that allow people to share at an early time in the presentation.

6. TIMING

A. *Plan well.* Experts plan for too much material, and some parts of the material are expendable. They prioritize activities so that parts may be deleted, if necessary.

B. *Practice, practice, practice.* Experts practice the material many times so they know where they should be at 15-minute intervals. They make sure there's a clock in the training room.

7. ADJUST INSTRUCTION

A. *Know group needs.* Experts determine the needs of the group at an early time in the training and structure activities and processes based on those needs.

B. *Request feedback.* Experts watch for signs of boredom and ask participants either during breaks or periodically during the session how they feel about the training.

C. *Redesign during breaks.* Experts find it helpful to have contingency plans and, if necessary, to redesign the program during a break. Redesigning during delivery is not advocated.

8. QUESTIONS

Answering Questions

A. *Anticipate questions.* Experts prepare by putting themselves in the participant's place and by writing out key questions learners might have.

B. *Paraphrase learners' questions.* Experts repeat and paraphrase participants' questions to ensure that everyone has heard the question and understands them.

C. *"I don't know" is okay.* Experts redirect questions they can't answer back to the group's expertise. They try to locate answers during breaks.

Asking Questions

A. *Ask concise questions.* Questions are a great tool for experts. They ask concise, simple questions and provide enough time for participants to answer.

9. FEEDBACK

A. *Solicit informal feedback.* Experts ask participants, either during class or at the break, if the training is meeting their needs and expectations. They also watch for nonverbal cues.

B. *Do summative evaluations.* Experts have participants fill out forms at the conclusion of training to determine if the objectives and needs of the group were met.

10. MEDIA, MATERIALS, FACILITIES

Media

A. *Know equipment.* Experts know how to fully operate every piece of equipment that they use.

B. *Have back-ups.* Experts carry a survival kit of extra bulbs, extension cords, markers, tape, etc. They also bring the information they are presenting in another medium.

C. *Enlist assistance.* Experts are honest with the group if there is a breakdown and ask if anyone can be of assistance.

Material

A. *Be prepared.* Experts have all materials ready and placed at each participant's workplace or stacked for distribution.

Facilities

A. *Visit facility beforehand.* Experts visit a new facility ahead of time, if possible, to see the layout of the room and to get an idea of where things are located and how to set up.

B. *Arrive early.* Experts arrive at least one hour in advance to ensure enough time for setting up and handling problems.

11. OPENINGS AND CLOSINGS

Openings

A. *Develop an "openings file."* Experts rely on the many sources for ice-breaker ideas. Through observation and experimentation, they develop ideas and keep a file of them.

B. *Memorize.* Experts develop a great opening and memorize it.

C. *Relax trainees.* Experts greet people as they enter, take time for introductions, and create a relaxed atmosphere.

Closings

A. *Summarize concisely.* Experts simply and concisely summarize the contents of the course, using objectives or the initial model.

B. *Thank participants.* Experts thank participants for their time and their contributions to the course.

12. DEPENDENCE ON NOTES

A. *Notes are necessary.* Experts recognize that no one completely outgrows the need for notes.

B. *Use cards.* Experts scale down their presentations to an outline or key words, which they write on note cards to use as prompts.

C. *Use visuals.* Experts make notes on frames of transparencies and on their copies of handouts.

D. *Practice.* Experts learn the script well so that they can deliver it from the keyword note cards.

SUMMARY

This study had three major focuses: (a) to determine what trainers considered to be the most frequent training delivery problems they faced as novices, (b) to determine how experts respond to these problems with solutions they have found to be effective, and to (3) present the findings in a useful manner for practitioners. The conclusions from each of the two distinct surveys within the study formed the research base for the major outcomes—the 12 most common training delivery problems novice trainers experience and expert solutions to these problems.

While advice and speculation abounds about best practices in training, little research is available about the practical problems novice trainers face. Other novice trainer problems should be researched following the general methodology of this study. They should pursue a specific and/or narrow frame of questions and use of open-ended questions which will likely result in the excellent response from both novices and experts. The resulting researcher's problem of dealing with large pools of qualitative data is lessened with new analysis methods such as the KJ Method.

Given the theory-to-practice gap that haunts the training profession, the general novice-expert methodology used in this study may be helpful in closing that gap.

REFERENCES

Chakiris, B. J., and Rolander, R. (1986). *Careers in Training and Development*. Alexandria, VA: American Society for Training and Development.

Gagne, R. M. (1987). "Introduction." In R. M. Gagne (Ed.), *Instructional Technology: Foundations* (pp. 1–9). Hillsdale, NJ: Erlbaum.

Jacobs, R. L. (1992). "Structured on-the-Job Training." In H. Stolovitch and E. Keeps, Eds. *Handbook of Human Performance Technology*. San Francisco; Jossey-Bass.

Knowles, M. (1984). *The Adult Learner: A Neglected Species*, 3rd ed. Houston: Gulf Publishing.

McLagan, P. A. (1983). *Models for Excellence*. Washington, DC: American Society for Training and Development (ASTD).

Mizuno, S. (Ed.). (1988). *Managing for Quality Improvement: The Seven New QC Tools.* Cambridge, MA: Productivity Press.

Pike, R. (1989). *Creative Training Techniques Handbook.* Minneapolis: Lakewood .

Sleezer, C. M. (1992). "Performance Analysis for Training." *Performance Improvement Quarterly.*

Smith, B. B. (1983a, April). Model and Rationale for Designing and Managing Instruction. *Performance and Instruction.* pp. 20–22.

Smith, B. B. (1983b, May). Designing and Managing Instruction. *Performance and Instruction.* pp. 27–30.

Swanson, R. (1982). "Industrial Training." In H.E. Mitzel (Ed.), *Encyclopedia of Educational Research,* New York: Macmillan, pp. 864–869.

Swanson, R. A. (1992). "Demonstrating Financial Benefits to Clients." In H. Stolovitch and E. Keeps, Eds. *Handbook of Human Performance Technology.* San Francisco: Jossey-Bass, pp. 602–618.

Thomas, R.(1988). "Conclusions and Insights Regarding Expertise in Specific Knowledge Domains and Implications for Research and Educational Practice. In R. G. Thomas (Ed.) *Thinking Underlying Expertise in Specific Knowledge Domains: Implications for Vocational Education* (p. 85–95). St. Paul, MN: University of Minnesota, Minnesota Research and Development Center.

Yelon, S. L. (1992). "Classroom Instruction." In H. Stolovitch and E. Keeps, Eds. *Handbook of Human Performance Technology,* San Francisco: Jossey-Bass, pp. 383–411.

Zemke, R., and Zemke, S. (1988). "Thirty Things We Know for Sure About Adult Learning." *Training,* 25(7), 57–61.

CHAPTER 16

A Model for Developing Employee Work Effectiveness in New Roles and Environments *

Employee careers consist of a series of boundary crossings, as people enter new work organizations, move from department to department, are promoted, become increasingly valued and trusted, or move from one company to another. What is critical from a performance improvement perspective is that each boundary crossing requires an employee to learn a new culture or subculture. Each boundary crossing thus creates a "new" employee with unique learning needs that must be met in order for that employee to move to high performance.

---

*This is a brief description of the Holton model for new employee development. A more complete description can be found in the following articles:

Holton, Elwood F. III, 1998 "Newcomer Entry Into Organizational Cultures: A Neglected Performance Issue." In P. Dean (Ed.) *Pursuing Performance Improvement*, Washington, DC: International Society for Performance Improvement.

Holton, Elwood F. III, 1998 In J. Gardner and G. Vander Veer, Editors *The Senior Year: A Beginning, not an End*. San Francisco: Jossey-Bass.

Holton, Elwood F. III, (1996) "New Employee Development A Review and Reconceptualization," *Human Resource Development Quarterly*, 7(3).

Improving performance of new employees crossing organizational boundaries requires a fundamental redefinition of what a new employee is, and a reconceptualization of new employee development. A new employee is defined here as *an employee who has crossed an organizational boundary that requires performance in a new organizational culture or subculture.* Conceptually, a fifteen-year employee who advances to a new level of management is little different from a new hire from outside the company. Both have crossed an organizational boundary into a new cultural context for performance.

New employee development (NED) is then defined as *all development processes organizations use to advance new employees to desired levels of performance.* It encompasses all developmental activities in which an organization engages, regardless of whether they are formal or informal, and whether they are planned or unplanned. The expected outputs of new employee development are: (a) an employee performing at a targeted level of performance and (b) that employee staying with the organizational unit.

Evidence suggests that properly designed programs for new employees can yield substantial returns (McGarrell, 1983). However, research also suggests that new employee turnover remains high (Leibowitz, Schlossberg, and Shore, 1991; Wanous, 1992) and is related to development processes during the first year. These factors, coupled with increasing layoffs and job changes in today's workplace, point to a need for increased focus on new employee development issues (Holton, 1996, 1995).

This chapter presents a brief description of a general model of new employee development that provides a conceptual framework for new employee develpment as a foundation for developing more comprehensive performance improvement interventions. It embraces the broad definition of new employee stated earlier, and is applicable to new employees in any type of organizational boundary crossing. Three key questions are addressed: (1) what *learning content* should be included in a comprehensive NED program; (2) what *learning strategies* are most effective to facilitate that learning; and (3) what should be *the role of educational institutions.*

A NEW EMPLOYEE LEARNING TAXONOMY

A basic assumption of this taxonomy and socialization in general is that organizations want employees who "fit" (Schein, 1992) and are quick to look for confirmation that a new employee will "fit in." Generally, greater fit leads to higher initial performance and increased opportunities for success because organizations prefer newcomers that fit the predominant culture, values, and norms (Chatman, 1991).

The taxonomy proposed here (Figure 16-1) is a systematic attempt to extend the macro structures and develop a comprehensive guide to the learning tasks of new employee development. It most closely follows Fisher (1986) in conceptualizing four content domains for new employee learning: *individual, people, organization,* and *work tasks.* The first three domains comprise what has traditionally been called socialization; the last domain consists of learning, traditionally called job training. Each domain is further subdivided into three learning tasks for a total of twelve learning tasks, which are defined and described below.

Figure 16-1. New employee development learning tasks.

Individual Domain

All new employees, regardless of experience level, bring with them accumulated learning, attitudes, and values that have been shaped by previous cultures and work experiences. Considering the highly interactive nature of the learning process and the emphasis on congruence between the individual and the organization, it is likely that this prior learning would impact upon entry success. The *individual* domain then encompasses important dimensions of pre-entry learning that are believed to impact socialization outcomes (Table 16-1). Despite occurring largely before work actually begins, they are important because organizations can influence them during the hiring process, entities preparing employees for work can influence them, and newcomers need to quickly evaluate if their prior learning in these areas might impede entry.

Table 16-1
Individual domain

1. **Attitude**	Identify personal values and attitudinal predispositions toward a professional career, job and organization; identify success-related attitudes in the organization; match personal attitudes to those desired by the organization.
2. **Expectations**	Develop appropriate expectations about the job, organization and themselves in the job; resolve frustrations due to expectation differences.
3. **Breaking in**	Become aware of the dynamics and importance of organizational entry; master the special skills and strategies required.

Attitudes. Outcomes might be affected by attitudes in two ways: by the newcomer's attitudes toward the organization, new role, new subunit or job; and by the newcomer's attitude toward the socialization and training process itself. Furthermore, attitudes are likely to affect social learning processes directly, perhaps through impressions created by visible behaviors resulting from newcomer's attitudes (discussed below). Attitudes also are a schema through which new learning and experiences are filtered and sorted (Ertmer and Newby, 1993). It is likely that new employee outcomes can be enhanced by identifying success-related attitudes in an organization and helping newcomers make attitude changes as appropriate.

Expectations. A common cause of problems is a mismatch between a newcomer's expectations and reality encountered in the organization, resulting in frustration and negative attitudes. A large body of research on realistic job previews (RJP) has consistently shown a strong correlation between met expectations and job attitudes (Premack and Wanous, 1985; Wanous and Colella, 1989). This research has rather conclusively showed that developing appropriate expectations is one of the foundation tasks for successful new employee development.

Breaking-in Skills. Newcomers must become aware of the importance of the breaking-in period (usually the first 9–12 months) and the special skills needed to successfully cross an organizational boundary and become accepted and respected as a member of a new team (Baum, 1990). Many new employees don't begin the process because their internal schema and scripts prevent them from seeing the need to do so. Newcomers must also understand how small groups react when new members are brought in, and must also understand the different stages associated with gaining membership and the demands placed on the newcomer (Moreland and Levine, 1982; Wanous, Reichers, and Malik, 1984).

People Domain

Learning to perform in new cultural contexts is fundamentally a social learning process (Katz, 1985). It is through interaction between the individual and the work environment that much of the information about the organization is obtained, acceptance is gained, and roles are learned (Ashford and Taylor, 1990; Louis, 1990). In fact, only a small amount of newcomer learning occurs in formal training or from written materials. Research clearly indicates that establishing relationships with people in the organization is a crucial phase of newcomer entry (Table 16-2).

Impression Management. The initial impressions newcomers make are instrumental in beginning what Schein (1969) calls the "success

Table 16-2
People domain

4. Impression Management	Become aware of the role impressions play in establishing the organization's initial evaluation; understand the impression-management process; learn what impressions will be viewed most favorably in the organization; and master the skills and strategies necessary to manage impressions.
5. Relationships	Understand the role relationships play in organizational success and the kinds of relationships that should be built; acquire skills necessary to build and maintain effective professional relationships and networks; and learn effective teamwork strategies.
6. Supervisor	Become aware of the importance of supervisor/subordinate relationships and their respective roles; identify supervisory style and requirements; build skills needed to be an effective subordinate and to manage the supervisor relationship for mutual gain; learn effective strategies for building a strong working relationship with a supervisor.

spiral." Coworkers use newcomers' initial behaviors to make attributions about their performance potential and fit, which in turn affects coworkers' expectations for future performance and their behavior toward the newcomer (Martinko and Gardner, 1987). If initial attributions are positive, newcomers are more likely to be given high visibility or important tasks. If they succeed at them, initial attributions are confirmed and increasingly important tasks are likely to follow. Existing employees are then more likely to establish relationships and help the newcomer succeed. The result is an upward spiral of success leading to more success and greater career opportunity.

Relationships. Positive working relationships with coworkers play many critical roles in successful adaptation and socialization. They help speed acceptance by groups (Baum, 1990); ameliorate the effects of unmet expectations (Major *et al.*, in press); and assist in learning culture (Louis, 1990). Most importantly, they provide the primary mechanism for social learning. Other important outcomes of building good relationships may include developing more successful organizational learning strategies and learning how to get things done through teamwork. The challenge for newcomers begins with all the usual problems of building interpersonal relationships. These problems may be particularly acute when the newcomer is perceived as different because he or she is disabled, of a different racial or ethnic background, or perhaps a different gender than is predominant in the organization.

Supervisor. Newcomers who build good relationships with supervisors can obtain more critical information, which has been found to result in greater satisfaction and commitment as well as less stress and intent to leave (Ostroff and Kozlowski, 1992). Weiss (1977) found that subordinates tended to adopt the work values of their immediate superiors and that supervisors were important role models for subordinates. Research in leader-member exchange (LMX) has linked the relationship between employees and supervisors to a variety of important job outcomes. Newcomers and supervisors have to move quickly and proactively to establish a positive relationship.

Organizational Domain

When newcomers establish strong, effective relationships with people in the organization, they can learn the complexities of the organization itself (Feldman, 1989). Table 16-3 represents the *organizational* domain. Recent studies have found a significant relationship between learning about non-task related dimensions of the organization and entry outcomes (Chao *et al.*, 1994; Copeland and Wiswell, 1994). This reinforces the notion that developing high performance new employees is a combination of task knowledge and knowledge about the organization, acquired through social learning processes.

Organizational Culture. Organizational culture is widely believed to be related to organizational success (Deal and Kennedy, 1982) and individual success when an individual's values match those of the predominant culture. Much critical information about an organization is contained in culture, which is not written down and is often not even formalized. A quick understanding of the norms, values, and work styles of the organization speeds adaptation and access to good assignments through the success spiral. Without a complete understanding of the organization's culture, a newcomer cannot understand

Table 16-3
Organization domain

7. **Organizational Culture**	Understand elements of organizational culture and how they affect performance; become aware of the importance of fitting into the organization's culture; acquire skills to learn key elements of culture that are not explicitly taught.
8. **Organizational Savvy**	Become aware of the informal organization and success factors in the organization; understand appropriate means for getting results through the informal organization; acquire skills to learn the informal organization and effectively use it to achieve desired results.
9. **Organizational Roles**	Locate oneself in the larger perspective of the organization's goals; understand the role and identity of a newcomer in the organization; learn what appropriate expectations and activities are for that role; accept role limits and realities, and reconcile role conflicts and ambiguity.

the informal systems, the roles people play, the "taboos" of the organization, why tasks are performed the way they are, or make sense of many of the other daily experiences of organizational life. Without culture understanding, a new employee may be ineffective even though technically competent at his or her task.

Organizational Savvy. Newcomers have to understand the many informal systems and methods that comprise the way things "really get done around here." Becoming an effective performer means developing the savvy to know how to work through an organization and its people to get results; learning informal procedures; understanding the politics of the organization; and learning to negotiate informal power structures and systems. Often called "learning the ropes," this is the process of using one's knowledge about culture to make sense of what happens in daily organizational activities (Louis, 1980) and to map relevant players in the power structure (Louis, 1982). Without an understanding of how to work within the organizational system, task competence can quickly be obscured by repeated violations of unwritten norms or political gaffes.

Organizational roles. Graen (1976) defines role making as having four components: acquiring knowledge about constraints and demands, receiving and sending persuasive communications about behavior in this role, accepting a particular pattern of behavior, and modifying this behavior over time. Systematic efforts to help newcomers understand their roles clearly, obtain information to reduce ambiguity, understand the organization's expectations, and learn ways to reduce role conflict in initial assignments should contribute to improved outcomes (Feldman, 1989).

Work Task Domain

The fourth domain is most familiar. There is no question that understanding the tasks of the job and having the correct knowledge, skills, and abilities is essential to new employee success (Table 16-4). Work savvy, described next, is less familiar but equally important.

Work Savvy. Incumbent employees quickly forget how important it is to develop a schema or system for understanding task assignments and for prioritizing, processing, and accomplishing the job. Information must be sorted to determine what is important, limited resources must be allocated, and skills learned in training applied to real work problems. While some may lump this under the more global construct of "learning the ropes," this taxonomy separates it because it deals with the *newcomer-work* interaction rather than the *newcomer-orga-*

Table 16-4
Work Task Domain

10. **Work savvy**	Understand how to apply knowledge and skills to the job, and acquire generic professional skills (for example, communication, time management) necessary to function in the job.
11. **Task knowledge**	Understand the basic tasks required on the job and ways to perform them successfully.
12. **Knowledge, skills and abilities**	Identify knowledge, skills, and abilities needed to perform tasks successfully, both now and in the future; develop formal and informal learning skills necessary to acquire the knowledge, skills, and abilities.

nization interaction. It is particularly significant for early careerists or career changers whose internal schema for getting work done may come from a significantly different environment.

Task Knowledge. Certainly mastery of the job tasks is necessary for success, but it is equally certain that it is insufficient by itself. It should be readily apparent from the previous discussion that complete task competence is impossible beyond a basic level without successful learning of all tasks. If task training is done in isolation, performance is problematic.

Knowledge, Skills, and Abilities. With a complete understanding of the tasks on the job and the newcomer's role, a new employee can see the entirety of the knowledge, skills, and abilities required to perform them. New employees may be prone to be overconfident about their knowledge prior to successful socialization. For many, one outcome of new employee development is "learning what they don't know." Some newcomers report a humbling experience when they realize they aren't as prepared as they thought they were (Holton, 1998).

NEW EMPLOYEE DEVELOPMENT SYSTEM

These twelve learning tasks are accomplished through four different learning venues: foundation learning programs (for example, schools), external job training (for example, post-secondary vocational education), employer based job training programs, and learning in the workplace. *Foundational learning* is defined as programs or institutions that provide foundation learning not directed at any specific job. *External job training* consists of programs or institutions that provide job training, but not for a specific employer. *Employer-based job training* programs are those activities offered by a specific employer for its employees and designed primarily to provide knowledge and skills necessary to complete job tasks. *Workplace* learning activities include all learning activities that occur in the workplace such as on-the-job training, social learning, and informal learning.

The twelve learning tasks and four interventions should be an integrated system to achieve new employee performance goals (see Figure 16-2). Potential employees engage in four types of interventions to complete twelve learning tasks, which, if completed successfully, should result in the new employee achieving targeted levels of perfor-

Figure 16-2. New employee development system.

mance and staying with the organization. The new employee development process is not conceptualized here as linear, but rather as a cyclical process, where newcomers may cycle through learning tasks and learning events repeatedly.

CHALLENGES FOR EDUCATIONAL INSTITUTIONS

Using this model as a framework, education should assume responsibility for four key aspects of development for their graduates beyond the task-related knowledge currently provided. These key aspects are develop the individual domain, teach basic skills in the people and organizational domain, build awareness of the entire scope of learning tasks, and develop organizational learning skills.

Develop the individual domain. There is little reason that education and job preparation institutions cannot take full responsibility for developing in their graduates sound work attitudes, realistic expectations, and an understanding of how to enter an organization. Clearly there will be certain organization-specific components that may need adjustment later, but the difficulties during the transition are more basic ones. For example, attitudes such as flexibility, a commitment to quality, working for the good of the team, a willingness to pay one's dues, and desire to learn, are often missing.

Teach basic skills in the people and organizational domains. These two domains are much more organization-specific, so education and training has a more limited role. However, basic skills in each domain should be taught so graduates can focus on the organization-specific components. For example, in the people domain, students can be taught principles of impression management and how to determine effective strategies in their new organization. They should certainly be taught how to build work relationships and networks. And, they can be taught basic skills of effective subordinates, how to determine effective subordinate skills in their new organization, and how to manage a boss.

In the organization domain, every graduate should understand what organizational culture is, how if affects their career, and how to decipher it. And, every graduate must understand something about organizational politics, how informal systems work in organizations, and how to use those systems to get results. Finally, they can be taught what the role of a newcomer is and how to make sure they meet role expectations.

Build awareness of the entire scope of learning tasks after employment. When teaching learning tasks in which students cannot be given all the answers, such as organizational culture or organizational savvy, colleges can at least teach students the questions to ask for advanced learning. Newcomers need to realize what they don't know about being successful in an organization, know what questions to ask, and be motivated to engage in the new learning.

Develop organizational learning skills. Frequently overlooked is the fact that most of the learning that occurs during organizational entry requires fundamentally different learning skills than are cultivated in college. First, many things can only be learned by interacting with other people, so *social learning* skills are most important. Second, the learning process is usually an *experiential* one, because the learning occurs while engaged in work projects. Third, *self-directed learning* becomes the norm since newcomers have to take the initiative to learn much beyond the task knowledge to do their jobs. Fourth, the learning is *unstructured* in that it has no definite beginning and ending point. And, it is *indeterminate* in that it may be difficult to tell when one has the "right" answers or when learning is completed, especially when dealing with complex or unusual problems. In short, it is a messy, but continuous, process.

REFERENCES

Ashford, S. J. and Taylor, M. S. "Adaptation to Work Transition: An Integrative Approach," in G. R. Ferris and K. M. Rowland (Eds.), *Research in Personnel and Human Resources Management:* vol 8, Greenwich, CN: JAI Press, 1990.

Baum, H. S. *Organizational Membership.* Albany, NY: State University of New York Press, 1990.

Chao, G. T., O'Leary-Kelly, A., Wolf, S., Klein, H. J., and Gardner, P.D. "Organization Socialization: Its Content and Consequences." *Journal of Applied Psychology, 79,* 1994, 450–463.

Chatman, J. A. "Matching People and Organizations: Selection and Socialization in Public Accounting Firms." *Administrative Science Quarterly, 36,* 1991, 459–484.

Copeland, S. T. and Wiswell, A. K. "New Employee Adaptation to the Workplace: A Learning Perspective." *Academy of Human Resource Development 1994 Proceedings,* 35–40.

Deal, T. E. and Kennedy, A. A. *Corporate Cultures: The Rites and Rituals of Corporate Life.* Reading, MA: Addison-Wesley, 1982.

Ertmer, P. A. and Newby, T. J. Behaviorism, Cognitivism, Constructivism: Comparing Critical Features from a Design Perspective. *Performance Improvement Quarterly, 6,* 1993, 50–72.

Feldman, D. C. Socialization, Resocialization, and Training: Reframing the Research Agenda, in I. L. Goldstein (Ed.), *Training and Development in Organizations.* San Francisco: Jossey-Bass, 1989, 376–416.

Fisher, C. D. Organizational Socialization: An Integrative Review, in G. R. Ferris and K. M. Rowland (Eds.), *Research in Personnel and Human Resources Management.* Greenwich, CN: JAI Press, vol. 4, 1986, 101–145.

Graen, G. B. Role-Making Processes within Complex Organizations, in M.D. Dunnette (Ed.), *Handbook of Industrial and Organizational Psychology.* Chicago: Rand McNally, 1976, 1201–1245.

Holton, E. F. *The New Professional*. Princeton, NJ: Peterson's Guides, 1991, 1998.

Holton, E. F. "College Graduates' Experiences and Attitudes during Organizational Entry." *Human Resource Development Quarterly*, 1995.

Holton, E. F. III. "New Employee Development: A Review and Reconceptualization." *Human Resource Development Quarterly*, vol. 7, 1996.

Holton, E. F. III. "Newcomer Entry into Organizational Cultures: A Neglected Performance Issue," in P. Dean (Ed.) *Pursuing Performance Improvement*, Washington, DC: International Society for Performance Improvement, 1998.

Holton, E. F. III, in J. Gardner and G. Van der Veer (Eds.) *The Senior Year: A Beginning, Not an End*. San Francisco: Jossey-Bass, 1998.

Katz, R. Organizational Stress and Early Socialization Experiences, in T. A. Beehr and R. S. Bhagat (Eds.), *Human Stress and Cognition in Organizations*. New York: John Wiley & Sons, 1985, 117–139.

Leibowitz, Z. B., Schlossberg, N. K., and Shore, J. E. "Stopping the Revolving Door." *Training and Development Journal*, Feb. 1991, 43–50.

Louis, M. R. Surprise and Sense Making: What Newcomers Experience in Entering Unfamiliar Organizational Settings. *Administrative Science Quarterly*, 25, 1980, 226–251.

Louis, M. R. "Managing Career Transition: A Missing Link in Career Development." *Organizational Dynamics, Spring*, 1982, 68–77.

Louis, M. R. "Acculturation in the Workplace: Newcomers as Lay Ethnographers," in B. Schneider (Ed.), *Organizational Climate and Culture*, San Francisco: Jossey-Bass, 1990, 85–129.

Major, D. A. Kozlowski, S. W. J., Chao, G. T., and Gardner, P. D. A Longitudinal Investigation of Newcomer Expectations, Early Socialization Outcomes, and the Moderating Effects. *Journal of Applied Psychology*, in press.

Martinko, M. J. and Gardner, W. L. "The Leader/Member Attribution Process," *Academy of Management Review*, 12, 1987, 235–249.

McGarrell, E. J., Jr. "An Orientation System that Builds Productivity." *Personnel*, 60, vol. 6, 1983, 32–41.

Moreland, R. L. and Levine, J. M. Socialization in Small Groups: Temporal Changes in Individual-Group Relations, in L. Berkowitz (Ed.). *Advances in Experimental Psychology*, New York: Academic Press, vol. 15, 1982, 137–192.

Ostroff, C. and Kozlowski, S. W. J. Organizational Socialization as a Learning Process: The Role of Information Acquisition. *Personnel Psychology*, vol. 45, 1992, 849–874.

Premack, P. L. and Wanous, J. P. A Meta-Analysis of Realistic Job Preview Experiments. *Journal of Applied Psychology*, vol. 70, 1985, 706–719.

Schein, Edgar H. Organizational Socialization and the Profession of Management. *Industrial Management Review*, Winter 1968, 1–16.

Schein, Edgar H. *Organizational Culture and Leadership, 2nd ed.* San Francisco: Jossey-Bass, 1992.

Wanous, J. P. *Organizational Entry: Recruitment, Selection, Orientation and Socialization of Newcomers, 2nd ed.* Reading, MA: Addison-Wesley, 1992.

Wanous, J. P. and Colella, A. "Organizational Entry Research; Current Status and Future Directions," in G. R. Ferris and K. M. Rowland (Eds.), *Research in Personnel and Human Resources Management*. Greenwich, CN: JAI Press, 1989, 59–120.

Wanous, J. P., Reichers, A. E., and Malik, S. D. Organizational Socialization and Group Development: Toward an Integrative Perspective. *Academy of Management Review*, vol. 9, 1984, 670–683.

Weiss, H. M. Subordinate Imitation of Supervisor Behavior: The Role of Modeling in Organizational Socialization. *Organizational Behavior and Human Performance*, vol. 19, 1977, 89–105.

CHAPTER 17

Linking Learning and Performance in HRD *

Performance is a multidimensional and poorly defined construct. For example, people say that individuals perform, departments perform, organizations perform, groups perform, animals perform, and machines perform. So, what do we mean by "performance" and performance improvement? More importantly, what should human resource development and performance improvement (HRD/PI) professionals mean when they talk about these constructs. The purpose of this chapter is to propose an integrated taxonomy of performance domains for HRD/PI that demonstrates the relationship between adult learning and performance in HRD.

AN INTEGRATED TAXONOMY OF PERFORMANCE DOMAINS FOR HRD/PI

Figure 17-1 presents an integrated taxonomy of performance system domains. From an HRD/PI perspective, four domains of performance are proposed: mission, process, critical performance subsystem, and individual.

Mission Domain

The purpose of HRD is to improve performance of the system in which it is embedded and which provides the resources to support it

---

*Holton, E. F. Adapted from *Advances in Developing Human Resources: The Theory and Practice of Performance Improvement*, R. Swanson (series editor) and R. Torraco (volume editor). Washington, D.C.: IS PI Press, 1999.

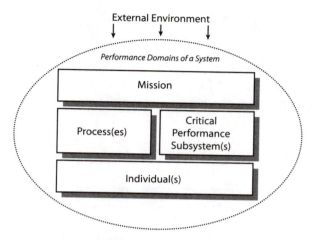

Figure 17-1. Performance system domains.

(Swanson and Arnold, 1997). All interventions and activities under-taken by HRD must ultimately enhance that system's performance. HRD/PI, like all professions, operates within an ethical frame that is larger than the system within which it is operating. Aside from gener-al ethical responsibilities, HRD's primary accountability is to the sys-tem within which it resides.

The system's mission, and the goals derived from it, specify the expected outcomes of that system. Every purposefully organized sys-tem operates with a mission, either explicitly or implicitly, and the role of the mission is to reflect the system's relationship with its *exter-nal* environment. For a business organization, the mission may reflect its relationship with its industry, society, and competitors. For a non-profit organization, its mission may reflect its relationship with the community and society. It is not necessary to specify in the taxonomy what the possible levels of impact outside the system are, because the mission will reflect that system's understanding of its responsibilities to the external environment.

It is important to note that the term *organization* is not used in lieu of the concept of the performance system. A mission may be defined for any system organized to accomplish some purpose. If the system has a purpose, then performance theory is applicable. In many instances, the mission level will be the same as the organization level, particularly in for-profit firms. However, for a trade association, the mission level may be an entire industry, or an entire profession for a professional association. For example, the Academy of Human Resource Development's mission is the advancement of the HRD profession through research. In other situations, the mission may include community outcomes or societal outcomes.

The particular system's definition of its performance relationship with the external environment is fully captured by the mission and goals of the organization. For business organizations, the metrics are likely to be dominated by traditional business outcome measures, including economic outcomes (more on metrics later). However, the mission level for a government organization may be dominated by metrics assessing societal benefits. The notion that the performance perspective only embraces economic returns as *the* system's mission (Bierema, 1997; Dirkx, 1997) is fundamentally flawed. Performance depends on the mission of the organization.

Process Domain

One of the positive outcomes of the quality and reengineering movements is the realization that managing and designing effective processes is an essential part of performance improvement. A number of performance models have clearly demonstrated the need for including the process level of performance (Juran, 1992; Hammer and Champy, 1993; Hronec, 1993; Kaplan and Norton, 1996; Rummler and Brache, 1995; Swanson, 1994). Readers desiring a deeper understanding of the importance of process to performance improvement should consult these sources.

Briefly, process is included in this model as a separate performance level because these levels often cut across multiple subsystems. A process can be defined as *a series of steps designed to produce a product or service* (Rummler and Brache, 1995, p. 45). Davenport (1993) further defines a process as *a specific ordering of work activities across time and place, with a beginning, and end, and clearly identified inputs and outputs: a structure for action (p. 5).* Rummler and Brache (1995) make these arguments for the importance of focusing on processes in performance systems:

☐ Process is the least understood and least managed level of performance.

☐ A process can be seen as a value chain, with each step adding value to the preceding steps.

☐ An organization is only as effective as its processes.

☐ Enhancing organizational and individual effectiveness will only improve performance as much as the processes allow.

☐ Strong people cannot compensate for a weak process (Rummler and Brache, 1995, p. 45).

Critical performance subsystem

This taxonomy includes a level for critical performance subsystem (CPS). A CPS is defined as a *internal* subsystem for which performance goals have been set that are derived from, and contribute to, the mission of the organization. Thus, the core difference between this domain and the mission domain is that the mission domain defines performance outcomes relative to the external environment, while the critical performance subsystem domain defines internal performance subsystems that do not always directly connect with the external environment.

One of the weaknesses of prominent integrated performance models (Rummler and Brache, 1995; Swanson, 1994) is that they do not appear to embrace productive subsystems within an organization. While it can be argued that integrated models can be applied to subsystems and then aggregated to the larger system, I argue that definitional confusion around this issue is one cause of the proliferation of performance models. That is, by appearing to ignore teams, divisions, departments, functions, etc., the integrated performance models appear to neglect organizational realities. In addition, they appear to neglect the interpersonal domain of teams and groups that is so central to many organizations today. In the case of structural subunits, it is easier to see how the organization level can be redefined to mean department or division rather than team performance, which has enough unique components to make the model fit less clearly.

The particular critical performance subsystem identified for a given system will vary considerably. For a team-based organization, the CPS may be teams; for a traditional organization, it may be department; for a community, it may be a neighborhood. Conversely, in a traditional organization, team performance may not be relevant if the performance system is built on department structure. Not all subsystems will be critical to accomplishment of the performance systems' mission, so it is not important that all subsystem performance be measured.

The crital performance subsystem is an important point of analysis. For example, the following questions may have to be answered:

- [ ] What are the subsystems that are critical to accomplishing the system's mission?
- [ ] What are the explicit critical performance subsystems? The implicit critical performance subsystems?
- [ ] Are the explicit and implicit CPSs congruent?
- [ ] Are the CPSs appropriate for the mission of the system?
- [ ] Are appropriate metrics in place?

Individual Domain

Human resource development and performance improvement has traditionally been at the individual level, reflecting the psychological roots of many in the field. The essence of HRD/PI practice has been the improvement of individual human performance, particularly through expanded expertise, which is believed to result in enhanced organizational performance. While there are differing opinions as to how best to accomplish this, there is broad agreement about the need to focus on individual performance improvement, particularly through learning and the guided development of expertise required to function in the system.

METRICS FOR PERFORMANCE DOMAINS

The purpose of this chapter is not to provide a complete taxonomy of performance metrics as has been well done by others (Hronec, 1993; Kaplan and Norton, 1996). However, as noted earlier, some performance models confuse domains of performance with measures. Thus, it is important to clarify the distinction between performance domains and measures.

Kaplan and Norton (1996) suggest two categories of performance measures: *outcomes* and *drivers.* Unfortunately, they do not offer concise definitions of either. For our purposes, *outcomes* are measures of effectiveness or efficiency relative to core outputs of the system, subsystem, process, or individual. The most typical outcomes are financial indicators (profit, ROI, etc.) and productivity measures (units of goals or services produced) and are often generic across companies. According to Kaplan and Norton, these measures tend to be lag indicators in that they reflect what has occurred or has been accomplished in relation to core outcomes.

Drivers measure elements of performance that are expected to sustain or increase system, subsystem, process, or individual ability and capacity to be more effective or efficient in the future. Thus, they are leading indicators of future outcomes and tend to be unique for particular business units. Together with outcome measures, they describe the hypothesized cause-and-effect relationships in the organization's strategy (Kaplan and Norton, 1996). Thus, drivers should predict future outcomes. For example, for a particular company, return on investment might be the appropriate outcome measure, which might be driven by customer loyalty and on-time delivery, which in turn might be driven by employee learning and therefore internal processes are optimized. In a government revenue department, an outcome measure might be percent of tax returns processed correctly within two weeks of receipt. A performance driver for that outcome might be number of quality improvement initiatives successfully implemented.

Kaplan and Norton (1996) go on to say that:

> Outcome measures without performance drivers do not communicate how the outcomes are to be achieved. . . . Conversely, performance drivers without outcomes measures may enable the business unit to achieve short-term operational improvements, but will fail to reveal whether the operational improvements have been translated into expanded business with existing and new customers, and, eventually, to enhanced financial performance. A good balanced scorecard should have an appropriate mix of outcomes (lagging indicators) and performance drivers (leading indicators) of the business unit's strategy (p. 31–32).

Thus, from this perspective, performance improvement experts who focus solely on actual outcomes, such as profit or units of work produced, are flawed in that they are likely to create short-term improvement, but neglect aspects of the organization that will drive future performance outcomes. However, experts who focus solely on performance drivers such as learning or growth are equally flawed in that they fail to consider the actual outcomes. Only when jointly considered will long-term performance change occur.

Typical Domains of Metrics for Measuring Performance

Domains of Performance	Performance Outcomes	Performance Drivers
Mission	Economic returns External metrics Market share Profitability Mortality rate Poverty level	Societal benefits Innovation Knowledge capital Management/leadership Strategy Social responsibility Organizational learning
Process	Customer Quality Cost Time Product features Market share (in product category)	Customer (needs satisfaction) Quality Innovation
Critial Performance Subsystem (team, department, etc.)	Team effectiveness Structural subunits performance Productivity (resource efficiency) Internal metrics Work outputs	Innovation Team/group climate Management/leadership Subsystem learning
Individual	Turnover Absenteeism Productivity Output	Knowledge and expertise Renewal and growth Individual learning Human relations Ethical performance

Figure 17-2. Performance domains for organizational systems.

Figure 17-2 presents some typical performance measures for each of the four performance domains, classified as performance outcome measures or performance driver measures.

It is important to note that some metrics could fall into either the outcome or driver category, depending on the nature of the performance system. Consider the case of societal benefits. For a profit-oriented corporation, this might well be defined as a performance driver because it affects the long-run opportunity for performance. For a government agency, this might be classified as a core performance outcome. Thus, the classification of a metric is dependent on the context of the specific performance system.

HRD/PI as Whole System Improvement

This chapter has presented an integrated taxonomy of performance domains and metrics. The taxonomy meets the criteria of being resourceful, situationally adaptable, able to embrace multiple organizational types and includes multiple measures of performance. More importantly, the taxonomy points to the unique role that human resource development and performance improvement plays in organizational science: performance improvement of the whole system.

Working across the system does not dismiss or reduce the importance of the individual. To the contrary, the performance perspective further enhances the individual in organizations by dismissing the common practice of trying to change the person before the system is changed, and by working to create healthy and effective organizational systems.

Disagreements in HRD/PI often revolve around the relative importance of different components of this taxonomy. One debate concerns levels. For example, strategic management experts consider strategy as the key performance driver while quality experts advocate process improvement as the path to organizational performance. Organization development experts often advocate group/team performance improvement. Educators advocate individual-level performance improvement, usually through learning.

Another debate centers around the importance of performance drivers versus outcomes. For example, adult educators view individual learning and development (a performance driver), as being the driver of all other levels and are critical of emphasis placed on outcomes

(Dirkx, 1997). Learning organization advocates place heavy emphasis on learning and development, and embrace multiple levels, but do not define expected performance outcomes. Because many HRD practitioners have developmental values and roots, the notion of performance outcomes and accountability for developmental processes is viewed with disdain and avoided.

The key point is this: all these perspectives are both correct—and wrong at the same time. They are correct in that strategy, team interventions, quality, and learning organization *may* improve performance. They are wrong in that they will improve performance *if and only if* that aspect of the system is the one in need of intervention. Said differently, if the whole system is not considered, a good solution may be applied to the wrong problem. The classic case in our discipline is the pervasive practice of trying to fix system problems with individual training. Each disciplinary view of performance has evolved to view its piece of the performance system as paramount for performance change, both as the entry point for interventions and as the core driver. Some disciplines arrive at this point with an awareness of the whole system, but with intellectual arrogance about their unique piece. Others arrive at this conclusion by ignoring the rest of the system.

These views (and others) violate the fundamental principles of systems theory that tell us that no one element of the system can be viewed separately from other elements. Intervening in only one element of the system without creating congruence in other parts of the system will not lead to systemic change. Furthermore, intervening in the whole system to improve outcomes or drivers alone is also flawed. Human performance technologists (Stolovich and Keeps, 1992) and needs assessors (Moore and Dutton, 1978) have understood the need to view the individual level in the larger organizational system in order to make individual-level performance improvement efforts more effective. HRD/PI goes a step further to analyze and improve performance of the whole system through a balanced approach of outcomes and drivers in the four performance domains.

REFERENCES

Bierema, L. L. (1997). "Development of the Individual Leads to a More Productive Workplace." In R. Rowden (Ed.), *Workplace Learning: Debating Five Critical Questions of Theory and Practice*, pp. 21–28. San Francisco: Jossey-Bass.

Bryk, A. S. and Raudenbush, S. W. (1992). *Hierarchical Linear Models.* Newbury Park, CA: Sage.

Campbell, J. P. (1990). "Modeling the Performance Prediction Problem in Industrial and Organizational Psychology." In M. Dunnette (Ed.) *Handbook of Industrial and Organizational Psychology,* pp. 678–732. Palo Alto, CA: Consulting Psychologists Press.

Cummings, T. G. and Worley, C. G. (1993). *Organization Development and Change, 5th Edition.* Minneapolis/St. Paul: West Publishing.

Dansereau, F. and Markham, S. E. (1982) "Levels of Aanalysis in Personnel and Human Resources Management." In M. D. Dunnette and E. A. Fleishman (Eds.), *Human Performance and Productivity: Human Capability Assessment,* 35–84, Hillsdale, NJ: Lawrence Erlbaum.

Davenport, T. H. (1993). *Process Innovation: Reengineering Work through Information Technology.* Boston: Harvard Business School Press.

Dirkx, J. M. (1997). "Human Resource Dvelopment as Adult Education: Fostering the Educative Workplace". In R. Rowden (Ed.), *Workplace Learning: Debating Five Critical Questions of Theory and Practice,* pp. 41–47. San Francisco: Jossey-Bass.

Edvinsson, L. and Malone, M. S. (1997) *Intellectual Capital: Realizing Your Company's True Value By Finding Its Hidden Brainpower,* New York: Harper Collins, 1997.

Gilbert, T. F. (1996). *Human Competence: Engineering Worthy Performance, Tribute edition.* Washington, DC: International Society for Performance Improvement.

Hammer, M. and Champy, J. (1993) *Reengineering the Corporation.* New York: Harper Collins.

Hitt, M. A., Ireland, R. D. and Hoskisson, R. E. (1997). Strategic Management: Competitiveness and Globalization. St. Paul, MN: West.

Hodson, R., and Sullivan, T. A. (1995). *The Social Organization of Work, 2nd Edition.* Belmont, CA: Wadsworth Publishing.

Holton, E. F. III (1997). "HRD Change Leadership in Organizations." In E. F. Holton III (Ed.) *In Action: Leading Organizational Change.* Alexandria, VA: American Society for Training and Development.

Holton, E. F. III, Bates, R. A., Leimbach, M. (1997). "Development and Validation of a Generalized Learning Transfer Climate Questionnaire: A Preliminary Report." In R. Torraco (Ed.), *Proceedings of the 1997 Academy of Human Resource Development Annual Conference.* Baton Rouge, LA: Academy of Human Resource Development.

Holton, E. F. III (1996). The Flawed Four-Level Evaluation Model. *Human Resource Development Quarterly, 7.*

Hronec, S.M. (1993) *Vital Signs: Using Quality Time and Cost Performance Measurements to Chart Your Company's Future,* New York: American Management Association.

Juran, J. M. (1992). *Juran on Quality by Design.* New York: The Free Press.

Kammeyer, K. C. W., Ritzer, G., and Yetman, N. R. (1997). *Sociology: Experiencing changing societies, 7th Edition.* Boston: Allyn and Bacon.

Kaplan, R. S. and Norton, D. P. (1996). *The Balanced Scorecard.* Boston: Harvard Business School Press.

Kaufmann, R., Rojas, A. M., and Mayer, H. (1993). *Needs Assessment: A User's Guide.* Englewood Cliffs, NJ: Educational Technologies.

Lewin, D. and Mitchell, D. J. B. (1995). *Human Resource Management: An Economic Approach, 2nd Edition.* Cincinnati, OH: South-Western.

McClernon, T. R. and Swanson, R. A. (1997). "Redefining HRD's Role in Organizations: A Case Study on Becoming a World-Class Business Partner." In E. F. Holton III (Ed.) *In action: Leading Organizational Change.* Alexandria, VA: American Society for Training and Development.

McGehee, W. and Thayer, P. W. (1961). *Training in Business and Industry.* New York: Wiley.

Moore, M. L. and Dutton, P. (1978) Training Needs Analysis: Review and Critique. *Academy of Management Review, 532–545.*

Morrow, C. C., Jarrett, M. Q., and Rupinski, M. T. (1997). *An Investigation of the Effect and Economic Utility of Corporate-Wide Training.* Personnel Psychology, 50, 91–119.

Osborne, D. and Gaebler, T. (1993). *Reinventing Government.* Reading, MA: Addison-Wesley.

Ostroff, C. and Ford, J. K. (1989). "Assessing Training Needs: Critical Levels of Analysis." In I. Goldstein and Assoc., *Training and Development in Organizations,* San Francisco: Jossey-Bass.

Porter, M. E. (1980) *Competitive Strategy: Techniques for Analyzing Industries and Competitors,* New York: The Free Press.

Reichheld, F. F. (1996). *The Loyalty Effect.* Boston, MA: Harvard Business School Press.

Rummler, G. and Brache, A. (1995). *Improving Performance: How to Manage the White Space on the Organization Chart.* San Francisco: Jossey-Bass.

Schneir, C. E. (1995). "Linking Business Strategy, Unit Goals, and Performance Management Systems." In H. Fisher and C. Fay (Eds.), *The Performance Imperative: Strategies for Enhancing Workforce Effectiveness,* 239–255. San Francisco: Jossey-Bass.

Silber, K. H. (1992) "Intervening at Different Levels in Organizations." In H. Stolovich (Ed.) *Handbook of Human Performance Technology,* 50–65. San Francisco: Jossey-Bass.

Sink, D. S., Tuttle, T. C. and DeVries, S. J. (1984). Productivity Measurement and Evaluation: What Is Available?, *National Productivity Review.*

Sleezer, C. M. (1991). Developing and Validating the Performance Analysis for Training Model. *Human Resource Development Quarterly,* 2(4), 355–372.

Stolovich, H. D. and Keeps, E. J. (1992). "What is Human Performance Technology?" In H. Stolovich and E. Keeps (Eds.), *Handbook of Human Performance Technology,* 3–13. San Francisco: Jossey-Bass.

Swanson, D. L. (1995). Addressing a Theoretical Problem by Reorienting the Corporate Social Responsibility Performance Model. *Academy of Management Review,* 20, 43–64.

Swanson, R. A. and Arnold, D. E. (1997). "The Purpose of HRD Is to Improve Performance." In R. Rowden (Ed.), *Workplace Learning: Debating Five Critical Questions of Theory and Practice,* pp. 13–19. San Francisco: Jossey-Bass.

Swanson, R. A. (1994). *Analysis for Improving Performance: Tools for Diagnosing Organizations and Documenting Workplace Expertise.* San Francisco: Berrett-Koehler.

Swanson, R. A. and Gradous, D. B. (1988). *Forecasting Financial Benefits of Human Resource Development.* San Francisco: Jossey-Bass.

Watkins, K. E. and Marsick, V. J. (1993). *Sculpting the Learning Organization.* San Francisco: Jossey-Bass.

Bibliography

Adams-Webber, J. R. *Personal Construct Theory: Concepts and Application.* New York: Wiley-Interscience, 1979.

Adult Education Association. *Adult Learning.* Washington, D.C.: Adult Education Association, 1965.

Adult Education Association. *Processes of Adult Education.* Washington, D.C.: Adult Education Association, 1965.

Adult Education Association. *Psychology of Adults.* Washington, D.C.: Adult Education Association, 1963.

Alford, H. J. *Continuing Education in Action: Residential Centers for Lifelong Learning.* New York: Wiley, 1968.

Allender, J. S. "New Conceptions of the Role of the Teacher." *The Psychology of Open Teaching and Learning.* Edited by M. L. Silberman, et al. Boston: Little, Brown, 1972.

Alliger, G. M. and Janak, E. A. "Kirkpatrick's Levels of Training Criteria: Thirty Years Later." *Personnel Psychology, 42,* 1989, 331–340.

Alliger, G. M., Tannenbaum, S. I., Bennett, W., Traver, H., Shotland, A. "A Meta-Analysis of the Relations Among Training Criteria." Personnel Psychology, 50, 1997, 341–358.

Allport, Gordon. *Becoming.* New Haven: Yale University Press, 1955.

Allport, Gordon. *Pattern and Growth in Personality.* New York: Holt, Rinehart, and Winston, 1961.

Allport, Gordon. *Personality and Social Encounter.* Boston: Beacon, 1960.

Anderson, C. R. Locus of Control, Coping Behaviors, and Performance in a Stress Setting: A Longitudinal Study. *Journal of Applied Psychology, 62,* 1977, 446–451.

Anderson, Scarvia, et al. *Encyclopedia of Educational Evaluation.* San Francisco: Jossey-Bass, 1974.

Apps, J. W. *Higher Education in a Learning Society.* San Francisco: Jossey-Bass, 1988.

Apps, J. W. *Improving Practice in Continuing Education.* San Francisco: Jossey-Bass, 1985.

Archer, R. P. "Relationships Between Locus of Control, Trait Anxiety, and State Anxiety:" An Interactionist Perspective. *Journal of Personality, 47,* 1979, 305–316.

Arends, R. I. and Arends, J. H. *System Change Strategies in Educational Settings.* New York: Human Sciences Press, 1977.

Argyris, Chris. *Increasing Leadership Effectiveness.* New York: Wiley Interscience, 1976.

Argyris, Chris. *Integrating the Individual and the Organization.* New York: John Wiley and Sons, 1964.

Argyris, Chris. *Interpersonal Competence and Organizational Effectiveness.* Homewood, Ill.: Dorsey, 1962.

Argyris, Chris. *Intervention Theory and Method: A Behavioral Science View.* Reading, Mass.: Addison-Wesley, 1970.

Argyris, C. *Reasoning, Learning and Action.* San Francisco: Jossey-Bass, 1982.

Argyris, C. and Schon, D. *Organizational Learning: A Theory of Action Perspective,* 1978.

ARL Inquiry, "Developing an Infrastructure for Individual and Organizational Change." In Proceedings of the 1996 Academy of Human Resource Development Annual Meeting. Baton Rouge, LA.

Arlin, P. K. "Adolescent and Adult Thought: A Structural Interpretation" In M.L. Commons, F.A. Richards and C. Armos (eds.) *Wisdom: its Nature, Origins, and Development.* Cambridge: Cambridge University Press, 1990.

Ashton-Warner, Sylvia. *Teacher.* New York: Simon and Shuster, 1963.

ASTD-USDL. *America and the New Economy.* Washington: DC American Society for Training and Development and the U.S. Department of Labor, 1990.

Ausubel, D. P. *Educational Psychology: A Cognitive View.* NY: Holt, Reinhart and Winston, 1968.

Ausubel, D. P. *The Psychology of Meaningful Verbal Learning: An Introduction to School Learning.* New York: Grime and Stratton, 1963.

Axford, R. W. *Adult Education: The Open Door.* Scranton, PA.: International Textbook Co., 1969.

Baldridge, J. V., et al. Policy Making and Effective Leadership: A National Study of Academic Management. San Francisco: Jossey Bass, 1978.

Baldridge, J. V. and Deal, T. S. *Managing Change in Educational Organizations.* Berkeley: McCutchan Publishing Corp., 1975.

Baldwin, T. T., Magjuka, R. J., Loher, B. T. "The Perils of Participation: Effects of Choice of Training on Trainee Motivation and Learning." Personnel Psychology, 44, 1991, 51–65.

Baltes, P. On the Incomplete Architecture of Human Ontogeny: Selection, Optimization, and Compensation as Foundations of Developmental Theory. *American Psychologist,* 52, 4, 1997, 366–380.

Baltes, P. B., Dittman-Kohli, F., and Dixon, R. "New Perspectives on the Development of Intelligence in Adulthood: Toward a Dual Process Conception and a Model of Selective Optimization with Compensation." In P. B. Baltes and O. G. Brim, Jr. (eds.), *Life-span Development and Behavior,* vol. 6, pp. 33–76. New York: Academic Press, 1984.

Baltes, Paul D. *Life-Span Development and Behavior.* vol. I. New York: Academic Press, 1978.

Bandura, Albert. *Principles of Behavior Modification.* New York: Holt, Rinehart and Winston, 1969.

Bandura, Albert. *Social Learning Theory.* Englewood Cliffs, NJ: Prentice-Hall, 1977.

Bandura, Albert and Walters, R. H. *Social Learning and Personality Development.* New York: Holt, Rinehart and Winston, 1963.

Bany, M. A. and Johnson, L. V. *Classroom Group Behavior.* New York: Macmillan, 1964.

Bard, R., Bell, C. R., Stephen, L., and Webster, L. *The Trainer's Professional Development Handbook.* San Francisco: Jossey-Bass, 1987.

Barker, Roger G. *Ecological Psychology: Concepts and Methods for Studying the Environment of Human Behavior.* Stanford, Cal.: Stanford University Press, 1968.

Barker, Roger G. (ed.). *The Stream of Behavior.* New York: Appleton-Century-Crofts, 1963.

Barker, Roger G. *Habitats, Environments, and Human Behavior.* San Francisco: Jossey-Bass, 1978.

Barker, Roger G. and Gump, P. V. *Big School, Small School: High School Size and Student Behavior*. Stanford, Cal.: Stanford University Press, 1964.

Barney, J. B. and Ouchi, W. G. *Organizational Economics*. San Francisco: Jossey-Bass, 1986.

Barrett, James H. *Gerontological Psychology*. Springfield, Ill.: Charles C. Thomas, 1972.

Barron, E. *Creativity and Psychological Health*. Princeton: Van Nostrand, 1963.

Bates, R., Holton, E., and Seyler D. "Factors Affecting Transfer of Training in an Industrial Setting." Richard Torraco (ed). *Academy of Human Resource Development 1997 Conference Proceedings: Baton Rouge, LA Academy of Human Resource Development*, 1996.

Baughart, E. W. *Educational Systems Analysis*. New York: Macmillan, 1969.

Becker, G. S. *Human Capital: A Theoretical and Empirical Analysis with Special Reference to Education, 3rd edition*. Chicago: University of Chicago Press, 1993.

Becker, J. (ed.). *Architecture for Adult Education*. Washington, D.C.: Adult Education Association, 1956.

Beckhard, R. *Organization Development: Strategies and Models*. Reading, Mass.: Addison-Wesley, 1969.

Beder, H. (ed.). "Marketing Continuing Education." *New Directions for Continuing Education* CE#31. San Francisco: Jossey-Bass, 1986.

Bee, H. L. *The Journey of Adulthood, 3rd edition*. Upper Saddle River, NJ: Prentice-Hall, 1996.

Bell, C. R. and Nadler, L. *The Client-Consultant Handbook*. Houston: Gulf Publishing Co., 1979.

Benack, S. and Basseches, M. A. "Dialectical Thinking and Relativistic Epistemology: Their Relation in Adult Development." In M. L. Commons, J. D. Sinnott, F. A. Richards and C. Armon (eds). *Adult Development*. N.Y.: Praeger, 1989.

Bengston, V. L. *The Social Psychology of Aging*. Indianapolis: Bobbs-Merrill, 1973.

Bennis, W. G. *Changing Organizations*. New York: McGraw-Hill, 1966.

Bennis, W. G. *Organization Development: Its Nature, Origins, and Prospects*. Reading, Mass.: Addison-Wesley, 1969.

Bennis, W. G., Benne, K. D., and Chin, R. *The Planning of Change.* New York: Holt, Rinehart and Winston, 1968.

Bennis, W. G. and Slater, P. E. *The Temporary Society.* New York: Harper and Row, 1968.

Bereiter, C. "Moral Alternatives to Education." *Interchange,* HI, 1972, 25–41.

Bergevin, P. *A Philosophy for Adult Education.* New York: Seabury, 1967.

Bergevin, P. and McKinley, J. *Participation Training for Adult Education.* St. Louis: Bethany Press, 1965.

Bette, N. R. "Individualizing Education by Learning Contracts." *New Directions for Higher Education,* no. 10, San Francisco: Jossey Bass, 1975.

Birren, James E. *The Psychology of Aging.* Englewood Cliffs, N.J.: Prentice-Hall, 1964.

Bischoff, L. L. *Adult Psychology.* New York: Harper and Row, 1969.

Blake, R. R. and Mouton, J. S. *Consultation.* Reading, Mass.: Addison-Wesley, 1976.

Blake, R. R. and Mouton, J. S. *The Managerial Grid.* Houston: Gulf Publishing Co., 1964.

Blank, W. E. *Handbook for Developing Competency-Based Training Programs.* Englewood Cliffs, N.J.: Prentice-Hall, 1982.

Block, J. H. *Mastery Learning: Theory and Practice.* New York: Holt, Rinehart and Winston, 1971.

Bloom, B. S., et al. "Taxonomy of Educational Objectives." *Handbook I: Cognitive Domain.* New York: McKay, 1956.

Bloom, B. S., Engelhart, M. D., Furst, E.J., Hill, W.H., and Krathwohl, D. R. Taxonomy of Educational Objectives." *The Classification of Educational Goals: Handbook 1: Cognitive Domain.* New York: Longmans, Green, 1956.

Bloom, B. S., Hastings, J. T., and Madaus, G, F. *Handbook on Formative and Summative Learning.* New York: McGraw Hill, 1969.

Bonham, L. A. (1988). "Learning Style Instruments: Let the Buyer Beware." *Lifelong Learning,* 1988, 11(6) 12–16.

Boone, Edgar, and Associates. *Serving Personal and Community Needs Through Adult Education.* San Francisco: Jossey-Bass, 1980.

Borich, Gary D. (ed.). *Evaluating Educational Programs and Products.* Englewood Cliffs, N.J.: Educational Technology Publications, 1974.

Botkin, J. W., Elmandjra, M., and Salitza, M. *No Limits to Learning. A Report to the Club of Rome.* New York: Pergamon Press, 1979.

Botwinick, J. *Cognitive Processes in Maturity and Old Age.* New York: Springer, 1967.

Boucouvalas, M. "Advances in the Neurosciences: Implications and Relevance for Lifelong Learning Professionals." Lifelong Learning Research Conference Proceedings. College Park, MD: University of Maryland, February, 1988, 16–20.

Boud, David. *Developing Student Autonomy in Learning.* New York: Nichols Publishing Co., 1981.

Bower, E. M. and Hollister, W. G. (eds.). *Behavioral Science Frontiers in Education.* New York: Wiley, 1967.

Boyd, R. D., Apps, J. W. and Associates. *Redefining the Discipline of Adult Education.* San Francisco: Jossey-Bass, 1980.

Bradford, L. P., Benne, K. D. and Gibb, R. *T-Group Theory and Laboratory Method.* New York: Wiley, 1964.

Brady, H. G. *Research Needs in Adult Education.* Tampa: University of South Florida, 1982.

Breivik, P.S. (ed.). "Managing Programs for Learning Outside the Classroom." *New Directions for Higher Education HE#56.* San Francisco: Jossey-Bass, 1986.

Brinkerhoff, R. O. *Achieving Results from Training.* San Francisco: Jossey-Bass, 1987.

Britton, Joseph H. and Britton, Jean O. *Personality Changes in Aging.* New York: Springer Publishing Co., 1972.

Brockett, R. G. (ed.). "Continuing Education in the Year 2000." *New Directions for Continuing Education CE#36.* San Francisco: Jossey-Bass, 1987.

Bromley, D. B. *The Psychology of Human Aging.* Baltimore: Penguin, 1966.

Bronfenbrenner, U. *The Ecology of Human Development.* Cambridge, MA: Harvard University Press, 1979.

Brookfield, S. D. *Developing Critical Thinkers.* San Francisco: Jossey-Bass, 1987.

Brookfield, S. D. *Understanding and Facilitating Adult Learning.* San Francisco: Jossey-Bass, 1986.

Brookfield, S. D. "Conceptual, Methodological and Practical Ambiguities in Self-Directed Learning" *Self-Directed Learning: Application and Theory. H.B. Long (ed).* Athens: GA University of Georgia Press, 1988.

Brown, G. *Human Teaching for Human Learning*. New York: Viking, 1971.

Bruner, J. S. "The Act of Discovery." *Harvard Educational Review*, XXXI (1961), 21–32.

Bruner, J. S. *The Process of Education*. Cambridge, Mass.: Harvard University Press, 1961.

Bruner, J. S. *Toward a Theory of Instruction*. Cambridge, Mass.: Harvard University Press, 1966.

Bruner, E. S. *An Overview of Adult Education Research*. Washington, D.C.: Adult Education Association, 1959.

Bryson, L. *Adult Education*. New York: American Book Co., 1936.

Bryson, L. *The Next America*. New York: Harper, 1952.

Buber, Martin. *I and Thou*, 2nd ed. New York: Scribner's, 1958.

Buford, T. O. *Philosophy for Adults*. Washington, D.C.: University Press of America, 1980.

Bullmer, K. *The Art of Empathy*. New York: Human Sciences Press, 1975.

Burnside, I. M. *Working with the Elderly: Group Process and Techniques*. Belmont, Calif.: Duxbury Press, 1978.

Burton, W. H. "Basic Principles in a Good Teaching-Learning Situation." *Readings in Human Learning*. L. D. and Alice Crow (eds.). New York: McKay, 1963, pp. 7–19.

Bushnell, D. and Rappaport, D. (eds.). *Planned Change in Education: A Systems Approach*. New York: Harcourt, Brace, Jovanovich, 1972.

Caffarella, R. and O'Donnell, J. "Research in Self-Directed Learning: Past, Present and Future Trends." *Self-Directed Learning: Application and Theory*. H.B. Long (ed). Athens: GA University of Georgia Press, 1988.

Campbell, J. P. "Training Design for Performance Improvement." *Productivity in Organizations*. San Francisco: Jossey-Bass, 1988, 177–215.

Candy, P. C. *Self-Direction for Lifelong Learning*. San Francisco: Jossey-Bass, 1991.

Carkhuff, Robert R. *Helping and Human Relations: A Primer for Lay and Professional Helpers*. 2 vols. New York: Holt, Rinehart and Winston, 1969.

Carnevale, A. P. *Human Capital: A High Yield Corporate Investment*. Washington, D.C.: American Society for Training and Development, 1983.

Carnevale, A. P., Gainer, L. J. and Meltzer A. S. *Workplace Basics: The Essential Skills Employers Want*. Alexandria, VA: American Society for Training and Development, 1990.

Cascio, W. F. *Costing Human Resources: The Financial Impact of Behavior in Organizations.* 2nd Ed. Boston, MA: Kent, 1987.

Casner-Loote, J. and Associates. *Successful Training Strategies.* San Francisco: Jossey-Bass, 1988.

Cattell, R.B. "Theory of Fluid and Crystallized Intelligence: A Critical Approach.: *Journal of Educational Psychology,* 1963, 54 (1), 1963, 1–22.

Cervero, R. M. *Effective Continuing Education for Professionals.* San Francisco: Jossey-Bass, 1988.

Cervero, R. M. and Wilson, A. L. *Planning Responsibly for Adult Education: A Guide to Negotiating Power and Interests.* San Francisco: Jossey-Bass, 1994.

Chakiris, B. J., and Rolander, R. *Careers in Training and Development.* Alexandria, VA: American Society for Training and Development, 1986.

Chalofsky, N. and Lincoln, C. I. *Up the HRD Ladder: A Guide for Professional Growth.* Reading, Mass.: Addison-Wesley, 1983.

Charters, A. N. and Associates. *Comparing Adult Education Worldwide.* San Francisco: Jossey-Bass, 1981.

Cheren, M. E. *Learning Management: Emerging Directions for Learning to Learn in the Workplace.* Columbus, OH: ERIC, National Center for Research in Vocational Education, 1987.

Chickering, A. *An Introduction to Experiential Learning.* New Rochelle, N.Y.: Change Magazine Press, 1977.

Chickering, A. and Associates. *The Modern American College.* San Francisco: Jossey-Bass, 1981.

Chickering, A. W. *Education and Identity.* San Francisco: Jossey-Bass, 1976.

Clark, C. S., Dobbins, G. H., Ladd, R. T. Exploratory Field Study of Training Motivation. *Group and Organization Management,* 18, 1993, 292–307.

Claxton, C. S. and Ralston, Y. *Learning Styles: Their Impact on Teaching and Administration.* Washington, D.C.: American Association of Higher Education.

Cleland, D. (ed.) *Systems, Organization Analysis, Management.* New York: McGraw-Hill, 1969.

Coan, A. W., et al. *The Optimal Personality.* New York: Columbia University Press, 1974.

Collins, Z. W. *Museums, Adults and the Humanities.* Washington, D.C.: American Association of Museums, 1981.

Combs, Arthur W., et al. *Helping Relationships: Basic Concepts for the Helping Professions.* Boston: Allyn and Bacon, 1971.

Combs, Arthur W. and Snygg, Donald. *Individual Behavior.* Rev. ed. NewYork: Harper, 1959.

The Commission on the Skills of the American Workforce. *America's choice: High Skills or Low Wages.* Rochester, NY: National Center on Education and the Economy, 1990.

Cookson, P.S. (ed.). *Recruiting and Retaining Adult Students. New Directions for Continuing Education CE#41.* San Francisco: Jossey-Bass, 1989.

Cornwell, J. M. and Manfredo, P. A. "Kolb's Learning Style Theory Revisited." *Educational and Psycholigical Measurement,* 54, 1994, 317–327.

Costa, P. T. and McCrae, R. R. *Revised NEO Personality Inventory (NEO-PI-R)* and *NEO Five-Factor Inventory (NEO0FFI) Professional Manual.* Odessa FL: Psycholofical Assessment Resources, 1992.

Craig, R. L. and Bittel, L. R. *Training and Development Handbook.* New York: McGraw-Hill, 1967, 1976.

Cranton, P. *Planning Instruction for Adult Learners.* Toronto: Wall and Thompson, 1989.

Cronbach, L. J. *Educational Psychology, 2nd ed.* New York: Harcourt, Brace and World, 1963.

Cronbach, L. J. *Toward Reform of Program Evaluation.* San Francisco: Jossey-Bass, 1980.

Cropley, A. J. *Towards a System of Lifelong Education.* Hamburg, Germany: UNESCO Institute for Education, 1980.

Cross, K. P. *Accent on Learning.* San Francisco: Jossey-Bass, 1976.

Cross, K. P. *Adults as Learners.* San Francisco: Jossey-Bass, 1981.

Crow, L. D. and Crow, A. (eds.). *Readings in Human Learning.* New York: McKay, 1963.

Crutchfield, R. S. "Nurturing Cognitive Skills of Productive Thinking." Silberman, M. L., Allender, J. S. and Yanoff, J. M. (eds.). *The Psychology of Open Teaching and Learning.* Boston: Little, Brown, 1972, pp. 189–196.

Crystal, J. C. and Bolles, R. N. *Where Do I Go From Here With My Life.* New York: Seabury Press, 1974.

Csikszentmihalyi, M. *Beyond Boredom and Anxiety.* San Francisco: Jossey-Bass, 1975.

Cummings, Thomas G. and Worley, Christopher. *Organization Development and Change, 6th ed.* Cincinatti, OH: Southwestern Publishing Co., 1997.

Daloz, L. A. *Effective Teaching and Mentoring*. San Francisco: Jossey-Bass, 1986.

Darkenwald, G. and Larson, G. (eds.). *Reaching Hard-to-Reach Adults*. San Francisco: Jossey-Bass, 1980.

Darkenwald, G. G. and Merriam, S. B. *Adult Education: Foundations of Practice*. New York: Harper and Row, 1982.

Dave, R. H. *Lifelong Education and School Curriculum. Monograph No. 1*. Hamburg, Germany: UNESCO Institute for Education, 1973.

Dave, R. H. (ed.). *Reflections on Lifelong Education and the School. Monograph No. 3*. Hamburg, Germany: UNESCO Institute for Education, 1975.

Davenport, J. and Davenport, J. A. (1985). A Chronology and Analysis of the Androgogy Debate. *Adult Education Quarterly*, 1985, 35, 152–159.

David, Thomas G. and Wright, B. D. (eds). *Learning Environments*. Chicago: University of Chicago Press, 1975.

Davis, G. A. and Scott, J. A. *Training Creative Thinking*. New York: Holt, Rinehart, and Winston, 1971.

Davis, R. C. *Planning Human Resource Development*. Chicago: Rand-McNally, 1966.

Dentwhistle, N. *Styles of Learning and Teaching*. New York: John Wiley and Sons, 1982.

Dewey, John. *Experience and Education*. New York: Macmillan, 1938.

Dewey, J. *How We Think*. Boston, MA: Heath and Company, 1933.

Dirkx, J. M. "Human Resource Development as Adult Education: Fostering the Educative Workplace." *Workplace Learning: Debating five critical questions of theory and practice*, R. W. Rowden (ed.) San Francisco: Jossey-Bass, 1996, pp. 41–47.

Di Vesta, F. J. "Cognitive Development." *Encyclopedia of Educational Research*, (5th ed.). New York: Macmillan and Free Press, 1982.

Dixon, G. *What Works at Work: Lessons from the Masters*. Minneapolis: Lakewood, 1988.

Dixon, N. Relationship Between Training Responses on Participant Reaction Forms and Post Test Scores. *Human Resource Development Quarterly*, 1(2), 1991, 129–137.

Dobbs, R. C. *Adult Education in America: An Anthological Approach*. Cassville, Mo.: Litho Printers, 1970.

Donahue, Wilma and Tibbitts, Clark. *The New Frontiers of Aging.* Ann Arbor: University of Michigan Press, 1957.

Dressel, Paul L. *Handbook of Academic Evaluation.* San Francisco: Jossey-Bass, 1976.

Drews, E. M. "Self-Actualization. A New Focus for Education." *Learning and Mental Health in School.* W. B. Waetjen and R. R. Leeper (eds.). Washington, D.C. Association for Supervision and Curriculum Development, N.E.A., 1966, pp. 99–124.

Drucker, P. E. *The Effective Executive.* New York: Harper and Row, 1967.

Dubin, R. and Raveggia, T. C. *The Teaching-Learning Paradox: A Comparative Analysis of College Teaching Methods.* Eugene, Ore.: Center for the Advanced Study of Educational Administration, University of Oregon, 1968.

Duffy, T. M. and Jonassen, D. H. *Constructivism and the Technology of Instruction: A Conversation.* Hillsdale, NJ: Lawrence Erlbaum and Assoc., 1992.

Dykes, A. R. *Faculty Participation in Academic Decision Making.* Washington, D.C.: American Council on Education, 1968.

Eble, Kenneth E. *The Craft of Teaching.* San Francisco: Jossey-Bass, 1976.

Edvinsson, L. and Malone, M. S. *Intellectural Capital.* New York: Harper-Collins, 1997.

Eiben, R. and Milliren, A. (eds.). *Educational Change: A Humanistic Approach.* La Jolla, CA: University Associates, 1976.

Elias, J. L. and Merriam, S. *Philosophical Foundations of Adult Education.* Huntington, N.Y.: Krieger, 1980.

Erikson, E. H. *Childhood and Society.* New York: W. W. Norton, 1950.

Erikson, E. H. *Identity and the Life Cycle.* New York: International Universities Press, 1959.

Erikson, E. H. *Insight and Responsibility.* New York: Norton, 1964.

Estes, W. J. "The Statistical Approach to Learning Theory." *Psychology: A Study of a Science.* S. Koch (ed.). vol. II. New York: McGraw-Hill, 1959.

Etzioni, Amatai. *Complex Organizations.* New York: The Free Press, 1961.

Etzioni, Amatai. *A Sociological Reader on Complex Organizations.* New York: Holt, Rinehart and Winston, 1969.

Eurich, N. P. *Corporate Classrooms: The Learning Business.* Lawrenceville, N.J.: Princeton University Press, 1985.

Even, M. J. "Adapting Cognitive Style Theory in Practice," *Lifelong Learning; The Adult Years,* 5(5), 1982, 14–16, 27.

Ewell, P. T. (eds.). *Assessing Educational Outcomes.* San Francisco: Jossey-Bass, 1985.

Farmer, D. W. *Enhancing Student Learning.* Wilkes-Barre, PA: King's College, 1988.

Faure, Edgar, et al. *Learning to Be: The World of Education Today and Tomorrow.* Paris: UNESCO, 1972.

Felker, D. W. *Building Positive Self-Concepts.* Minneapolis: Burgess Publishing Co., 1974.

Feur, D. and Gerber, B. "Uh-oh . . . Second Thoughts about Adult Learning Theory," *Training,* vol. 25, No 12, 1988, 125–149.

Fingeret, A. and Jurmo, P. (eds.). *Involving Learners in Literacy Education.* San Francisco: Jossey-Bass, 1989.

Flanders, N. A. and Simon, A. *Teacher Influence, Pupil Attitudes, and Achievement.* U.S. Department of Health, Education and Welfare, Office of Education. Cooperative Research Monograph No. 12 (OE-25040). Washington, D.C., Government Printing Office, 1965.

Flannery, D. D. "Global and Analytical Ways of Processing Information." Daniele D. Flannery (ed.) *New Directions in Adult and Continuing Education: Applying Cognitive Learning Theory to Adult Learning.* San Francisco: Jossey-Bass, 1993.

Flavell, J. H. "Cognitive Changes in Adulthood." Goulet, L. R. and Baltes, P. B. (eds.). *Life-Span Development Psychology.* New York: Academic Press, 1970, pp. 247–253.

Freedman, R. D. and Stumpf, S. A. Learning Style Theory: Less Than Meets the Eye. *Academy of Management Review,* 5, 1980, 445–447.

Friere, Paulo. *Pedagogy of the Oppressed.* New York: Herder and Herder, 1970.

Froland, C., et al. *Helping Networks and Human Services.* Beverly Hills, CA: Sage Publications, 1981.

Gage, N. L. *Teacher Effectiveness and Teacher Education.* Palo Alto, Cal.: Pacific Books, 1972.

Gage, N. L., Berliner, D.C. (1988). *Educational Psychology,* 4th ed. Houston, TX: Houghton Mifflin.

Gagne, R. M. *The Conditions of Learning.* New York: Holt, Rinehart and Winston, 1965.

Gagne, R. M. "Domains of Learning." *Interchange,* 1972, pp. 1–8.

Gagne, R. M. "Policy Implications and Future Research. A Response." *Do Teachers Make a Difference?* A Report on Research on Pupil Achievement. U.S. Department of Health, Education and Welfare, Office of Education. Washington, D.C., Government Printing Office, 1970.

Gagne, R. M. "Introduction." *Instructional Technology: Foundations.* Hillsdale, NJ: Erlbaum, 1987, 1–9.

Gagne, R., Briggs, L., and Wager, W. *Principals of Instructional Design,* 3rd ed. New York: Holt, Reinhart and Winston, 1988.

Gale, R. *The Psychology of Being Yourself.* Englewood Cliffs, N.J.: Prentice-Hall, 1974.

Gambrill, Eileen D. *Behavior Modification: Handbook of Assessment, Intervention, and Evaluation.* San Francisco: Jossey-Bass, 1977.

Gardner, John. *Self-Renewal: The Individual and the Innovative Society.* New York: Harper and Row, 1963.

Gardner, H. *Frames of Mind.* New York: Basic Books, 1983.

Garrision, D. R. Self-Directed Learning: Toward a Comprehensive Model. *Adult Education Quarterly,* 48, 1997, 18–33.

Gessner, R. (ed.). *The Democratic Man: Selected Writings of Eduard C. Lindeman.* Boston: Beacon, 1956.

Getzels, J. W. and Jackson, P. W. *Creativity and Intelligence.* New York: Wiley, 1962.

Getzels, J. W., J. M. Lipham, and Campbell, R. F. *Educational Administration as a Social Process.* New York: Harper and Row, 1968.

Gibbons, M. A Working Model of the Learning How to Learn Process. in R. Smith and Associates, *Learning How to Learn Across the Life Span.* San Francisco: Jossey-Bass.

Gill, S. J. Shifting Gears for High Performance, *Training and Development,* 49 (5), May 1995, 25–31.

Gilley, J. and Eggland, S. A. *Principles of Human Resource Development.* Reading, MA: Addison-Wesley, 1989.

Glaser, R. (ed.). *Training Research and Education.* Pittsburgh: University of Pittsburgh Press, 1962.

Goble, F. *The Third Force: The Psychology of Abraham Maslow.* New York: Pocket Books, 1971.

Godbey, G. C. *Applied Andragogy: A Practical Manual for the Continuing Education of Adults.* College Station, PA: Continuing Education Division, Pennsylvania State University, 1978.

Goldstein, K. M. and Blackman, S. *Cognitive Style: Five Approaches and Relevant Research.* New York: Wiley-Interscience, 1978.

Goodlad, J. I. *The Dynamics of Educational Change.* New York: McGraw-Hill, 1975.

Gordon, Ira J. *Criteria for Theories of Instruction.* Washington, D.C.: Association for Supervision and Curriculum Development, N.E.A., 1968.

Gould, Samuel, chairman, Commission on Nontraditional Study. *Diversity By Design.* San Francisco: Jossey-Bass, 1973.

Goulet, L. R. and Baltes, P. B. *Life-Span Developmental Psychology.* New York: Academic Press, 1970.

Gowan, J. C., et al. *Creativity: Its Educational Implications.* New York: John Wiley and Sons, 1967.

Gowan, J. C. and Associates. *Preparing Educators of Adults.* San Francisco: Jossey-Bass, 1981.

Grabowski, S. M. (ed.). *Adult Learning and Instruction.* Syracuse: ERIC Clearinghouse on Adult Education, 1970.

Grabowski, S. M. and Mason, Dean W. *Learning for Aging.* Washington, D.C.: Adult Education Association of the U.S.A., 1974.

Grace, Andre P. *Striking a Critical Pose: Andragogy–Missing Links, Missing Values,* 1996.

Granick, S. and Patterson, R. D. *Human Aging II.* U.S. Department of Health, Education, and Welfare, National Institute of Mental Health. (HSM 71-9037). Washington, D.C., Government Printing Office, 1971.

Grant, G., et al. *On Competence.* San Francisco: Jossey-Bass, 1979.

Grattan, C. H. *In Quest of Knowledge: A Historical Perspective of Adult Education.* Chicago: Follett, 1955.

Greiner, L. E. (ed.). *Organizational Change and Development.* Homewood, Ill.: Irwin, 1971.

Griffiths, D. E. (ed.). *Behavioral Science and Educational Administration.* Sixty-Third Yearbook of the National Society for the Study of Education. Chicago: NSSE, 1964.

Gross, Ronald. *The Lifelong Learner: A Guide to Self-Development.* New York: Simon and Schuster, 1977.

Grippin, P. and Peters, S. *Learning Theory and Learning Outcomes.* New York: University Press of America, 1984.

Gross, Ronald. *Invitation to Lifelong Learning.* Chicago: Follett Publishing Co., 1982.

Grow, G. O. "Teaching learners to be self-directed." *Adult Education Quarterly,* 41, 1991, 125–149.

Guba, E. G. and Lincoln, Y. S. *Effective Evaluation.* San Francisco: Jossey-Bass, 1981.

Gubrium, Jaber E. (ed.). *Time, Roles, and Self in Old Age.* New York: Human Sciences Press, 1976.

Gubrium, Jaber E. and Buckholdt, D. R. *Toward Maturity: the Social Processing of Human Development.* San Francisco: Jossey-Bass, 1977.

Guilford, J. P. *The Nature of Human Intelligence.* New York: McGraw-Hill, 1967.

Haggard, E. A. "Learning A Process of Change." *Readings in Human Learning.* L. D. and A. Crow (eds.). New York: McKay, 1963, pp. 19–27.

Hall, G. E. and Jones, H. L. *Competency-Based Education: A Process for the Improvement of Education.* Englewood Cliffs, N.J.: Prentice-Hall, 1976.

Handy, H. W. and Hussain, K. M. *Network Analysis for Educational Management.* Englewood Cliffs, N.J.: Prentice-Hall, 1968.

Hare, Paul. *Handbook of Small Group Research.* New York: Free Press of Glencoe, 1962.

Hare, Paul. *Small Group Process.* New York: Macmillan, 1969.

Hare, Van Court, Jr. *Systems Analysis. A Diagnostic Approach.* New York: Harcourt, Brace, and World, 1967.

Harman, D. *Illiteracy: A National Dilemma.* New York: Cambridge, 1987.

Harrington, Fred H. *The Future of Adult Education.* San Francisco: Jossey-Bass, 1977.

Harris, D. and Bell, C. *Assessment and Evaluation for Learning.* New York: Nichols, 1986.

Harris, P. R. and Moran, R. T. *Managing Cultural Differences,* 4th ed. Houston: Gulf Publishing, 1996.

Harris, T. L. and Schwahn, W. E. *Selected Readings on the Learning Process.* New York: Oxford University Press, 1961.

Hartley, H. I. *Educational Planning-Programming-Budgeting: A Systems Approach.* Englewood Cliffs, N.J.: Prentice-Hall, 1968.

Hartree, A. "Malcolm Knowles' Theory of Andragogy: A Critique." *International Journal of Lifelong Education*, 3, 1984, 203–210.

Havighurst, Robert. *Developmental Tasks and Education, 2nd ed.* New York: David McKay, 1972.

Hayes, C. D. *Self-University.* Wasilla, AK: Autodidactic Press, 1989.

Heerman, B. (ed.). *Personal Computers and the Adult Learner.* San Francisco: Jossey-Bass, 1986.

Heerman B. (ed.). *Teaching and Learning With Computers.* San Francisco: Jossey-Bass, 1988.

Hefferlin, J. B. L. *Dynamics of Academic Reform.* San Francisco: Jossey-Bass, 1969.

Heifernan, J. M., Macy, E. L. and Vickers, D. E. *Educational Brokering: A New Service for Adult Learners.* Washington, D.C.: National Center for Educational Brokering, 1976.

Hendrickson, A. (ed.). *A Manual for Planning Educational Programs for Older Adults.* Tallahassee, Fla.: Department of Adult Education, Florida State University, 1973.

Herzberg, Frederick. *Work and the Nature of Man.* Cleveland: The World Publishing Co., 1966.

Herzberg, Frederick, et al. *The Motivation to Work.* New York: John Wiley and Sons, 1959.

Hesburgh, T. M., Miller, P. A. and Wharton, C. R. Jr. *Patterns for Lifelong Learning.* San Francisco: Jossey-Bass, 1973.

Heyman, Margaret M. *Criteria and Guidelines for the Evaluation of Inservice Training.* Washington, D.C.: Social and Rehabilitation Service, Department of Health, Education and Welfare, 1967.

Hickcox, L. K. "Learning Styles: A Survey of Adult Learning Style Inventory Models." In Ronald R. Sims and Serbrenia J. Sims (eds.) *The Importance of Learning Styles: Understanding the Implications for Learning, Course Design, and Education.* Westport, CN: Greenwood Press, 1995.

Hicks, W. D. and Klimoski, R. J. "Entry into Training Programs and Its Effects on Training Outcomes: A Field Experiment." *Academy of Management Journal*, 30, 1987, 542–552.

Hiemstra, R. and Sisco, B. *Individualizing Instruction: Making Learning Personal, Empowering, and Successful.* San Francisco: Jossey-Bass, 1990.

Hilgard, E. R. and Bower, G. H. *Theories of Learning.* New York: Appleton-Century-Crofts, 1966.

Hill, J. E. and Nunhey, D. N. *Personalizing Educational Programs Utilizing Cognitive Style Mapping.* Bloomfield Hills, Mich.: Oakland Community College, 1971.

Holton, E. F. "Performance Domains: Bounding the Theory and Practice." In R. Swanson (series ed.) and R. Torraco (vol. ed.). *Advances in Developing Human Resources.* Washington, D.C.: ISPI Press, 1998.

Holton, Elwood F. III. "New Employee Development: A Review and Reconceptualization." *Human Resource Development Quarterly,* 7, 1996, 233–252.

Holton, E., Bates, R., Seyler, D. and Carvalho, M. "Toward Construct Validation of a Transfer Climate Instrument." *Human Resource Development Quarterly,* 8, 1997.

Horn, J. L. and Cattell, R. B. "Refinement and Test of the Theory of Fluid and Crystallized Intelligence." *Journal of Educational Psychology,* 57, 1966, 253–270.

Horney, Karen. *Feminine Psychology.* New York: W.W. Norton, 1967.

Hornstein, H. A., et al. *Social Intervention: A Social Science Approach.* New York: The Free Press, 1971.

"Hospital Continuing Education Project." *Training and Continuing Education.* Chicago: Hospital Research and Educational Trust, 1970.

Houle, Cyril O. *Continuing Your Education.* New York: McGraw-Hill, 1964.

Houle, Cyril O. *The Design of Education.* San Francisco: Jossey-Bass, 1972.

Houle, Cyril O. *The Effective Board.* New York: Association Press, 1960.

Houle, Cyril O. *The External Degree.* San Francisco: Jossey-Bass, 1973.

Houle, Cyril O. *Governing Boards.* San Francisco: Jossey-Bass, 1989.

Houle, Cyril O. *The Inquiring Mind.* Madison: University of Wisconsin Press, 1961.

Houle, Cyril O. *Continuing Learning in the Professions.* San Francisco: Jossey-Bass, 1980.

Houle, Cyril O. *Patterns of Learning:* New Perspectives on Life-Span Education. San Francisco: Jossey-Bass, 1984.

Houle, C. O. *The Literature of Adult Education: A Bibliographic Essay.* San Francisco: Jossey-Bass, 1992.

Howe, M. J. A. *Adult Learning: Psychological Research and Applications.* New York: John Wiley and Sons, 1977.

Huber, R. L. "Memory Is Not Only About Storage." *Applying Cognitive Learning Theory to Adult Learning,* D. D. Flannery (ed.). San Francisco: Jossey-Bass, 1993, pp. 35–46.

Hultsch, D. F. and Deutsch, E. *Adult Development and Aging: A Life Span Perspective.* New York: McGraw-Hill, 1981.

Hunt, Morton. *The Universe Within: A New Science Explores the Human Mind.* New York: Simon and Schuster, 1982.

Hunkins, Francis P. *Involving Students in Questioning.* Boston: Allyn and Bacon, 1975.

Hutchings, P. and Wutzdorff, A. (eds.). *Knowing and Doing: Learning through Experience.* New Directions for Teaching and Learning TL#35. San Francisco: Jossey-Bass, 1988.

Ickes, W. and Knowles, E. S. *Personality, Roles, and Social Behavior.* New York: Springer-Verlag, 1982.

Illich, Ivan. *Deschooling Society.* New York: Harper and Row, 1970.

Illich, Ivan. Tools for Conviviality. New York: Harper and Row, 1973.

Illsley, P. (ed.). *Improving Conference Design and Outcomes.* San Francisco: Jossey-Bass, 1985.

Ingalls, John. *Human Energy: The Critical Factor for Individuals and Organizations.* Reading, Mass.: Addison-Wesley, 1976.

Ingalls, J. D. and Arceri, J. M. *A Trainers Guide to Andragogy.* Social and Rehabilitation Service. U.S. Department of Health, Education, and Welfare. (SRS 72-05301). Washington, D.C., Government Printing Office, 1972.

Iscoe, I. and Stevenson, W. W. (eds.). *Personality Development in Children.* Austin, Texas: University of Texas Press, 1960.

Jacobs, R. L. Structured On-the-Job Training. *In Handbook of Human Performance Technology* (H. Stolovitch and E. Keeps, eds.). San Francisco; Jossey-Bass, 1992.

Jacobs, R. L. and Jones, M. J. *Structured On-the-Job Training.* San Francisco: Berrett-Koehler, 1995.

James, W. B. and Blank, W. E. "Review and Critique of Available Learning-Style Instruments for Adults." *Applying Cognitive Learning Theory to Adult Learning,* D. D. Flannery (ed.). San Francisco: Jossey-Bass, 1993.

James, W. B. and Galbraith, M. W. "Perceptual Learning Styles: Implications and Techniques for the Practitioner." *Lifelong Learning,* 8, 1985, 20–23.

Jaques, D. *Learning in Groups.* Dover, N. H.: Croom Helm, 1984.

Jensen, G., Liveright, A. A. and Hallenbeck, W. *Adult Education: Outlines of an Emerging Field of University Study.* Washington, D.C.: Adult Education Association, 1964.

John, M. T. Geragogy: *A Theory for Teaching the Elderly.* Reading, MA: Addison-Wesley, 1987.

Johnson, D. W. and Johnson, E. P. *Learning Together and Alone: Cooperation, Competition, and Individualization.* Englewood Cliffs, N.J.: Prentice-Hall, 1975.

Johnstone, J. W. C. and Rivera, William. *Volunteers for Learning: A Study of the Educational Pursuits of American Adults.* Chicago: Aldine, 1965.

Jonassen, D. H. and Grabowski, B. L. *Handbook of Individual Differences, Learning, and Instruction.* Hillsdale, NJ: Lawrence Erlbaum, 1993.

Jones, G. Brian, et al. *New Designs and Methods for Delivering Human Developmental Services.* New York: Human Sciences Press, 1977.

Jones, H. E. "Intelligence and Problem Solving." *Handbook of Aging and the Individual.* J. E. Birren (ed.). Chicago: University of Chicago Press, 1959, pp. 700–738.

Jones, K. *Simulations: A Handbook for Teachers.* New York: Nichols, 1980.

Jones, R. M. *Fantasy and Feeling in Education.* New York: New York University Press, 1968.

Joughin, G. "Cognitive Style and Adult Learning Principles." *International Journal of Lifelong Education,* 11(1), 1992, 3–14.

Jourard, S. M. "Fascination. A Phenomenological Perspective on Independent Learning." *The Psychology of Open Teaching and Learning.* M. L. Silberman, et al. (eds.). Boston: Little, Brown, 1972, pp. 66–75.

Joyce, Bruce and Weil, Marsha. *Models of Teaching.* Englewood Cliffs, N.J.: Prentice-Hall, 1972.

Jung, Carl. *The Nature of the Psyche.* Trans. by R. E C. Hull. Bollingen Series XX, Vol. 8. Princeton, N.J.: Princeton University Press, 1969.

Kabanoff, B. and O'Brien, G.E. Work and Leisure: A Task Attributes Analysis. *Journal of Applied Psychology,* 65, 1980, 596–609.

Kagan, J. (ed.). *Creativity and Learning.* Boston: Houghton-Mifflin, 1967.

Kagan, J. and Moss, H. A. *Birth to Maturity: A Study in Psychological Development.* New York: John Wiley and Sons, 1962.

Kahle, L.R. "Stimulus Condition Self-Selection by Males in the Interaction of the Locus of Control and Skill-Chance Situations." *Journal of Personality and Social Psychology,* 38, 1980, 50–56.

Kaplan, Abraham. *The Conduct of Inquiry.* San Francisco: Chandler, 1964.

Kast, F. E. and Rosenzweig, J. E. *Organization and Management: A Systems Approach.* New York: McGraw-Hill, 1970.

Kastenbaum, Robert (ed.). *New Thoughts on Old Age.* New York: Springer Publishing Co., 1964.

Kastenbaum, Robert (ed.). *Contributions to the Psycho-Biology of Aging.* New York: Springer Publishing Co., 1965.

Katz, D. and Kahn, R. L. *The Social Psychology of Organizations.* New York: Wiley, 1966.

Kaufman, R. *Educational System Planning.* Englewood Cliffs, N.J.: Prentice-Hall, 1972.

Kaufman, A. S. *Assessing Adolescent and Adults Intelligence.* Boston: Allyn and Bacon, 1990.

Keeton, Morris T., et al. *Experiential Learning: Rationale, Characteristics, and Assessment.* San Francisco: Jossey-Bass, 1976.

Kelly, G. S. *The Psychology of Personal Constructs.* New York: W. W. Norton, 1955.

Kember, D. and Murphy, D. The Impact of Student Learning Research and the Nature of Design on ID Fundamentals. In B.B. Seels (ed.). *Instructional Design Fundamentals: A Reconsideration.* Englewood Cliffs, NJ: Educational Technologies, 1995.

Kempfer, H. H. *Adult Education.* New York: McGraw-Hill, 1955.

Kidd, J. R. *How Adults Learn.* New York: Association Press, 1959, 1973.

Kidd, J.R. *How Adults Learn.* Englewood Cliffs, NJ: Prentice-Hall, 1978.

Kingsley, H. L. and Garry, R. *The Nature and Conditions of Learning,* 2nd ed. Englewood Cliffs, N.J.: Prentice-Hall, 1957.

Kirkpatrick, Donald L. *Evaluating Training Programs.* Madison, Wis.: American Society for Training and Development, 1975.

Kirkpatrick, Donald L. *A Practical Guide for Supervisory Training and Development.* Reading, Mass.: Addison-Wesley, 1971.

Knowles, Malcolm S. *The Adult Education Movement in the United States,* 2nd ed. Huntington, N.Y.: Krieger Publishing Co., 1977.

Knowles, Malcolm S. *The Modern Practice of Adult Education: From Pedagogy to Andragogy.* Englewood Cliffs: Cambridge, 1980.

Knowles, Malcolm S. *Self-Directed Learning: A Guide for Learners and Teachers.* New York: Association Press, 1975.

Knowles, Malcolm S. *Andragogy In Action.* San Francisco: Jossey-Bass, 1984.

Knowles, Malcolm S. *Informal Adult Education*. New York: Association Press, 1950.

Knowles, Malcolm S. *The Modern Practice of Adult Education: Andragogy versus Pedagogy*. New York: Association Press, 1970, 1980.

Knowles, Malcolm S. *Using Learning Contracts*. San Francisco: Jossey-Bass, 1986.

Knowles, Malcolm S. *The Adult Learner: A Neglected Species*, 4th ed. Houston, TX: Gulf Publishing Co., 1990.

Knowles, Malcolm S. and Knowles, Hulda. Introduction to Group Dynamics. New York: Cambridge University Press, 1972.

Knowles, Malcolm S. *The Making of an Adult Educator*. San Francisco: Jossey Bass, 1989.

Knowles, Malcolm S. and Hulda, F. *Introduction to Group Dynamics*. Chicago: Follett, 1973.

Knox, Alan B. *Adult Development and Learning*. San Francisco: Jossey-Bass, 1977.

Knox, Alan B. *Helping Adults Learn*. San Francisco: Jossey-Bass, 1986.

Knox, Alan B., and Associates. *Developing, Administering, and Evaluating Adult Education*. San Francisco: Jossey-Bass, 1980.

Kohlberg, L. "Continuities in Childhood and Adult Moral Development Revisited." In *Developmental Psychology: Personality and Socialization*. P. Baltes and K. Schaie (eds.). Orlando, FL: Academic Press, 1973.

Kohler, W. *Gestalt Psychology*. New York: Meridian, 1947.

Kolb, D. A. *Experiential Learning: Experience as the Source of Learning and Development*. Englewood-Cliffs: Prentice-Hall, 1984.

Kolb, D. A. (1981). Experiential Learning Theory and the Learning Style Inventory: A reply to Freedman and Stumpf. *Academy of Management Review*, 6, 1981, 289–296.

Kolb, D. A. *The Learning Style Inventory*. Boston: McBer, 1976.

Kramer, D. A. Development of an Awareness of Contradiction Across the Life Span and the Question of Postformal Operations. In *Adult Development*, Commons, M. L., Sinnott, J. D., Richards, F. A., and Armon, C. (ed.). NY: Praeger Publishers and the Dare Association, Inc., 1989, 133–157.

Kreitlow, B. W. and Associates. *Examining Controversies in Adult Education*. San Francisco: Jossey-Bass, 1981.

Labouvie-Vief, G. *Models of Cognitive Functioning in the Older Adult: Research Need in Educational Gerontology.* In *Introduction to Educational Gerontology*, 3rd ed. Sherron, R. H. and Lumsden, D. B. (eds.). NY: Hemisphere Publishing Corp., 1990, 243–263.

Latham, G. P. Behavioral Approaches to the Training and Learning process. In *Training and Development in Organizations* I.L. Goldstein and Associates (ed.). San Francisco, CA: Jossey-Bass Publications, 1989, 256–295.

Laughary, J. W. and Rippley, T. M. *Helping Others Help Themselves.* New York: McGraw-Hill, 1979.

Leagans, J.P., Copeland, H. G. and Kaiser, G. E. *Selected Concepts from Educational Psychology and Adult Education for Extension and Continuing Educators.* Syracuse: University of Syracuse Press, 1971.

Lefcourt, Herbert M. *Locus of Control: Current Trends in Theory and Research.* New York: John Wiley and Sons, 1976.

Leibowitz, Z. B., Farren, C. and Kaye, B. L. *Designing Career Development Systems.* San Francisco: Jossey-Bass, 1986.

Lengrand, Paul. *An Introduction to Lifelong Education.* Paris: UNESCO, 1970.

Lenning, Frank W. and Many, W. A. (eds.). *Basic Education for the Disadvantaged Adult: Theory and Practice.* Boston: Houghton Mifflin, 1966.

Leonard, G. B. *Education and Ecstasy.* New York: Delacorte, 1968.

Leonard-Barton, D. *The Wellspring of Knowledge: Building and Sustaining the Sources of Innovation.* Boston: HBR Press, 1995.

Levering, R. and Moskowitz, M. *The 100 Best Companies to Work for in America.* New York: NAL-Dutton, 1994.

Levinson, D. J. *The Season's of a Man's Life.* New York: Knopf, 1978.

Levinson, D. J. "A Theory of Life Structure Development in Adulthood." In *Higher Stages of Human Development.* C. N. Alexander and E. J. Langer (eds.). New York: Oxford University Press, 1978, 35–54.

Levinson, D. J. "A Conception of Adult Development." *American Psychologist*, 41, 1986, 3–13.

Levinson, H., et al. *Men, Management, and Mental Health.* Cambridge, Mass.: Harvard University Press, 1963.

Lewin, Kurt. *Field Theory in Social Science.* New York: Harper, 1951.

Lewis, L. H. (ed.). *Experiential and Simulation Techniques for Teaching Adults.* San Francisco: Jossey-Bass, 1986.

Lewis, L. H. and Williams, C. J. Experiential Learning: Past and Present. In *Experiential Learning: A New Approach* L. Jackson and R. S. Caffarella (eds.). San Francisco: Jossey-Bass, New Directions for Adult and Continuing Education, 62, 1994, 5–16.

Leypoldt, M. M. *Forty Ways to Teach in Groups.* Valley Forge, Penn.: Judson Press, 1967.

Likert, R. *The Human Organization: Its Management and Value.* New York: McGraw-Hill, 1967.

Likert, R. *New Patterns of Management.* New York: McGraw-Hill, 1961.

Lindeman, Eduard C. *The Meaning of Adult Education.* New York: New Republic, 1926.

Lippitt, G. L. *Organization Renewal.* New York: Appleton-Century-Crofts, 1969.

Lippitt, G. L. *Visualizing Change.* Somerset, N.J.: John Wiley and Sons, 1978.

Lippitt, G. L. and Lippitt, R. *The Consulting Process in Action.* La Jolla, CA: University Associates, 1978.

Loevinger, J. *Ego Development: Concepts and Theories.* San Francisco: Jossey-Bass, 1976.

London, M. *Change Agents: New Roles and Innovative Strategies for Human Resource Professionals.* San Francisco: Jossey-Bass, 1988.

Long, Huey B. *Are They Ever Too Old to Learn?* Englewood Cliffs, N.J.: Prentice-Hall, 1971.

Long, Huey B. *The Psychology of Aging: How It Affects Learning.* Englewood Cliffs, N.J.: Prentice-Hall, 1972.

Long, Huey B. et al. *Changing Approaches to Studying Adult Education.* San Francisco: Jossey-Bass, 1980.

Long, Huey B. and Associates. *Self-Directed Learning: Application and Theory.* Athens, GA: Department of Adult Education, University of Georgia, 1988.

Luiten, J., Ames, W., and Ackerman, G. A Meta Analysis of the Effects of Advance Organizers on Learning and Retention. *American Educational Research Journal.* 17, 1980, 211–218 and 291, 405.

Lumsden, D. B. and Sherron, R. H. *Experimental Studies in Adult Learning and Memory.* New York: John Wiley and Sons, 1975.

McClelland, D. C. *Power: The Inner Experience.* New York: McGraw-Hill, 1960.

McClelland, D. C., Atkinson, J. W., Clark, R. A. and Lowell, E. I. *The Achievement Motive.* New York: Appleton-Century-Crofts, 1953.

McDonald, F. J. "The Influence of Learning Theories on Education." *Theories of Learning and Instruction.* Sixty-third Yearbook of the National Society for the Study of Education, Part I. E. R. Hilgard (ed.). Chicago: University of Chicago Press, 1964, pp. 126.

McGregor, D. *The Human Side of Enterprise.* New York: McGraw Hill, 1960.

McGregor, D. *Leadership and Motivation.* Cambridge, Mass.: The Massachusetts Institute of Technology Press, 1967.

McKenzie, L. *The Religious Education of Adults.* Birmingham, Ala.: Religious Education Press, 1982.

McLagan, P. A. *Models for Excellence.* Washington, D.C.: American Society for Training and Development (ASTD), 1983.

McLagan, P.A. "Models for HRD Practice." *Training and Development,* 43 (9), 1989, 49–59.

Mager, R. E. *Preparing Instructional Objectives.* Palo Alto, Cal.: Fearon, 1962.

Mager, R. E. *Goal Analysis.* Palo Alto, Cal.: Fearon, 1972.

Mager, R. E. and Pipe, P. *Analyzing Performance Problems,* Palo Alto, Cal.: Fearon, 1970.

Mangham, I. *Interactions and Interventions in Organizations.* New York: John Wiley and Sons, 1948.

Marquardt, M. J. *Building the Learning Organization.* New York: McGraw Hill, 1996.

Marrow, A. J., Bowers, D. G. and Seashore, S. E. *Management By Participation.* New York: Harper and Row, 1968.

Martorana, S. V. and Kuhns, E. *Managing Academic Change.* SanFrancisco: Jossey-Bass, 1975.

Maslow, A. H. *Motivation and Personality.* New York: Harper and Row, 1970.

Maslow, A. H. "Defense and Growth." *The Psychology of Open Teaching and Learning.* M. L. Silberman, et al. (eds.). Boston: Little, Brown, 1972, pp. 43–51.

Menges, R. J. and Mathis, B.C. *Key Resources on Teaching, Curriculum, and Faculty Development.* San Francisco: Jossey-Bass, 1988.

Merriam, S. B. "Adult Learning: Where Have We Come From? Where Are We Headed?" *New Directions for Adult and Continuing Education, no. 57.* San Francisco: Jossey-Bass, 1993.

Merriam, S. *Case Study Research in Education.* San Francisco: Jossey-Bass, 1988.

Merriam S. and Caffarella, R. S. *Learning in Adulthood.* San Francisco: Jossey-Bass, 1991.

Merriam S. and Cunningham, P. M. (eds.). *Handbook of Adult and Continuing Education.* San Francisco: Jossey-Bass, 1989.

Merrill, M. D. Constructivism and Instructional Design. In *Constructivism and the Technology of Instruction.* T. M. Duffy and D. H. Jonassen (eds.). Hillsdale, NH: Lawrence Erlbaum, 1992.

Messick, S. The Nature of Cognitive Styles: Problems and Promise in Educational Practice. *Educational Psychologist,* 19, 1984, 59–74.

Messick, S., et al. *Individuality in Learning.* San Francisco: Jossey-Bass, 1976.

Mezirow, J. "A Critical Theory of Adult Learning and Education." *Adult Education,* 32 (1), 3–27, 1981.

Mezoff, B. "Cognitive Style and Interpersonal Behavior: A Review with Implications for Human Relations Training." *Group and Organization Studies,* 7:1, 1982, 13–34.

Michael, Donald. *On Learning to Plan and Planning to Learn: The Social Psychology of Changing Toward Future-Responsive Societal Learning.* San Francisco: Jossey-Bass, 1973.

Miles, M. W. and Charters, W. W., Jr. *Learning in Social Settings.* Boston: Allyn and Bacon, 1970.

Millenson, J. R. *Principles of Behavioral Analysis.* New York: Macmillan, 1967.

Miller, H. L. *Teaching and Learning in Adult Education.* New York: Macmillan, 1964.

Millett, J. D. *Decision Making and Administration in Higher Education.* Kent, Ohio: Kent State University Press, 1968.

Millhollan, Frank and Forisha, B. E. *From Skinner to Rogers.* Lincoln, Nebraska: Professional Educators Publications, 1972.

Moore, M. G. and Willis, N. P. (eds.). *New Developments in Self-Directed Learning. New Directions in Continuing Education* CE#42. San Francisco: Jossey-Bass, 1989.

Mizuno, S. (ed.). *Managing for Quality Improvement: The Seven New QC Tools.* Cambridge, MA: Productivity Press, 1988.

Moos, R. E. *Evaluating Educational Environments.* San Francisco: Jossey-Bass, 1979.

Moos, R. E. *The Human Context: Environmental Determinants If Behavior.* New York: Wiley, 1976.

Moos, R. E. and Insel, P. M. *Issues in Social Ecology:* Human Milieus.

Moran, R. T. and Harris, P. R. *Managing Cultural Synergy.* Houston: Gulf Publishing Co., 1982.

Moustakas, C. *Finding Yourself, Finding Others.* Englewood Cliffs, N.J.: Prentice-Hall, 1974.

Mouton, J. S. and Blake, R. R. *Synergogy: A New Strategy for Education, Training, and Development.* San Francisco: Jossey-Bass, 1984.

Nadler, Leonard and Nadler, Zeace. *The Conference Book.* Houston: Gulf Publishing Co., 1977.

Nadler, Leonard and Nadler, Zeace. *Developing Human Resources.* Houston: Gulf Publishing Co., 1970.

Nadler, Leonard and Nadler, Zeace. *Designing Training Programs: The Critical Events Model,* 2nd ed. Houston: Gulf Publishing Company, 1994.

Nadler, Leonard and Nadler, Zeace. *Corporate Human Resource Development.* New York: Van Nostrand Reinhold, 1980.

Nadler, Leonard and Nadler, Zeace and Wiggs, G. *Managing Human Resources Development.* San Francisco: Jossey-Bass, 1986.

Neimi, J. A. and Gooler, D. D. (eds.). *Technologies for Learning Outside the Classroom.* San Francisco: Jossey-Bass, 1987.

Neugarten, Bernice L. (ed.). *Personality in Middle and Later Life.* New York: Atherton Press, 1964.

Neugarten, Bernice L. (ed.). *Middle Age and Aging.* Chicago: University of Chicago Press, 1968.

Noe, R. A, Hollenbeck, J. R., Gerhart, B. and Wright, P. M. *Human Resource Management: Gaining a Competitive Advantage.* Burr Ridge, IL: Irwin. Palo Alto, CA: National Press Books, 1994.

Norris, N. A. (ed.). *Community College Futures: From Rhetoric to Reality.* Stillwater, OK: New Forums Press, 1989.

Optnet, S. *Systems Analysis for Business and Industrial Problem Solving,* Englewood Cliffs, N.J.: Prentice-Hall, 1965.

Ormrod, J. *Human Learning Principles, Theories, and Educational Applications.* Columbus, OH: Merrill, 1990.

Osborn, Ruth H. *Developing New Horizons for Women.* New York: McGraw-Hill, 1977.

Parker, B. K. *Health Care Education: A Guide to Staff Development.* Norwalk, CT: Appleton-Century-Crofts, 1986.

Parsons, T. *The Social System.* New York: Free Press of Glencoe, 1951.

Pascual-Leone, J. "Growing into Maturity: Toward a Metasubjective Theory of Adulthood Stages." In P. B. Baltes and O. G. Brim Jr (eds.), *Lifespan Development and Behavior, vol. 5.* New York: Academic Press, 1983.

Patton, M. Q. *Creative Evaluation.* Beverly Hills, CA: Sage Publications, 1981.

Patton, M. Q. *Practical Evaluation.* Beverly Hills, CA: Sage Publications, 1982.

Patton, M. Q. *Qualitative Evaluation.* Beverly Hills, CA: Sage Publications, 1980.

Pearlin, L. I. "Life Strains and Psychological Distress Among Adults." In Themes of Work and Love in Adulthood. N. J. Smesler and E. H. Erikson (eds.). Cambridge, MA: Harvard University Press, 1980, 174–92.

Perry, W. "Cognitive and Ethnical Growth: The Making of Meaning." In: *Forms of Intellectual and Ethnical Developments with the College Years: A Scheme,* NY: Holt Rinehart and Winston, 1970, 76–116.

Perry, P. and Downs, S. "Skills, Strategies, and Ways of Learning." *Programmed Learning and Educational Technology.* 22, 1985, 177–181.

Peters, J. M. and Associates. *Building an Effective Adult Education Enterprise.* San Francisco: Jossey-Bass, 1980.

Pfeiffer, William J. and Jones, John E. *A Handbook of Structured Experiences for Human Relations Training.* Vols. I, II, III, IV, V. San Diego: University Associates Press, 1969–1976.

Phares, E. J. Locus of Control in Personality. Morristown, NJ: General Learning Press, 1976.

Phillips, J. J. *Handbook of Training Evaluation and Measurement Methods,* 3rd ed. Houston: Gulf Publishing Co., 1997.

Piaget, Jean. *Science of Education and the Psychology of the Child.* New York: Viking, 1970.

Pike, R. *Creative Training Techniques Handbook.* Minneapolis: Lakewood, 1989.

Pittenger, O. E. and Gooding, C. T. *Learning Theories in Educational Practice*. New York: Wiley, 1971.

Pollack, O. *Human Behavior and the Helping Professions*. New York: John Wiley, 1976.

Postman, N. and Weingartner, C. *Teaching as a Subversive Activity*. New York: Dell, 1969.

Powell, J. W. *Learning Comes of Age*. New York: Association Press, 1956.

Powers, D. R., Powers, M. E, and Aslanian, C. B. *Higher Education in Partnership with Industry*. San Francisco: Jossey-Bass, 1988.

Pratt, D. D. "Andragogy after Twenty-Five Years." *New Directions for Adult and Continuing Education*, no. 57. San Francisco: Jossey-Bass, 1993.

Pratt, D. D. "Andragogy as a Relational Construct." *Adult Education Quarterly*, 38, 1988, 160–181.

Pressey, S. L. and Kuhlen, R. G. *Psychological Development Through the Life Span*. New York: Harper and Row, 1957.

Raths, Louis, et al. *Teaching for Learning*. Columbus, Ohio: Charles E. Merrill, 1967.

Raths, Louis, Harmin, H. and Simon, Sidney. *Values and Teaching*. Columbus, Ohio: Charles E. Merrill, 1966.

Rae, L. *How to Measure Training Effectiveness*. New York: Nichols, 1986.

Rankel, P., Harrison, R., and Runkel, M. *The Changing College Classroom*. San Francisco: Jossey-Bass, 1969.

Rasmussen, W. D. *Taking the University to the People: 75 Years of Cooperative Extension*. Ames, Iowa: Iowa State University Press, 1989.

Reber, R. A. and Wallin, J. A. "The Effects of Training, Goal Setting, and Knowledge of Results on Safe Behavior: A Component Analysis." *Academy of Management Journal*, 27, 1984, 544–560.

Reese, H. W. and Overton, W. E. "Models of Development and Theories of Development." *Life-Span Developmental Psychology*. L. R. Gottlet and P. B. Baltes (eds.). New York: Academic Press, 1970, pp. 115–145.

Reynolds, M. "Learning Styles: A Critique." *Management Learning*. 28, 1997, 115–133.

Richey, R. C. Instructional Design Theory and a Changing World. In *Instructional Design Fundamentals: a Reconsideration*. B.B. Seels (ed.). Englewood Cliffs: NJ: Educational Technologies, 1995.

Riegel, K. F. "The Dialectics of Human Development." *American Psychologist*, 31, 1976, 689–700.

Robertson, D. L. *Self-Directed Growth*. Muncie, IN: Accelerated Development, 1988.

Robinson, D. and Robinson, J. S. *Training for Impact*. San Francisco: Jossey-Bass, 1989.

Robinson, A. G. and Stern, S. Corporate Creativity: How Innovation and Improvement Actually Happen. San Francisco: Berrett-Koehler, 1997.

ROCOM. *Intensive Coronary Care Multimedia System Program Coordinator's Manual*. Nutley, N. J.: Hoffman-LaRoche, 1971.

Rogers, C. R. *Client-Centered Therapy*. Boston: Houghton-Mifflin, 1951.

Rogers, C. R. On Becoming a Person. Boston: Houghton-Mifflin, 1961.

Rogers, C. R. *Freedom to Learn*. Columbus, Ohio: Merrill, 1969.

Rogers, C. R. A Way of Being. Boston: Houghton Mifflin, 1980.

Rosenblum, S. and Darkenwald, G. G. "Effects of Adult Learner Participation in Course Planning on Achievement and Satisfaction." *Adult Education Journal*, 20 (2), 1983, 67–87.

Rosenshine, B. "Enthusiastic Teaching. A Research Review." *School Review*, LXXVIII, 1970, 499–514.

Rosenshine, B.V. "Effective Teaching in Industrial Education and Training." *Journal of Industrial Teacher Education*, 23, 1986, 5–19.

Rosenthal, R. and Jacobson, L. *Pygmalian in the Classroom*. New York: Holt, Rinehart and Winston, 1968.

Rosow, J. M. and Zager, R. *Training—The Competitive Edge*. San Francisco: Jossey-Bass, 1988.

Rossi, P. H. and Biddle, B. J. *The New Media and Education*. Chicago: Aldine, 1966.

Rossing, B. E. and Long, H. B. "Contributions of *Curiosity* and Relevance to Adult Learning Motivation." *Adult Education*, 32 (1), 1981, 25–36.

Rotter, J. B. "Internal Versul External Control of Reinforcement: A Case History of a Variable." *American Psychologist*. 45 (4), 1990, 489–493.

Rotter, J. B. "Generalized Expectations for Internal Versus External Control of Reinforcement." *Psychology Monographs*. 80 (1), 1966, 1–28.

Rountree, D. *Teaching Through Self-Instruction: A Practical Handbook for Course Developers*. New York: Nichols, 1986.

Rudwick, B. H. *Systems Analysis for Effective Planning*. New York: Wiley, 1969.

Rummelhart, D. E. and Norman, D. A. "Accretion, Tuning and Restructuring: Three Models of Learning." In *Semantic Factors in Cognition*. J. W. Cotton and R. LO. Klatzky (eds.). Hillsdale, NJ: Erlbaum, 1978.

Rummler, G. A. and Brache, A. P. Improving Performance: How to Manage the White Space on the Organization chart, 2nd ed. San Francisco: Jossey-Bass, 1995.

Savery, John R. and Duffy, Thomas M. "Problem Based Learning: An Instructional Model and Its Constructivist Framework." In Brent G. Wilson (ed.). *Constructivist Learning Environments: Case Studies in Instructional Design,* Englewood Cliffs, NJ: Educational Technology Publications, 1996.

Schaie, K. W. "The Course of Adult Intellectual Development." *American Psychologist,* 49, 1994, 304–13.

Schein, E. *Process Consultation. Its Role in Organization Development.* Reading, Mass.: Addison-Wesley, 1969.

Schein, E. and Bennis, W. G. *Personal and Organizational Change through Group Methods.* New York: Wiley, 1965.

Schindler-Rainman, Eva and Lippitt, Ronald. *The Volunteer Community: Creative Use of Human Resources.* Washington, D.C.: Center for a Voluntary Society, 1971.

Schlossberg, N. K., et al. *Perspectives on Counseling Adults.* Monterey, CA: Brooks/Cole, 1965.

Schlossberg, N. K., Lynch, A. Q., and Chickering, A. W. *Improving Higher Education Environments for Adults.* San Francisco: Jossey-Bass, 1989.

Schon, Donald A. *Beyond the Stable State.* San Francisco: Jossey-Bass, 1971.

Schon, Donald A. *Educating the Reflective Practitioner.* San Francisco: Jossey-Bass, 1987.

Schuttenberg, E. "The Development of a General Purpose Organizational Output Instrument and Its Use in Analysis of an Organization." Unpublished doctoral dissertation Boston University School of Education, 1972.

Schwab, J. J. "The Practical: Arts of Eclectic." *School Review,* LXXIX, August 1971, 493–542.

Seay, Maurice F., et al. *Community Education: A Developing Concept.* Midland, Mich.: Pendell Publishing Co., 1974.

Seiler, J. A. *Systems Analysis in Organizational Behavior.* Homewood, ILL.: Irwin and Dorsey, 1967.

Senge, P. The Fifth Discipline: The Art and Practice of the Learning Organization. NY: Doubleday, 1990.

Seyler D., Holton E. and Bates, R. "Factors Affecting Motivation to Use Computer-Based Training." *The Academy of Human Resources 1997 Conference Proceedings.* Richard J. Toracco (ed.). Baton Rouge, LA Academy of Human Resources, 1997.

Shaw, N. (ed.). *Administration of Continuing Education*. Washington, D.C.: National Association for Public and Continuing Education, N.E.A., 1969.

Sheehy, Gail. *Passages: Predictable Crises of Adult Life*. New York: E. P. Dutton, 1974.

Silberman, C. E. *Crisis in the Classroom*. New York: Vintage, 1971.

Silberman, M. L., Allender, J. S. and Yahoff, J. M. *The Psychology of Open Teaching and Learning: An Inquiry Approach*. Boston: Little, Brown, 1972.

Sillars, R. *Seeking Common Ground in Adult Education*. Washington, D.C.: Adult Education Association of the U.S.A., 1958.

Simerly, R. G. and Associates. *Handbook of Marketing for Continuing Education*. San Francisco: Jossey-Bass, 1989.

Simerly, R. G. and Associates. *Strategic Planning and Leadership in Continuing Education*. San Francisco: Jossey-Bass, 1987.

Simon, H. A. *Administrative Behavior*. New York: Macmillan, 1961.

Simon, Sydney, Howe, L. W. and Kirschenbaum, H. *Values Clarification*. New York: Hart Publishing Co., 1972.

Skinner, B. F. "The Science of Learning and the Art of Teaching." *Harvard Educational Review*. 24, 1954, 86–97.

Skinner, B. F. *The Technology of Teaching*. New York: Appleton-Century-Crofts, 1968.

Sleezer, C. M. "Performance Analysis for Training." *Performance Improvement Quarterly,* 1992.

Smith, B. B. "Model and Rationale for Designing and Managing Instruction." *Performance and Instruction*. April 1983, 20–22.

Smith, B. B. Designing and Managing Instruction. *Performance and Instruction*. May 1983, 27–30.

Smith, Maury. *A Practical Guide to Value Clarification*. La Jolla, Cal.: University Associates, 1977.

Smith, P. L and Ragan, T. J. Instructional Design. NY: Merrill, 1993.

Smith, R. M. Learning How to Learn. Englewood Cliffs, NJ: Cambridge, 1982.

Smith, R. M., Aker, G. E, and Kidd, J. R. (eds.). *Handbook of Adult Education*. New York: Macmillan, 1970.

Smith R. M. (ed.). *Theory Building for Learning How To Learn*. Chicago: Educational Studies Press, 1988.

Snow, R. E. Aptitude-Treatment Interaction as a Framework for Research on Individual Differences in Learning. In *Learning and Individual Differences: Advances in Theory and Research*. P. L. Ackerman, R. J. Sternberg, and R. Glaser (eds.). New York: W. H. Freeman and Co., 1989.

Solomon, L. and Berzon, B. (eds.). *New Perspectives on Encounter Groups*. San Francisco: Jossey-Bass, 1972.

Sorenson, Herbert. *Adult Abilities*. Minneapolis: University of Minnesota Press, 1938.

Spector, P. A. "Behavior in Organization as a Function of Employee's Locus of Control." *Psychological Bulletin*. 91(30), 1982, 482–497.

Spelman, M. S. and Levy, P. Knowledge of Lung Cancer and Smoking Habits. *British Journal of Social and Clinical Psychology*, 5, 1966, 207–210.

Srinivasan, Lyra. *Perspectives on Nonformal Adult Learning*. New York: World Education, 1977.

Stanage, S. M. *Adult Education and Phenomenological Research*. Malabar, FL: Krieger, 1987.

Steele, Sara M. and Brack, Robert E. *Evaluating the Attainment of Objectives: Process, Properties, Problems, and Projects*. Syracuse: Syracuse University Publications in Continuing Education, 1973.

Stephens, J. M. *The Process of Schooling*. New York: Holt, Rinehart and Winston, 1967.

Sternberg, R. J. The Concept of Intelligence and Its Role in Lifelong Learning and Success. American Psychology, 52, 1997, 1030–1037.

Sternberg, R. J. *The Triachic Mind: A New Theory of Human Intelligence*. NY: Viking, 1988.

Stevens-Long, J. *Adult Life: Developmental Processes*. Palo Alto, CA: Mayfield Publishing Co., 1979.

Stewart, D. W. *Adult Learning in America: Eduard Lindeman and His Agenda for Lifelong Education*. Malabar, FL: Krieger, 1987.

Stewart, T. A. Intellectual capital: The New Wealth of Organizations. NY: Doubleday, 1997.

Stokes, Kenneth (ed.). *Faith Development in the Adult Life Cycle*. New York: William H. Sadlief, 1983.

Storey, W. D. *Orientation to Your Career Development Program*. Ossining, N.Y.: General Electric Company Management Development Institute, 1972.

Stumpf, S. A. and Freedman, R. D. The Learning Style Inventory: Still Less than Meets the Eye. Academy of Management Review, 6, 1981, 297–299.

Suchman, Edward A. *Evaluative Research: Principles and Practice in Public Service and Social Action Programs.* New York: Russell Sage Foundation, 1967.

Suchman, J. R. "The Child and the Inquiry Process." *The Psychology of Open Teaching and Learning.* M. L. Silberman, et al. (eds.). Boston: Little, Brown, 1972, pp. 147–159.

Swanson, R.A. *Analysis for Improving Performance: Tools for Diagnosing Organizations and Documenting Workplace Expertise.* San Francisco, CA; Berrett-Koehler, 1996.

Swanson, R. A. Human Resource Development: Performance is Key. *Human Resource Development Quarterly,* 6 (2), 1995, 207–213.

Swanson, R. "Industrial Training." In *Encyclopedia of Educational Research,* H. E. Mitzel (ed.). New York: Macmillan, 1982, pp. 864–869.

Swanson, R. A. "Demonstrating financial benefits to clients." In *Handbook of Human Performance Technology.* H. Stolovitch and E. Keeps, eds. San Francisco: Jossey-Bass, 1992, pp. 602–618.

Swanson, R. A. Ready-Aim-Frame. *Human Resource Development Quarterly,* 2 (3), 1991, 203–205.

Swanson, R. A and Arnold, D. E. "The Purpose of Human Resource Development Is to Improve Organizational Performance. In *Debating the Future of Educating Adults in the Workplace,* R.W. Rowden (ed.). San Francisco: Jossey-Bass, 1996, pp. 13–19.

Swanson, R. A. and Fentress, J. "The Effects Influential Tactics on Instructor Ratings. *Journal of Industrial Teacher Education,* 13 (1), 1975, pp. 5–16.

Swanson, R. A. and Gradous, D. B. *Forecasting Financial Benefits of Human Resource Development.* San Francisco: Jossey-Bass, 1988.

Swanson, R. A. and Holton, E. F. *Human Resource Development Handbook: Linking Research and Practice.* San Francisco: Berrett-Koehler, 1997.

Taba, H. *Curriculum Development Theory and Practice.* New York: Harcourt, Brace and World, 1962.

Tannenbaum, S. I., Mathieu, J. E., Salas, E., and Cannon-Bowers, J. A. Meeting Trainees' Expectations: The Influence of Training Fulfillment on the Development of Commitment, Self-Efficacy, and Motivation. *Journal of Applied Psychology,* 76, 1991, 739–769.

Taylor, Bernard, and Lippitt, Gordon L. *Management Development and Training Handbook.* New York: McGraw-Hill, 1975.

Tedeschi, J. T. (ed.). *The Social Influence Process.* Chicago: Airline-Atherton, 1972.

Tennant, M. and Pogson, P. *Learning and Change in the Adult Years: A Developmental Perspective.* San Francisco: Jossey-Bass, 1995.

Tessmer, M. and Richey, R. C. "The Role of Context in Learning and Instructional Design. *Educational Technology Research and Development,* 45, 1997, 85–115.

Thayer, Louis (ed.). *Affective Education: Strategies for Experiential Learning.* La Jolla, Cal.: University Associates, 1976.

Thomas, R. Conclusions and Insights Regarding Expertise in Specific Knowledge Domains and Implications for Research and Educational Practice. In *Thinking Underlying Expertise in Specific Knowledge Domains: Implications for Vocational Education* R. G. Thomas (ed.). St. Paul, MN: University of Minnesota, Minnesota Research and Development Center, 1988, 85–95.

Thompson, J. R. "Formal Properties of Instructional Theory for Adults." *Adult Learning and Instruction.* S. M. Grabowski (ed.). Syracuse: ERIC Clearing House on Adult Education, 1970, pp. 28–45.

Thorndike, Edward L. *Adult Interests.* New York: Macmillan, 1935.

Thorndike, Edward L. *Adult Learning.* New York: Macmillan, 1928.

Toffler, A. (ed.). *Learning for Tomorrow: The Role of the Future in Education.* New York: Random House, 1974.

Tolman, E. C. "Principles of Purposive Behavior." In *Psychology: A Study of a Science,* Vol. 2. S. Koch (ed.). New York: McGraw-Hill, 1959.

Torraco, R. J. "Theory Building Research Methods." In *Human Resource Development Research Handbook.* R. A. Swanson and E. F. Holton III (eds.). San Francisco: Berrett-Koehler, 1997, 114–137.

Torraco, R. J. and Swanson, R. A. "The Strategic Roles of Human Resource Development." *Human Resource Planning.* 18 (4), 1995, 11–21.

Tough, A. *The Adult's Learning Projects.* Toronto: Ontario Institute for Studies in Education, 1971, 1979.

Tough, A. *Learning Without a Teacher.* Toronto: Ontario Institute for Studies in Education, 1967.

Tough, A. *Intentional Changes: A Fresh Approach to Helping People Change.* Chicago: Follett, 1982.

Totshen, K. P. *The Mastery Approach to Competency-Based Education.* New York: Academic Press, 1977.

Tracey, William R. *Managing Training and Development Systems.* New York: American Management Associations, 1974.

Trecker, H. B. *Citizen Boards at Work*. New York: Association Press, 1970.

Tyler, L. *Individuality: Human Possibilities and Personal Choice in the Psychological Development of Men and Women*. San Francisco: Jossey-Bass, 1978.

Tyler, R. W. *Basic Principles of Curriculum and Instruction*. Chicago: University of Chicago Press, 1950.

Van Maanen, J. and Dabbs, J. M. *Varieties of Qualitative Research*. Beverly Hills, CA: Sage Publications, 1982.

Vermilye, Dyckman W. (ed.). *Lifelong Learners—A New Clientele for Higher Education*. San Francisco: Jossey-Bass, 1974.

Verner, C. and Booth, Alan. *Adult Education*. New York: Center for Applied Research in Education, 1964.

Verner, C. *A Conceptual Scheme for the Identification and Classification of Processes*. Washington, D.C.: Adult Education Association, 1962.

Von Bertalanffy, L. *General System Theory*. New York: Braziller, 1968.

Vroom, V. H. *Work and Motivation (classic reprint)*. San Francisco: Jossey-Bass, 1995.

Waetjen, W. B. and Leeper, R. R. (eds.). *Learning and Mental Health in the School*. Washington, D.C.: Association for Supervision and Curriculum Development, N.E.A., 1966.

Walberg, Herbert J. (ed.). *Evaluating Educational Performance: A Sourcebook of Methods, Instruments, and Examples*. Berkeley, Cal.: McCutchan, 1974.

Watkins, K. and Marsick, V. "The Case for Learning." In *Academy of Human Resource Development 1995 Conference Proceedings*, E.F. Holton (ed.). Austin, TX.: AHRD, 1995.

Watkins, K. E. and Marsick, V. J. *Sculpting the Learning Organization*. San Francisco: Jossey-Bass, 1993.

Watson, G. (ed.). *Concepts for Social Change*. Washington, D.C.: National Training Laboratories Institute for Applied Behavioral Science, N.E.A., 1967.

What Do We Know About Learning? Teachers College Record, 1960–61, pp. 253–257.

Weiler, Nicholas W. *Reality and Career Planning: A Guide for Personal Growth*. Reading, Mass.: Addison-Wesley, 1977.

Weinstein, C. E. and Mayer, R. E. "The Teaching of Learning Strategies." In Handbook of Research on Teaching, 3rd ed., M. C. Wittrock (Ed.). New York: Macmillan, 1986.

White, R. H. "Motivation Reconsidered. The Concept of Competence." *Psychological Review,* LXVI, 1959, 297–333.

Willems, E. P. and Rausch, H. L. (eds.). *Naturalistic Viewpoints in Psychological Research.* New York: Holt, Rinehart and Winston, 1969.

Wislock, R. F. "What Are Perceptual Modalities and How Do They Contribute to Learning?" In *Applying Cognitive Learning Theory to Adult Learning,* Daniele D. Flannery (ed.). San Francisco: Jossey-Bass, 1993.

Wiswell, B. and Ward, S. "Combining Constructivism and Andragogy in Computer Software Training." In *Proceedings of the 1997 Academy of Human Resource Development Annual Conference.* R. Torraco (ed.). Baton Rouge, LA: Academy of Human Resource Development.

Witkin, H. A., Monroe, O. A., Goodenough, D. R. and Cox, P. W. "Field-Dependent and Independent Cognitive Styles and Their Educational Implications." *Review of Educational Research,* vol. 47, no. 1, 1977, 1–64.

Wlodowski, R. J. *Enhancing Adult Motivation to Learn.* San Francisco: Jossey-Bass, 1985.

Woodruff, Diana S. and Birren, J. E. (eds.). *Aging.* New York: D. Van Nostrand Co., 1975.

Yelon, S. L. "Classroom Instruction." In *Handbook of Human Performance Technology.* H. Stolovitch and E. Keeps. (eds.). 1992.

Zadeh, L. *Systems Theory.* New York: McGraw-Hill, 1969.

Zahn, J. C. *Creativity Research and Its Implications for Adult Education.* Syracuse: Library of Continuing Education, Syracuse University, 1966.

Zander, A. *Groups at Work.* San Francisco: Jossey-Bass, 1977.

Zander, A. *Making Groups Effective.* San Francisco: Jossey-Bass, 1982.

Zemke, R., and Zemke, S. Thirty Things We Know for Sure about Adult Learning." *Training,* 25(7), 1988, 57–61.

Zurcher, L. A. *The Mutable Self: A Concept for Social Change.* Beverly Hills, CA: Sage, 1977.

Author Index

Subject Index